BUSINESS ISSUES TODAY

Alternative Perspectives

BUSINESS ISSUES TODAY

Alternative Perspectives

Robert B. Carson
State University College, Oneonta, New York

St. Martin's Press
New York

Library of Congress Catalog Card Number: 83–61610
Copyright © 1984 by St. Martin's Press, Inc.
All Rights Reserved.
Manufactured in the United States of America.
87654
fedcb
For information, write St. Martin's Press, Inc.,
175 Fifth Avenue, New York, N.Y. 10010

cover design: Darby Downey
cover photo: Hazel Hankin/Stock, Boston

cloth ISBN: 0–312–10904–0
paper ISBN: 0–312–10905–9

ACKNOWLEDGMENTS

ISSUE 1
William E. Simon, "The System Works—If Given a Chance." From *A Time for Truth* by William E. Simon. Copyright 1978 by William E. Simon. Reprinted by permission of McGraw-Hill Book Company.
Felix G. Rohatyn, "The System Needs Help." From "Alternatives to Reaganomics" by Felix Rohatyn, *New York Times* Magazine, December 5, 1982. © 1982 by The New York Times Company. Reprinted by permission.

ISSUE 2
Milton Friedman, "The Social Responsibility of Business Is to Increase Its Profits." From *New York Times* Magazine, September 13, 1970. © 1970 by The New York Times Company. Reprinted by permission.
Richard T. DeGeorge, "Business Has Social Responsibilities." From *Business Ethics* by Richard T. DeGeorge. Copyright © 1982 by Macmillan Publishing Company.
Albert Z. Carr, "Can an Executive Afford a Conscience?" From *Harvard Business Review*, July–August 1970. Copyright © 1970 by the President and Fellows of Harvard College; all rights reserved. Reprinted by permission of the Harvard Business Review.

Acknowledgments and copyrights continue at the back of the book on pages 346–348, which constitute an extension of the copyright page.

For James and Sarah and their generation,
who will be making the difficult choices very soon

Preface

Over the past half dozen years, the number of students interested in business studies in American universities and colleges has exploded. At most of these institutions, business is the largest and fastest-growing undergraduate major. The growth of interest in business doubtless reflects the employment realities in an economy that has grown very slowly over the past decade and the understandable concern of students for improving their job prospects. Of course, it may also reflect a deeper and more genuine interest in business subjects among contemporary college students than existed a decade or more ago. Whatever the reason, more college students today want to learn about business than at any time in the past.

Ironically, the business institutions that these students choose to study so intently are undergoing searching reexamination and criticism. American business enterprise is in the midst of revolutionary change. Over the past ten years of economic contraction, old business values and practices have come under attack, even from business itself. One need only turn to the business and financial pages of newspapers or news weeklies to see the extent of this debate. How can Americans raise productivity? What can they learn from Japanese styles of management? Are mergers getting out of hand? What is the proper role for government in a business economy? Does the United States need an "industrial policy"? Will "high tech" replace the "smokestack" industrial foundations of the American economy? Such questions are not matters of idle curiosity but reflect the soul searching now going on in business as it attempts to come to terms with a whole new agenda of management, marketing, and financial problems.

Regrettably, many of the business textbooks used by students fail to examine in much detail these current debates over key business-policy issues. Instead, most texts follow a tried and safe approach of neutrally surveying business organizations, rarely commenting on the changing trends in philosophy and practice. In my own classes, I found that even the best business texts sidestepped or ignored most of the issues that my students were reading about in the paper or hearing about on television. More important, the average text was not preparing students for important real-world business situations in which they would be involved after college.

My response is this collection of readings on thirteen contemporary business issues. Its objective is to bring the current debates over business policy into the introduction-to-business or introduction-to-management classrooms. To keep the discussion lively and to confront students with the diversified and sometimes contradictory points of view that flourish in the business community, I have tried to select readings that exemplify controversy and division of opinion. I approach each issue with the object of helping students evaluate and choose from among differing points of view. The readings and the end-of-issue discussion questions are meant to show beginning students that business is not the monolithic and unchanging institution that the textbooks often present and to invite them to develop their own philosophies or perspectives on crucial business-policy matters. I do not advocate a particular point of view here. Rather I present representative points of view from which the reader can make his or her own choice. I hope that such an exercise in studying business-policy alternatives will heighten students' awareness of the hard choices they will soon face in their own professional lives.

Accompanying this volume is a carefully prepared Instructor's Manual designed to aid instructors in using the readings in the classroom. The manual includes a chart correlating the issues covered in this book with eight leading introduction-to-business texts.

I would like to thank the following reviewers for their helpful suggestions as the book took final shape: G. Vaughn Johnson of the University of Nebraska, Emerson N. Milligram of Carlow College, Lewis M. Stewart of Georgia Southern College, Noel G. Powell of West Georgia College, Allen D. Mason of Stephens College, Walter W. Perlick of California Polytechnic State University, V. Wayne Klemin of Central Washington University, Barry L. Van Hook of Arizona State University, Dr. Ella W. Van Fleet of Texas A & M University, Terry Marion of Missouri Southern State College, Charles W. Schilling, Ph.D., of the University of Wisconsin-Platteville, Jim Hackett of Southern California College, and George M. Wenstrup. Special thanks are due to Michael Weber of St. Martin's Press for having faith in the project and to Emily Berleth and Ron Aldridge for putting it in its final shape. Charlize Fazio again served bravely as my typist. Fred Puritz provided outstanding aid and support in preparing the Instructor's Manual and in offering critical advice on the text.

Contents

BUSINESS ISSUES TODAY

Alternative Perspectives

PART 1

INTRODUCTION

The Contours of Change in American Business Development

Throughout most of American history—with the possible exceptions of the Depression years of the 1930s and the protest years of the 1960s—business institutions, business values, and business leaders have enjoyed a high popular regard. Comparatively few Americans have ever disagreed with President Calvin Coolidge's observation that the "business of America is business." Few could deny that over the long haul the business system has worked reasonably well, delivering the goods, the jobs, and the standard of living acceptable to the vast majority of the population. Moreover, the traditional American virtues of independence and hard work have seemed safely embodied in the entrepreneurial activities and instincts of a business society. However, by the 1980s the American business system seems to have entered a new and uncomfortable period.

Recent Reexaminations of the Business System

For more than a decade now, the American economy has performed badly. The nation has experienced four major recessions, a prolonged and painful episode of rising prices, rising levels of unemployment, steady increases in business and personal bankruptcies, and a general decline in both the growth of our national output and the efficiency with which we turn out goods and services. Since business *is* the economy, the economic decline has raised a number of serious questions about the future of American private enterprise.

3

As a result, a growing literature has appeared over the last few years, analyzing the problems of contemporary business and offering a wide range of suggested solutions. Revisionist critics from within and without business have directed their inquiry and criticism into every area of business's functional activities: research and production, finance, marketing, and, most significantly, management practices in general. To the casual observer, many of these critiques may seem unduly harsh and the suggested solutions nothing short of revolutionary. More surprising is the fact that the harshest critics and the most "revolutionary" proposals come not from the small band of political radicals who have always opposed the capitalist production-for-profit system; they come from the ranks of business enterprise.

Almost every aspect of business behavior has been held up for close scrutiny. Business has been criticized for being too narrowly and immediately profit directed, thereby failing to invest in long-term product development and to lay out long-term operational strategies. Financing and accounting techniques, with their apparent bias toward making stockholders happy through creative but dangerous financial methods, also have drawn fire. Personnel managers have been attacked for their failure to motivate workers and their too-frequent dependence upon wages alone as an inspirational device to spur workers' output. Along with their failure to plan for the long run, upper management has been charged with evading necessary research and development commitments and failing to use the newest and best production technology. Meanwhile, in what has become a familiar refrain, the Japanese, our strongest competitors, have been cited constantly as a model that American enterprise might pattern itself after in the development of new industrial and business policies.

As we shall see in the following readings, the list of charges against recent business practices and of recommendations for change is long and growing. Nor is there much unanimity in the complaints and the proposed cures. At first glance, the entire situation seems to be confusing and contradictory: businesspeople attacking accepted business practices and talking about "revolutionary change." However, the contradictions disappear if we take a longer, historical view of American enterprise. In fact, *change*, not permanence, and *adaptation*, not mindless opposition to change, have always been dominant characteristics in the development of the American business system. Indeed, American business enterprise has always been in a kind of "permanent revolution." To understand this point and to put into proper focus our examination of the current debate over the directions and content of modern business policy, a short detour through American business history is in order.

The Permanent Revolution

While past practices and conditions may not be very useful in choosing among future strategies, a longer view of American business institutions and operations does provide two important insights: First, it clearly points up the evolutionary and changing character of business as an institution, thus putting the shrillness of much of the current debate in a proper and a somewhat calming perspective. No less than in our own era have past shifts in the direction and organization of business enterprise seemed about to destroy all that was "good and desirable." Second, a trip through American business history allows for some understanding of how technical, social, and economic forces make change inevitable.

An excursion into the past necessarily leads to the arbitrary identification of certain landmarks and epochs in business development. Four watershed periods have been selected for study: (1) the era of merchant capitalists, colonial times up to 1860; (2) the rise of big business, 1860–1900; (3) the development of the modern corporation, 1900–1929; and (4) the maturing of a mixed enterprise system, 1929 to the present. The reader is encouraged to examine each of these eras with several questions in mind: What were the dominant characteristics of business institutions and behavior? What forces emerged that forced change upon the business environment? What adaptations actually took place, and how successful were they?

The Era of Merchant Capitalists: Colonial Times up to 1860

To appreciate the significance and dimensions of change in American business institutions, we need only contrast the extent and complexity of modern enterprise with the crude and underdeveloped business system that existed in colonial times. The wealth of productive power now taken for granted did not exist for the early American colonists. The land and climate were hostile, the native population was unfriendly (and for good reason), and epidemics frequently decimated settlements. Although there were a few cities during the colonial period, Americans were primarily farmers, farm workers, or slaves tied to farming. Business activities already common in England or on the continent were comparatively slow to develop.

The official position of the British administrators of the colonies was to pursue the policies of *mercantilism*, which subordinated the colonies to the needs of the mother country. Colonial production efforts were directed to raising crops or providing raw materials that could be exported directly to England. Meanwhile, colonial manufacturing was to be kept to a minimum. Finished goods, except for a few farm tools made by local blacksmiths, had to be purchased from British suppliers. Trade among the colonies was officially discouraged. Under mercantilism, the colonies were both a captive market for British merchants and a supplier of cheap raw materials.

Small wonder, then, that such arrangements eventually produced the stirrings of revolution and the demand for separation from England. The small merchants and the frontier farmers of the Northeast and the plantation operators of the South all found the exploitative and restrictive policies of mercantilism outrageous. It was not purely a matter of "taxation without representation" that produced the war of independence; it was a common desire to sweep aside all external controls.

Fracturing political and economic connections with England did not immediately stimulate business growth. Although the new nation was rich in land and raw materials, labor was in short supply. In 1790 the population stood at 3.9 million, about 90 percent working in agricultural pursuits (20 percent of the population were southern plantation slaves). Capital was also in critically short supply. With the combined shortage of labor and capital, the growth of business enterprise, especially manufacturing establishments, was very slow. There was little risk capital and there were few urban workers available for industrial purposes. Independent artisans and home manufacturing supplied the bulk of finished product needs.

THE EARLY MERCHANT CAPITALISTS

What businesses did exist were usually commercial or financial enterprises. All were small and invariably organized as partnerships or proprietorships. The early merchant proprietors were not business specialists. They doubled in shipping, warehousing, retailing and wholesaling, insurance, and banking—apparently no single activity produced sufficient profit or was demanding enough to absorb all of the entrepreneur's time.

Business administration simply did not exist as we know it today. Indeed, business was carried on in a most haphazard way. Usually no administrative hierarchy existed, with accountants, clerks, and apprentices reporting directly to the owner. Business was rarely brisk, even on good days, and most employees worked at their own pace. The proprietors themselves were not very hard drivers. Even the very successful John Jacob Astor (one of our first millionaires) was rarely in the office before nine in the morning or after two in the afternoon. In their private lives the more successful merchants tried to copy the lifestyle of English aristocrats, spending much of their day in leisure—reading, writing, and dining.

Business operated without benefit of any of the specialists common today. There were no management consultants, no public relations experts, no public accountants, no personnel specialists, and so on. Insurance companies operated without actuaries to calculate probable losses. Banks, which did not really exist until the later years of the eighteenth century, usually maintained only single-entry bookkeeping and frequently were guilty of incredible mathematical errors in keeping their accounts.

However, for all these shortcomings the merchant capitalist served an important task. Ever so slowly they did accumulate profits that in turn provided the basis for manufacturing development. Early industrial entrepreneurs, such as Samuel Slater in textiles, the Brown brothers in candles, and Samuel Colt in firearms, obtained their *start-up capital* from merchant capitalist investors.

THE IMPACT OF INVENTIONS

Complementing the accumulation of capital in the early nineteenth century were a number of important inventions. Eli Whitney's cotton gin created an industry by making it possible for the first time to clean cotton faster than it could be picked. Whitney also developed the technique of producing standardized and interchangeable parts in the manufacture of firearms, a practice that quickly spread to most new machine industries and spelled ruin to the craftsmen who made each machine part with tender loving care but at great expense. Francis Lowell introduced the power loom to spin yarn. Robert Fulton applied the steam engine to water transportation. Before the Civil War Elias Howe had invented the sewing machine, Samuel Morse had introduced the telegraph, and Cyrus McCormick had perfected a mechanical reaper to replace the hand cutting of grain crops. Invention produced new invention. Between 1790 and 1811 the U.S. Patent Office averaged seventy-seven inventions annually. Between 1850 and 1860 it averaged more than 2,500 a year.

THE BEGINNINGS OF THE FACTORY SYSTEM

The flood of inventions and the increased availability of capital, however, did not produce a manufacturing society overnight. Home production of such goods as clothes, foodstuffs, and many tools continued. Per capita income was not much over $100 per year, and consumer demand for goods was of necessity quite low.

Nevertheless, the factory system did take root. The model for all that was to come later sprang up in the 1830s and 1840s in the Connecticut River Valley. Using the water power of the river to operate the looms and spinning machines, a crude assembly line process was developed. Work was specialized and divided among specific tasks on a continuous production basis. Labor, still a productive factor in short supply in the United States, was recruited from the surrounding farming areas. Often forgotten is the fact that the earliest industrial workers were women. The entrepreneurs enticed the daughters of New England farmers to the mill towns with promises of clean working conditions and the provision of reading circles and other "intellectual" pursuits after their work hours. Meanwhile, their virtue was to be protected by "housemothers" in company-operated boarding houses. The girls came by the thousands. It was doubtless an exciting change from the boredom of farm life where they worked and waited (hopefully) until marriage provided an escape from home. Their fathers were probably equally enthusiastic. Daughters were not highly prized among offspring, and the absence of another mouth at the table was desirable. The new girls usually worked a few years, saved a modest dowry, and left with better marriage prospects. From a management viewpoint the high turnover rate was not a problem. Skills were quickly learned, and enthusiastic fifteen-to-twenty-year-olds were highly productive workers.

Although production organization has matured and become vastly more complex since the 1840s, the key concepts of continuous production and division of labor have endured since the first factory models of

New England. Other contributions to the business system by the early enterprisers were less impressive. A few firms were organized as limited liability corporations, but, like the merchant capital enterprises before them, most remained proprietorships or partnerships. Ownership and management were inherited family rights and obligations. There was little opportunity to move up, and, as with most family firms, there was great reluctance to try new business methods. These changes in the business system would have to come later.

GOVERNMENT IMPACT ON BUSINESS

Today, the popular perception of government's impact on business is mostly negative; however, this was not true in the early stages of business development. Business correctly saw government as an active partner in the process of development. Government did intervene in the economy, but only to stimulate private initiative and to create a legal framework hospitable to business. In the areas of banking, money, and credit, the federal government maintained stable currency and financial conditions that were essential to business affairs. Tariffs on foreign goods were enacted to protect native industry. Canals, highways, and harbors were built to encourage trade and commerce. Public land policy was developed to encourage both agricultural expansion and the exploitation of raw materials. Government was also an important source of capital. Subsidies and bounties were paid by the federal government as seed money to shipping, small arms manufacturing, fishing, and railroad industries.

The courts were equally helpful. Business successfully sought legal protection from labor unions (which the courts found to be illegal conspiracies). The rights of contract were protected, and the power of individual states to regulate business was greatly restricted. Meanwhile, there was virtually no direct regulation of business by the federal government.

Such policies were as important to business in the early stages of development as the process of capital accumulation, new invention, and the creation of a manufacturing system.

The Rise of Big Business: 1860–1900

Despite the increasingly hospitable climate for business, the nation remained largely rural, agrarian, and nonindustrial up to the Civil War.

Then a sudden explosion of business and economic activity propelled the United States to leadership in world industrial production.

THE CIVIL WAR AND BUSINESS DEVELOPMENT

Although the war between the states took half a million lives, devastated half the nation, and slowed national growth, nevertheless, it had some positive effects in building a business society. In the North, huge government outlays for military goods and provisions created new firms and industries almost overnight. Providing an army with food, firearms, gunpowder, cannon, kerosene lanterns, uniforms, and wagons demanded enlarged and more technical production facilities. Because government contracts usually specified precise standards and calibrations for equipment procured, producers had to develop standardized production methods. All of these wartime demands compelled the development of business and production methods that were vastly more mature than anything the society had experienced earlier.

Government purchases also created a national market for many goods that before had been produced only for local or regional consumption. Entrepreneurs quickly understood the possibilities of reaching beyond their local markets. Men like Gustavus Swift in meat packing and Charles Pillsbury in flour were to profit from the lesson. When the war ended, they quickly applied the concepts of a national market to the development of their own firms. Why, indeed, should entrepreneurial enterprise be limited merely to local markets?

Perhaps the war had its greatest impact on financial affairs. Before the conflict, bankers, brokerage firms, and other financial institutions had been quite small; however, with vast federal borrowing to finance the war, financial houses enjoyed a brisk and profitable business selling government bonds. Meanwhile, sizable concentrations of capital were put together by a number of enterprising government contractors. Men like Commodore Vanderbilt, Daniel Drew, Jay Gould, and J. P. Morgan amassed considerable fortunes that were to be put to other uses after the war.

THE AGE OF THE ENTREPRENEUR

After the Civil War there was a flood of new inventions. The Bessemer process for making steel, the typewriter, the cash register, the lino-

CHANGES IN CORPORATE STRUCTURE AND STRATEGY: THE 3 Ds

Following Andrew Carnegie's dictum that it was "a good idea to put all your eggs in one basket," nineteenth-century business had focused on one product. Business energies concentrated on lowering production costs. There was little interest in marketing or management strategies, as it was assumed the product would sell itself. Meanwhile, administrative decisions were made by one or a comparative handful of entrepreneurs at the corporate top. In the early twentieth century, this management approach was challenged by new concepts of *diversification, development,* and *decentralization,* known affectionately today as the *3 Ds.*

Diversification meant that industries began production of a number of product lines. Such a course of action, of course, required firms to become deeply involved in product development—to go out and develop new lines of goods. In the early years of the century, meat packers like Swift branched into soap making, electrical machinery manufacturers such as GE started production of a broad range of household appliances, and the old gunpowder firm of DuPont went into paints, fertilizers, and industrial chemicals. Diversification and development seemed to promise greater profits to a firm. By using byproducts of the firm's main line of goods, production facilities as well as management and technical skills could be shared among a number of goods, thus keeping costs down and profits up. Alas, at first it did not work that way.

At DuPont, when diversification and product development were first employed intensively, the result was enormous business losses. The problem was soon attributed to the old tactic of concentrating business decision making at the top of the firm. The trouble was that the top level of leadership, despite its general business abilities, lacked the specific knowledge of new products and new markets needed to make proper business decisions. Decentralization was the answer. In 1921, DuPont reorganized its management structure into five autonomous divisions (cellulose, paint, purolin, dyestuffs, and, of course, explosives). Each division had its own head responsible to central management, but central management no longer had much influence on day-to-day decisions. Within a few years, DuPont was earning large profits in each of its divisions. Meanwhile, the DuPont model of decentralized management con-

type machine, the telephone, the electric light bulb, and the internal combustion engine were but a few. Each invention opened up enormous business prospects. With comparatively little capital, an enterprising and lucky entrepreneur with a new idea could build a giant firm.

Beginning his business career as a $35-per-month secretary to the superintendent of the Pennsylvania Railroad, young Andrew Carnegie obtained a $217.60 bank loan to buy part interest in a railroad sleeping car company. Within a year Carnegie was earning $5,000 on his investment. From this venture, Carnegie moved into steel and brought a half interest in a steel mill on a loan of $71,000. Thirty years later the investment was worth more than $150 million.

John D. Rockefeller began as a bookkeeping clerk, formed a partnership working as a commission agent, and just happened to be present in the 1860s at the beginning of the oil discoveries in western Pennsylvania. With a few thousand dollars earned securing produce for the government during the Civil War, Rockefeller began a long and complicated career developing Standard Oil. By 1900 his corporation controlled over 90 percent of the production and refining of oil in the United States. It is said that Standard Oil refined everything except the Pennsylvania Legislature (which it simply bought off), but most of all it refined millionaires. At one time old John D. was estimated to be worth $850 million (this was after he had already given $750 million away). However, Standard Oil also produced dozens of other millionaires whose names now are largely forgotten.

Only a handful of entrepreneurs enjoyed the success of Carnegie and Rockefeller, but there were enough "rags to riches" stories to hold the public's attention and to permit business to gain considerable respect. During the freewheeling 1870s and 1880s, newspapers and churches heaped tributes on the new "captains of industry," and a generation of schoolboys learned in their daily lessons that the virtues of hard work and struggle would produce material rewards.

CORPORATE ORGANIZATION

Individual "captains of industry" were widely celebrated, but in reality the "one-man company" was coming to an end. Most large firms, such as Standard Oil, Dupont, and the Carnegie Steel Works, employed many "lieutenants" in determining strategies and in running various aspects of the corporation. As early as the 1870s, Rockefeller introduced a committee system (himself and his chief aides, Henry Flagler and Samuel Anderson) to carry on long-range planning and day-to-day scrutiny of operations.

The legal form of business enterprise also underwent change. During the last two decades of the nineteenth century the incorporation laws of most states were eased considerably. Partnerships and proprietorships were abandoned in favor of the corporate form, which offered the possibility of raising large amounts of capital through stock sales and limited the stockholder's financial responsibility to the amount of his investment. Stock ownership, however, remained very narrow. Few ordinary citizens had the means to invest in stock, and most large corporations were limited to a handful of very wealthy and powerful stockholders.

THE COMING OF THE TRUSTS

While the advocates of business spoke glowingly about the virtues and rewards of the competitive struggle, the facts of competition were a great deal different. Few thoughtful men of industry, then or now, have seriously believed that "struggle" was its own reward. For instance, Carnegie and Rockefeller succeeded precisely because they had learned to suppress competition. Carnegie absorbed his smaller rivals in mergers, and when that failed drove them from business by price cutting and other tactics. Rockefeller's favored device for ending competition was the *trust*. By establishing the Standard Oil Trust as a single corporation to buy controlling stock in competing companies, all of these concerns were brought under a single board of trustees.

In the basic industries, such as steel, oil, coal, sugar, and railroads, concentration and monopoly progressed hand in hand with the rise of great business fortunes. By the late 1880s the abuse of monopolistic power was so common that public reaction demanded restraints on the industrial giants.

In 1887, the railroad industry was subjected to federal regulation with the creation of the Interstate Commerce Commission. Three years later, Congress enacted the Sherman Antitrust Act. This act declared that monopoly and conspiracies to "restrain trade" were illegal. Some years were to pass before the Sherman Act was applied seriously to business, but it signaled the end of unrestricted business activity. Fortunes were still to be made, but things would never be the same again.

THE PROBLEMS OF LABOR

While fortunes were being made and business grew, labor's position deteriorated. Wage workers and artisans, all in short supply, had commanded good wages before the Civil War. Labor's share declined, however, precisely as the labor supply grew. Millions of Americans left their farms for urban employment, and after the 1870s millions of immigrants flooded into the country. As the expanded use of machine production reduced the need for skilled labor and as the pool of labor grew, wages were held down.

By 1900, for a fairly average 60- to 70-hour work week, a male worker received about $9 and children got as little as $2. This was more than workers in any other industrial nation received, but that was small comfort for a family where husband, wife, and children all worked just to make ends meet.

Labor turned increasingly to unions to improve wages and abominable working conditions. Every step of the way the corporations fought back. The closing decades of the century produced massive strikes and industrial violence. The other side of the growth of corporations and the creation of great fortunes was a growing legacy of labor–capital animosity. By the closing years of the century many business and political leaders recognized that this conflict would have to be dealt with soon, before it tore the social fabric of the system apart.

The Development of the Modern Corporation: 1900–1929

Four important developments imposed themselves on the business system during the first thirty years of the twentieth century. First, the giant enterprises underwent important overhauling in management, marketing, and production practices. Second, goods production shifted increasingly from basic industries such as steel, railroads, coal, and o toward new consumer oriented goods. Third, government regulation business and economic affairs vastly increased. Fourth, the period end in a long economic depression.

trol quickly spread to other firms and industries. The modern concept of the multiline, multidivision corporate giant had emerged.

THE RISE OF CONSUMER GOODS MARKETS

The development of large numbers of consumer products was not directly a business invention. Businesses would doubtless have been happy to sell consumer goods in the nineteenth century. The problem was that consumer income was so low that few markets existed. Between 1900 and 1929, however, per capita income in the United States more than tripled. At the same time, the population shifted from its traditional rural base to a solid urban foundation. By 1920 more than half of all Americans lived in cities, and city dwellers did not as a rule make their own soap, grow their own food, or sew their own clothes. Urbanites needed iceboxes, stoves, pots, pans, clothing, and foodstuffs. In addition, they wanted radios, furniture, baby carriages, toys, and all manner of other products. And of course there was the grand consumer product—the automobile.

The revolutionary rise in consumer goods, both durable goods (such as refrigerators and autos) and nondurables (prepared foods and clothing), had an important impact on business. Whole new industries appeared almost overnight. The retailing business, which had been quite modest in the nineteenth century, grew to incredible size, producing such giant chains as A & P, Woolworth's 5 and 10, J. C. Penney's, Sears & Roebuck, and Montgomery Ward.

Competition for the consumer dollar demanded whole new marketing strategies. No consumer goods producer could expect product success without newspaper and magazine advertising. In the 1920s the radio was to become a veritable chatterbox of commercial advertising. The idea was to fix the consumer's mind on a brand name: Lucky Strike cigarettes, Morton's salt, Ivory soap, Coca-Cola, Nabisco crackers, and so on. Meanwhile, consumer durables producers introduced warranties and service agreements in efforts to go the competition one better.

To stimulate consumer buying, credit purchasing was encouraged in the 1920s. Although automobiles and new home purchases accounted for most of the growth of consumer debt, many retail stores and some chains began to permit "buying on time" or installment purchase agreements. By 1929, 15 percent of all consumer buying was paid for through credit arrangements of some kind.

THE BEGINNING OF GOVERNMENT REGULATION

Certainly many business leaders hoped that the Interstate Commerce Commission (1887) and the Sherman Antitrust Act (1890) were merely passing lunacies, but that was not to be the case. In the first two decades of the twentieth century, government regulation of business affairs greatly increased.

The ugly working conditions of the mines and mills caused many state governments to enact legislation that shortened working hours and set minimum wages. The use of child labor was curtailed sharply, and commissions were established to monitor work conditions. At the same time the growing militancy of labor unions led the federal government to pass legislation (Clayton Act, 1914) that exempted labor unions from prosecution as monopolies or conspiracies. Union organizers had been stymied in the courts for years by this legal interpretation of union activity. Now there was a weak mandate that allowed labor the right to organize. Business's old domination of workers was ending, but the industrial strife of the 1880s and 1890s also began the decline. To many thoughtful business leaders this did not seem a bad bargain.

Less impressive, however, was the growing attack upon corporate size and power. In three landmark cases involving Standard Oil, American Tobacco, and DuPont Gunpowder, the Supreme Court not only upheld the Sherman Act but went further. Monopoly firms were broken up and restructured to create more competition. In 1914 the Federal Trade Commission was established to increase federal surveillance of mergers, combinations, and other business practices. The Clayton Act (1914) broadened the Sherman Act interpretation of monopoly behavior by making it illegal for a firm to acquire the assets of competing companies or to have any of its board of directors sit on competing companies' boards.

Regulatory attention was not limited to the issue of business concentration and size. In 1905, Upton Sinclair's novel above life and work conditions in the Chicago meatpacking business produced a wave of public sentiment that the food industry be "cleaned up." Sinclair had intended *The Jungle* to raise public concern for the plight of the workers. Instead his nauseating descriptions of meat production practices hit

Americans in their stomachs. The passage of the Pure Food and Drug Act in 1906 was a direct result. Under this act the federal government established standards for food and drug preparation and appointed inspectors to maintain standards in food processing plants throughout the nation. Although the full implications of such actions were not yet understood, the consumer movement had been born.

THE GREAT CRASH

Of all the bewildering changes taking place in the business environment during the first third of the twentieth century, the most perplexing was the general economic collapse after 1929. The boom–bust rhythm of economic activity had long been observed and had been more or less accepted as a fact of business life. Hard times usually would appear in eight-to-twelve-year intervals. Economists had studied the business cycle in considerable detail and had a number of explanations for the gradual swings from prosperity to recession or depression and back to prosperity again. No one, however, had a very convincing explanation of why the economy continued to dribble downward after 1929.

The decade of the 1920s had begun with the highest of hopes among business leaders. New goods, new investment opportunities, and improved business organization all seemed to signal continued prosperity. The collapse of the stock market usually is cited as the most obvious culprit for this sudden change of affairs. During the closing years of the 1920s there had begun, at first slowly and then at a hectic pace, a rising demand for corporate securities. Practically any kind of financial instrument would do: common stock, preferred stock, or bonds. And almost any corporation's stock was acceptable to speculators. As buying drove up stock prices, firms rushed to print up more paper by issuing new stock or splitting old shares. In just a few years (1925–1929), the number of shares traded on the New York Stock Exchange grew from 400 million to over 1 billion. The rising demand for stock caused prices to rise, and the expectations that they would continue to rise caused even greater demand. There seemed to be no end to the boom, of "making it" simply by buying stock, watching its market value continually rise, and then selling it to another buyer with the same dreams.

The traditional rule of thumb for estimating the value of a share of stock was "ten times earnings." In 1929, many stocks were selling at more than fifty times earnings. Even the ordinarily cautious banking and investment community let itself be drawn into the superspeculation. They sold the flimsiest of securities and bonds to their customers and bought paper themselves that was only slightly more stable. Meanwhile, many firms took the capital raised from their own stock sales and poured it back into the market by speculating on other companies' stocks.

It could not go on forever. Sooner or later at some astronomical price there would not be buyers for all the stocks offered for sale. Prices would have to go down. But when prices did begin to fall, sellers would greatly outnumber buyers, as expectations for continued price increases ceased. This would have to produce panic selling and the quick explosion of the speculative bubble. It might be expected that thoughtful people, especially economists, businesspeople, and bankers, must have known that this would have to be the inevitable scenario. Surprisingly, almost no one did. Black Tuesday, October 29, 1929, the day when sellers finally outnumbered buyers, came as an incredible shock. Within a matter of hours the bubble burst and billions of dollars of paper wealth and profits evaporated into the air.

The crash did not by itself cause the Great Depression. Later it would become evident that many other factors played a larger contributory role. (Economists disagree among the precise causes, but some of the reasons offered are too much consumer borrowing, the decline of foreign trade, inadequate business investment, and wrong government policies.) Nevertheless, in people's minds at the time and later on, the crash and the Depression were inseparably tied together. Moreover, both events commonly were interpreted as business's fault. Businesspeople and business institutions, which for a hundred years or more had enjoyed the highest public confidence and respect, fell from public favor. The decade that had begun with business confidence and dominance ended in disillusion and disenchantment with the business system.

The Maturing of the Business System: 1929 to the Present

There has been a "mixed bag" of economic events since the crash: Depression followed by war, followed by a long prosperity period, followed by the recent uncertainties of inflation, unemployment, and energy shortages. For business it has been a time for adapting and adjusting old tactics and experimenting with new strategies.

ADJUSTING TO THE MIXED ECONOMY

The power and reach of government greatly expanded during the Depression. Under President Franklin Roosevelt's New Deal, new federal agencies, such as the Federal Power Commission, the Securities and Exchange Commission, the Federal Communications Commission, and the Civil Aeronautics Board, were created as watchdogs over certain industries. The National Labor Relations Act gave unions the right to organize and to bargain collectively on behalf of workers. Broad social legislation protected workers in their old age (Social Security Act) and from the ills of unemployment (Unemployment Insurance Act). Minimum-wage laws and welfare programs were constructed to aid the very poor. In the postcrash atmosphere, such programs were extremely popular with most Americans. Business was less than enthusiastic about these changes, but business was then seen as the enemy, the author of all the Depression ills.

Although there was much grumbling about "creeping socialism" and "that dictator Roosevelt," the business system eventually came to accept most of these changes. Only among small enterprisers, those who found the cost of government regulation and of government programs the hardest to bear, did strong antigovernment feeling persist to any great degree.

When World War II mobilization demanded that businesses subordinate their individual corporate strategies to the war effort, the adjustment was made easily. Wartime output and price controls and considerable central planning of production provoked no important criticism, the massive spending for war goods put plants and workers back to work and, not to be overlooked, produced very sizable corporate profits. Almost unnoticed at the time was the fact that government spending and deficits were growing to astronomical levels.

With recollections of the Depression fresh in mind, efforts to stabilize the economy through government spending and taxing actions (fiscal policy) and through the control of money and interest rates (monetary policy) grew after the war. Business adapted fairly quickly to these stabilization activities of government. By the 1960s most business leaders responded quite favorably to the concept of government managing the general economic conditions affecting employment, prices, and economic growth rates. In the general prosperity of the 1950s and 1960s, the stabilization efforts seemed to have ended the cruel downswings of the business cycle.

By the early 1970s, however, there was a change of attitude. Now the economy suffered the twin plagues of unemployment and inflation. (This double-headed monster was dubbed "stagflation.") Many economists and business observers now pointed to excessive government interference as the cause of the new economic problems. The old popularity of government stabilization policies, as well as direct government regulation of the economy, began to ebb. In 1980 Ronald Reagan captured the presidency on a broadly popular platform of pledging to trim government spending and government interference in the economy. The appeal was attractive not only to business but to virtually all sectors of the population.

CHANGES IN CORPORATE STRUCTURE

After World War II, most large business firms returned to the early strategy of increasing their size through mergers and corporate expansion. The objective was to obtain greater *economies of scale* (reductions in per-unit costs through greater efficiency) and to capture larger shares of the market. Corporations also continued their policy of diversification. Now, however, whole new product lines were added that were totally unrelated to each other. Through merger, a firm in one industry, such as tobacco, might penetrate an unrelated industry, such as apparel or the record industry. The objective in this case was to develop a broad mix of products that would insulate the firm from a sudden change of fortune in any particular market. If cigarette smoking fell from style among the young, there would still be designer jeans and rock music. (We shall examine those "conglomerate" mergers in more detail in issue 8.)

The expansion activities of big business produced greater concentration. As a result between 1948 and 1972 the largest 200 corporations increased their share of all corporate assets from 48 percent to 60 percent. Surprisingly, government did not return to a vigorous opposition to corporate growth. Antitrust prosecutions were kept to the very minimum.

Many firms also began to look beyond national markets and national production bases during this period. Naturally, American business had always been interested in expanding foreign trade; however, the rebuilding European and Japanese economies and the potential untapped income from Third World countries suggested a new approach. Rather than merely exporting American-made goods, many enterprises found it desirable to export capital.

American firms in growing numbers acquired overseas subsidiaries or built overseas plants to be closer to their markets. Others sought the advantages of cheaper foreign labor or raw materials for producing goods for American markets. By 1970 more than 3,500 American firms could qualify as *multinational businesses* (firms having their headquarters in one nation but carrying out production and direct sales operations in more than one country). By 1980 multinationals were accounting for about 25 percent of the total output of the noncommunist world.

CHANGES IN TECHNOLOGY AND PRODUCTION

The recent era witnessed startling technological changes. New inventions and innovations, many associated with the growing military and space industries, produced brand-new firms and industries in synthetics, electronics, telecommunications, and computers. Older businesses applied new technology to produce new products or to turn out old products in new ways. Firms devoted more and more of their financial resources and management talents to research and development of new products. Henry Ford may have been able to build his Model "T" the same way for fourteen years, but no modern firm with a plan to survive the competition in technology dared to be so complacent.

The increased production of more sophisticated products also demanded a change in production methods. Practically all firms shifted production techniques to a greater use of machines and less hand labor. More automatic processes (automation) were introduced in the production and assembly of goods.

The most important technological change was of course the rise of the computer. From a comparatively unwieldy and slow-reacting device for making business calculations and storing data in the late 1950s, the computer was transformed within two decades into the very centerpiece of business operations. With the development of the microprocessor, that quarter-square-inch sliver of silicon capable of holding up to 540,000 separate calculations, the intelligence of the computer and its uses within business began to grow exponentially. Once out of the bottle, the computer genie left little unchanged. Production moved beyond mere automation to CAD/CAM (Computer Assisted Design/Computer

Assisted Manufacturing). Robots—really computerized welding and assembly machines—put together autos and other goods that had actually been designed using computer technology.

Meanwhile, management practices were transformed as new computerized information systems were designed for gathering, storing, and interpreting vast amounts of data on virtually every aspect of the firm's operations. This required taking new approaches in the making of business decisions. It is no surprise that the computer boom made computer technology the nation's new growth industry, with computer related industries forging ahead of steel, autos, and the other old industrial standbys as the major employer and recipient of investment funds.

Such changes had profound effects upon the demand for labor and capital in manufacturing industries. Many older, skilled occupations were destroyed by the new technology, while other skills, such as using the computer and servicing the complex machines, were created. Evergreater amounts of capital were needed to carry out production; in fact, the capital requirements were an important contributory factor to the growth of corporate concentration that we examined in the last section.

CHANGES IN MARKETING AND MARKETS

After World War II, consumer incomes began a long period of steady growth. With both income and leisure time expanding, consumers had both the money and the time for "discretionary spending" (buying goods and services not really essential to filling the basic needs of food, clothing, and shelter). Business competition for these discretionary dollars grew very rapidly. New consumer products and services had to be developed and, most important, they had to be sold. With the advent of television, new product marketing took a giant leap forward and advertising came of age. Almost instantly, millions sitting before the tube could be informed of some new object, device, or substance (each sold by trade name, of course) with the claim that it would improve their lives. Whether or not consumers really believed the claims is unimportant; consume they did, as thousands of new products were introduced each year.

The rise in consumer spending also stimulated the growth of service-oriented industries. Services, strictly speaking, are an "intangible" commodity—such as E. F. Hutton's financial advice or H. & R. Block's tax preparation. In a broader sense, the quick food palaces, motels, and entertainment industries that spread along the accesses to interstate highways were also service suppliers to a nation of vacationers and travelers. The intangible was quickness, convenience, pleasure, or thrills. Until unemployment and inflation bit deep into consumers' discretionary income in the 1970s, the demand for "intangibles" made the service industry the fastest-growing sector of the American economy.

Looking Ahead

While our excursion through past business epochs may have illustrated the continuing role of change and adaptation in business affairs, the history lesson should not be improperly learned. It should not be concluded that just any old change will be good. There have been bad changes in the past that have cost business enterprise, workers, and citizens dearly. For instance, the quick and extensive introduction of new chemical-based technologies in the first half of this century produced a broad range of useful and profitable products—plastics, polymers, pesticides, and the like. However, we have learned recently that producing such products, at least producing them in the way we did, created havoc with the environment, with workers' health, and even with the well-being of consumers. Similarly, the emergence of the giant, multiproduct, multidivisioned, multinational corporation greatly lowered business production and marketing costs but also created serious management problems of control and raised questions as to whether merger decisions are really in the best interests of the owners. These and other current business problems might well have been avoided if business had adapted to past changes in different ways. Thus, while change may be inevitable and even greatly desired, it cannot be approached thoughtlessly.

The following selection of issues has been made with an eye toward focusing on the more important and more interesting changes that are being forced upon corporate agendas. For the most part they reflect issues that are not likely to go away very quickly. Each issue commences with a short introduction intended to set up the topic, to put the issue within the historical and present context of American business institutions. The selections chosen in each issue represent divergent and salient themes of business thought on each topic; however, the reader is cautioned that space prohibits more than a small sampling of the differing opinions.

Except where the issue does not lend itself to such an organization, the structure of the readings is intended to appear as a kind of debate. Even where the readings are not set in direct opposition to one another, the end-of-issue discussion questions are constructed to create a debating situation. As the reader will see very quickly, this book is about *choices*. At this point, some may recall Woody Allen's old admonition about choices, delivered in his take-off on a traditional commencement address: "More than any other time in history, mankind faces a crossroad. One path leads to despair and utter hopelessness, the other to total extinction. Let us pray we have the wisdom to choose correctly." Hopefully the reader will not see the choices in the following business issues as between "hopelessness" and "extinction" but simply as a range of reasonable alternatives for dealing with a current business problem.

In examining the readings, the student is cautioned not to conclude that the articles are set up in such a way that the "correct" view is obvious and the other views are set out as straw men. Indeed, there is no attempt in the readings selection to take a favored position. Rather, the different arguments and opinions are offered so that the reader should form an individual opinion as to which view (if any) is a good analysis of the problem or a good strategy for American enterprise.

Discussion and Review Questions

1. In what ways did the early merchant capitalist differ from the later industrial capitalist? Why was there such a difference in style?

2. Compare and contrast government's role in business affairs in the mid nineteenth century with the role played in the mid twentieth century. How do you react to the charge that "government is always antibusiness"?

3. How do you account for the rise of giant corporations?

4. How did the "3 Ds" strategy of early-twentieth-century corporations differ from the approach of the nineteenth-century industrial capitalist?

5. How do you account for the rise of consumer goods markets?

6. Looking back over the past one hundred years, what do you rate as the two or three most important factors in the development of the American business system? Defend your choices.

7. Pull out your crystal ball for a moment. What do you think will be the most important changes in business over the next one hundred years?

PART 2

THE ORGANIZATION AND STRUCTURE OF MODERN BUSINESS

ISSUE 1

How Well Is American Capitalism Working?

Before turning directly to the question posed in this issue, we first must attempt to answer a couple of more basic questions: What is capitalism? What is the nature of the modern American version of this social and economic system? Only then can we turn to an evaluation of how well our system is performing.

As we saw in our historical survey of American business, the social and economic framework within which business operates has undergone enormous changes over the past 200 years. As conceived in 1776 by the great Scottish economist and philosopher, Adam Smith, capitalism was to be the ultimate expression of economic and individual freedom. With a few strokes of a pen, Smith sought to set aside almost 1,500 years of economic ideas and institutions. Until only a century or two before Smith's *Wealth of Nations* appeared, traditional medieval economic and social thought, under the cloak of religious doctrine and the power of feudal institutions, had maintained a static economic order.

Adam Smith and the Rise of a Business Philosophy

For a world that had long known only restrictions and controls upon individual economic activity and which was dominated by aristocratic and inherited privilege, Smith proposed a new concept of economic freedom. His plan was simple enough: Allow everybody to pursue his own economic interests without interference or direction. The result would not be chaos and anarchy but the development of an orderly and rational market economy. Smith called this process "the invisible hand."

27

This would be possible if the following conditions were encouraged:

1. All individuals (Smith really meant only men) were permitted to acquire and hold property freely, the state acting only to protect the private property rights of individuals.
2. All individuals were free to select their own occupation or means of employing their wealth.
3. Business enterprises were free to hire resources and produce goods (or to withdraw from markets) according to their own choice. Profit seeking, of course, would be the guiding consideration in all these decisions, not the requirements of the state or the church.
4. Free competition among businesses and among individuals was to be sustained. No monopoly privileges should be granted to business, nor should labor be able to exercise monopolistic power through trade unions.
5. In the marketplace, buyers and sellers would act rationally, always attempting to buy as cheaply as possible and sell as dearly as possible. This haggling eventually would produce a price acceptable to all parties, or no sale would take place.
6. Meanwhile, government should play only the most minimal role by maintaining law and order and not interfering in the free competitive forces of the marketplace.

It is not surprising that Smith's economic ideas caught on and, in fact, are still popular among the most rugged economic individualists. With the market serving as both the carrot and the stick in economic behavior, there was little need for external regulation. *Capitalism* and *freedom* were one and the same in the minds of many. For the bright and the diligent (as well as anyone who might possess plain good luck), the unfettered economy provided incredible opportunities for success in commerce, finance, and manufacturing. In the United States, as we have seen already, the nineteenth century produced literally thousands of successful entrepreneurs who prospered in an essentially pure capitalist environment. Even today, the hope of entrepreneurial accomplishment induces tens of thousands of individuals to launch new business ventures each year (see issue three); yet, the modern capitalist environment is a far cry from the world of Adam Smith.

The Coming of the Mixed Economy

In surveying the American business system it is obvious that competition still exists; however, it is not a perfect competition. Often it is not price competition at all. With the possible exception of some farm markets where there are still large numbers of producers of similar and undifferentiated products (wheat, for instance), virtually every producer of goods and services has some control over price. The degree of control varies from industry to industry and between firms within an industry. Nevertheless, it does exist and it amounts to an important modification in our model of a free-enterprise economy.

The second important modification in the basic market model has been the growth of government in the economy. To Adam Smith government was to be limited to maintaining law and order at home, protecting the nation from invasion, and supplying certain *public goods* (roads, canals, and harbor improvements, for instance) that the market would not find profitable to produce. However, over the past two hundred years, government has been increasingly utilized to regulate markets, control output, direct resource use, tax, subsidize, and carry on a wide range of activities aimed at "balancing" the economy. The justification for these elaborations of government power, put in the simplest possible argument, is that a *mixture* of government intervention and private market decision making offers the best of the two worlds of central direction and individual freedom.

To see just how far we have moved from Adam Smith's neat little world, the following characteristics of our "mixed economy" might be contrasted with the preceding list by Smith:

1. While individuals can acquire and control property, this property may be taxed and regulated in use by government.
2. While individuals are free to choose their occupation, government, through student loans, higher education aid, antidiscrimination programs, training programs, subsidies to business, and so on, considerably directs labor participation in the economy.
3. Business enterprises' freedom to hire and use resources in their quest for profits has been limited by minimum wage laws, social legislation protecting workers, income taxes, and environmental and energy constraints.
4. Government antimonopoly law and government regulatory agencies closely monitor business's pricing and output decisions.
5. Apart from these direct economic interventions by government, the state also has assumed responsibility for the general performance of the economy through fiscal policy (government taxing and spending activities) and monetary policy (control over interest rates and borrowing). Government attempts to control the general level of economic activity by restraining inflation and reducing unemployment. Indeed, these fis-

cal and monetary policy activities by government are an explicit indication that the market model as it is understood by most Americans is not expected to work by itself.

The Two Visions Reconsidered

Which vision of capitalism, the traditional perspective of Adam Smith or the current mixed capitalist approach, serves the American business system best? At first glance, the traditional view of unregulated markets might seem to be the obvious answer. At least this would seem to be the case if only the louder public utterances of business leaders were listened to. However, the matter is not so simple.

Not only have the contours of the business economy changed, as we saw in the introductory chapter, but a great many business leaders have more or less cheerfully adapted to these changes. Many would not wish to return to the unstable and unpredictable days of *laissez faire* competition. While big government and big labor unions may restrict some of business's freedom, many business leaders are willing to accept these restraints to obtain the security that a more intensively controlled business environment provides.

The modern division of opinion among businesspeople on the question of the degree of market freedom is easily apparent in the two representative arguments that follow. The first, by William Simon, Secretary of the Treasury under President Nixon, urges a return to the older habits of traditional *laissez faire* capitalism; the second, by investment banker Felix Rohatyn, rejects Smith's world. In particular, Rohatyn opposes the conservative economic philosophy of the Reagan administration and calls for more control, planning, and government intervention. The point at issue is not a minor matter of philosophical debate. It represents a basic point of disagreement among contemporary business leaders—whether or not the nation would be better served by an "industrial policy" that integrates business and government planning or by less government intervention. It is probably the single most important controversy confronting American business today. Yet for all the disagreement between these opposing business perspectives, there is a major point of agreement: Both sides, although for different reasons, do not see American capitalism as working very well.

1.1   The System Works—If Given a Chance

WILLIAM E. SIMON

Our Founding Fathers must have read *The Wealth of Nations* with great satisfaction, for, as Smith himself observed, the American colonies had been practicing what he preached for more than a century. In their dedication to individual liberty, the earliest leaders of this nation were determined to leave citizens free to seek their fortunes with a minimum of state interference, and a free-market system rooted in "natural law" had been the brilliant result. From its very birth America was a natural laboratory for the liberty-loving philosophies of such men as Locke and Smith, and this country proved to be the noblest experiment ever devised by man. Not coincidentally, it also proved to be the form of society that produced a degree of wealth and a standard of living for the "common man" that had never before been seen. America was by the very definition of its founders a capitalist nation.

In sum, individual liberty *includes* the individual's economic freedom, and the Founding Fathers knew it. They had good reason to leave the productive activities of men as free as possible. Their calculations, like those of Adam Smith, were correct. When men are left free by the state to engage in productive action, guided by self-interest above all, they do create the most efficient and powerful production system that is possible to their society. And the greatest misfortune in America today is that most people do not understand this. They don't understand our traditional economic system precisely because it is not, in the ordinary sense, a system at all—meaning a conscious organization or detailed plan. Essentially, as always, what they don't understand is how, in the *absence* of conscious planning, millions of men can function efficiently together to produce wealth. But it is precisely that *absence* of conscious planning that accomplishes the miracle! To this very day—

obscured by a tragic amount of government intervention since the thirties—it is *still* Adam Smith's "invisible hand" and "the system of natural liberty" that are producing our goods and services, creating our jobs, paying our salaries, financing our government, and generating American wealth.

The enormously complex and productive system known as a free market operates without conscious supervision and direction. It works as follows: Day in and day out, people engage in economic activities called businesses—small individual ones and gigantic ones held together by a tissue of voluntary individual contracts. They organize and allocate resources by selling and buying in markets which respond sensitively to the wishes of individuals. Each consumer "votes," in effect, with his dollar in untold thousands of market "elections," and his vote is automatically translated into shifts of resources into the desired products and services. The products for which people are willing to pay an adequate price are produced; things for which people are not willing to pay an adequate price are not produced.

The free market is nothing but the sum of these interacting individual decisions. It is the most individualistic and the most democratic economic system conceivable. It works with no conscious direction. There is no single purpose or goal. Each "voter" has his own purposes and goals; he seeks to maximize his rewards, to avoid or to cut his losses. There are literally billions of purposes, billions of decisions, billions of adjustments every day as inventors, entrepreneurs, middlemen, employers, workers, buyers, and sellers pursue their own respective self-interests.

And what is the end result of these billions of individual decisions? It is the torrential outpouring of man-made wealth that characterizes the history of American capitalism—in which 28 percent of the total production of the human race is created by only 5 percent of the world's population. American capitalism has generated the most astounding flood of imaginative goods and services ever to have appeared on the face of the globe—goods and services produced in inconceivable variety and abundance and (until the relatively recent invasion of government into the marketplace) with maximum efficiency. This is the system that has endowed the average American with the highest standard of living in the world and in history—even if the job of eliminating the last pocket of poverty is not yet completed. That is what Adam Smith said would happen if men were left free by the state to produce, and that is exactly what happened. Paul McCracken, former chairman of the Council of Economic Advisers, observes: "Great masses of the world's people do not . . . have a material level of living significantly better than did their ancestors a generation ago. . . . But we have been doubling the material levels of living for the average American roughly every 40 years."

Defenders of the free enterprise system, struggling in the face of growing antagonism and noisy heresies, often seek to defend it by reeling off statistical evidence of the productivity of the free market. For example, a memo that landed on my desk in the Treasury Department contained these figures to illustrate the "success of the free enterprise system":

- 96 percent of all American homes have a telephone;
- 50 percent of all Americans own at least one automobile;
- 96 percent of all American homes have at least one television;
- after American farmers finish feeding the U.S., they export 60 percent of their wheat and rice; 50 percent of their soybeans; one quarter of their grain sorghum and one fifth of their corn. The U.S. provides half the world's wheat.
- American farms produce this despite the fact that since 1940 the number of U.S. farms and farm workers has decreased by two thirds. During that time, however, agricultural output has increased by 75 percent.

Now all this is very true, and indeed, it doesn't scratch the surface of what one could say about the American economy, if one wished to make such lists. The extraordinary wealth of our nation is well known throughout the world. The statistics which record the tangible results of that system nevertheless miss the invisible dimension. The single most awe-inspiring thing about our economic system lies in what is *absent*, what is *not* perceivable to the naked eye. It is the fact that the flood of wealth emerges from the lack of any direction of the economic process, from the lack of government control, from the lack of state-imposed or "national" purposes and goals. The capitalist miracle occurred in the United States, the politically freest nation in the world, precisely because this explosion of wealth is uniquely a result of *individual liberty*. That is the true defense of capitalism. That is what most people do not understand—and that is what deserves to be shouted from the rooftops. . . .

There is nothing subjective or biased about this view that political and economic freedom are inextricably related. It is conceded as objective fact by even the most interventionist of economists. Arthur Okun, for example, a liberal economist who was chairman of Lyndon Johnson's Council of Economic Advisers, readily grants the integral relationship of a free market and political freedom. He says:

> A market economy helps to safeguard political rights against encroachment by the state. Private ownership and decision-making circumscribe the power of the government—or, more accurately, of those who run the government—and hence its ability to infringe on the domain of rights. In the polar case of a fully collectivized economy, political rights would be seriously jeopardized. If the government commanded all the productive resources of the society, it could suppress dissent, enforce conformity and snuff out democracy.[1]

Ironically, this connection between political and economic freedom is perfectly understood by totalitarians. Their "understanding," however, has a morbid cast. The communist theoretician knows precisely how to *destroy* individual freedom; he destroys economic freedom, and the job is done. More specifically, he expropriates private property, the means of production, and he forbids profits. He places the entire production–exchange–consumption chain under the direct rule of the state, which means, of course, that he places the physical life of each individual at the mercy of the state. That is the essence of tyranny. . . .

Despite our comparative wealth, our situation is unusually ominous, for cultural, as well as economic, reasons. In the United States a population accustomed to historically unprecedented liberty is now ruled, almost exclusively, by a political–social–intellectual elite that is committed to the belief that government can control our complex marketplace by fiat better than the people can by individual choice and that is ideologically committed to social democracy or democratic socialism. So blinding is this commitment that this intellectual elite can watch the social democracies slide into stagnation and chaos around them and never question the interventionist assumptions which have caused that stagnation and chaos—assumptions they share. They believe, tragically, that one can drastically mix polar political opposites, that, to quote *Newsweek*, one can fuse the dynamics of "communism and capitalism within one society with no evil consequences. . . ."

During my tenure at Treasury I watched with incredulity as businessmen ran to the government in every crisis, whining for handouts or protection from the very competition that has made this system so productive. I saw Texas ranchers, hit by drought, demanding government-guaranteed loans; giant milk cooperatives lobbying for higher price supports; major airlines fighting deregulation to preserve their monopoly status; giant companies like Lockheed seeking federal assistance to rescue them from sheer inefficiency; bankers, like David Rockefeller, demanding government bailouts to protect them from their ill-conceived investments; network executives, like William Paley of CBS, fighting to preserve regulatory restrictions and to block the emergence of competitive cable and pay TV. And always, such gentlemen proclaimed their devotion to free enterprise and their opposition to the arbitrary intervention into our economic life by the state. Except, of course, for their own case, which was always unique and which was justified by their immense concern for the public interest.

My own response to such businessmen was harsh, and I warned those with whom I discussed these practices that they were indeed, as Lenin had predicted, braiding the rope that would be used to hang them. FDR used to laugh scornfully at the businessmen who came creeping to him, hat in hand, to obtain government favors while they preached about the sanctity of free enterprise. But I am not amused by businessmen of this type. They have supplied powerful ammunition to those who are anxious to demonstrate that the free market and freedom itself are intrinsically flawed.

Businessmen, too, have intensified the despotic regulatory trends by their secretive attempts to fight them—not by means of courageous open battle, but by the pathetically short-range and cowardly attempts to bribe those with political power over their destinies. As economist Murray Weidenbaum has pointed out, much, if not all, of the corruption of the business ethic that has come to light, at home and abroad, is a direct "solution" to the problem of irrational government intervention. Bribes in particular are usually attempts by businessmen to appease the bureaucrats on all levels of the government, federal, state, and local, who wield an extortionist power over trade and production. And many campaign contributions and bribes to politicians are perceived by businessmen as "insurance policies" against this extortionist power. Such actions by business are not just unlawful and unethical—which is sufficient reason not to take them—but also impractical. Revelations of these bribes have reinforced antibusiness attitudes and fed the ideological portrayal of capitalism as a criminal phenomenon. I was appalled by the flood of bribery cases which emerged while I was in office and spoke out strongly against such businessmen. I was not only angered by the lack of ethics, but also horrified by the certainty that such conduct would inevitably bring more punitive and destructive regulation upon our productive system. And it did.

Having said all this, however, I still believe it is obvious that business, seen as a whole, is more sinned against than sinning. This view clashes, of course, with the conventional liberal wisdom that business is "really" controlling the regulatory agencies. It is easy enough to arrive at an objective assessment of where the power "really" lies. Just ask yourself if the dictatorial and destructive situation I have described in the regulatory agencies could possibly exist if business "really" controlled these agencies. Would men who "controlled" them inflict 57,027 pages of new regulations on themselves in one year? Would they inflict costs mounting to the billions on themselves? Would they incessantly ban their own products? Would they drag out for years crucial decisions on which their financial lives depend? Would they devour their investment capital, destroy their own productivity, restrict their innovative capacity? Would they drive themselves into bankruptcy? Obviously not. The balance of power—and the balance of terror—lie on the side of the regulators. *Some* businessmen do indeed extract advantage from the situation, but the victimization of *all* businessmen in America is incessant. And the one crime of businessmen as a group, to which few call attention but which I condemn profoundly, is that business, on the whole, has been gripped by cowardly silence in the face of this consistent violation of its liberty and interests. It is its final, and possibly its worst, betrayal of the free enterprise system.

Note

1. Okun, Arthur. *Equality and Efficiency: The Big Tradeoff.* The Brookings Institution, 1965, p. 38.

1.2   The System Needs Help

FELIX G. ROHATYN

I have been in business for 34 years and I believe we are facing the most dangerous worldwide economic situation of my professional experience. We are facing it with a political philosophy that appears to be uncaring and backward and without a governmental process worthy of the name. We are facing it with less international cooperation than at any time since World War II.

All over the world, trade and economic activity is contracting, unemployment is growing and financial structures are getting weaker. In America, a victory over inflation (which may turn out to be Pyrrhic) has been achieved at a very high cost in terms of unemployment, a collapse of investment and a polarization of our political system. The present best-case scenario for 1983 calls for a slow recovery for the economy. That will not be good enough for our basic industries, not good enough for investment in public-works projects, not good enough for employment and not good enough for the health of a seriously strained international banking system. . . .

The Reagan philosophy construes government to be the source of most evils; virtue is reserved for the theoretical free marketplace. Since such a philosophy does not believe in government, it has no process with which to govern. The incoherence of the program combined with the absence of a means to carry it out aggravates rather than diminishes many of our more serious difficulties.

One of the strongest lessons that we have learned from the economic failures of the past decade is that the *way* we reach and implement a program or policy is fully as important as its theoretical and substantive design. The problems we face cannot be solved without cooperation, and the price of that cooperation is involvement in the decision-making process.

My conservative Republican friends take me to task for what they consider my dangerously interventionist, liberal views. But I believe that large social, economic and political problems can be handled only when there is a conviction that government has not only a right but a duty to intervene when imbalances become too great. The process must accommodate the bargaining and all the constituencies must be heard in order to find solutions. This is particularly true in times of economic strain, when sacrifice has to be negotiated; over the long run, it cannot be legislated.

Our most urgent national objective has to be the reduction of unemployment through high economic growth rates and low interest rates. Our objectives for growth must be raised from their present modest rates and coordinated with Europe and Japan. A coherent program to bring this about must begin with a bipartisan social contract involving the Executive, the Congress, business and labor, and the Federal Reserve in an effort to bring about a balanced budget within five years and maintain low interest rates. . . .

We must then face the issue of employment. We cannot stimulate our economy sufficiently and reduce unemployment without major investment in industry and rebuilding the infrastructure. To reach those sectors that normal market forces or government policy have neglected, new structures should be created, notably a modern version of the Reconstruction Finance Corporation of the 1930's.

The original R.F.C., set up by Herbert Hoover and energized by Franklin Roosevelt, functioned essentially from 1932 to 1945, though it lasted until 1953. During that period, it saved thousands of banks, railroads and businesses, financed public works and ultimately defense plants in World War II. It created organizations functioning today, such as the Commodity Credit Corporation and the Rural Electrification Administration, and it returned a profit of $500 million to the taxpayers.

The 1980's are different from the 1930's, of course, but the basic principles of a modern R.F.C. would be the same. The R.F.C. would be the investment and development bank of the Government, publicly accountable, but sheltered from political pressures. It would be a focus of American commitment to our basic industrial underpinning as well as to rebuilding cities, harbors, transportation systems—the complex of facilities known as infrastructure.

A commitment to basic industry would not be easy, but it is important. A major world power like America cannot be credible without a strong, competitive manufacturing base.

Today, high technology is a very glamorous notion; basic industries such as automobiles and steel are not. But the auto industry is one of the largest customers of microprocessors as well as of industrial robots and many other high-technology products. In the future, we will employ far fewer workers per automobile or per ton of steel. But that does not mean that those same workers, with proper training, cannot make the robots, the machine tools and the many products of tomorrow that will go into a car or a ton of steel. That will not happen, however, if we take the position that we do not care about the survival of our auto industry as long as we make better semiconductors. This year the American auto industry will manufacture roughly 5,000,000 cars; the Japanese will manufacture 7,000,000 cars, of which we will buy about 1,700,000. What would the Japanese minister of industry say to a suggestion to cut his auto industry in half in order to invest in biotechnology? Obviously, retraining for the industries of the future has to be part of any economic and social program, but we must first save what we have today.

At the same time, there is much talk in Washington today of a need to invest in public infrastructure, partly to create jobs and partly to fill a real need. The program proposed by the Administration calls for a five-year, $32.9 billion highway and mass-transit investment, to be financed largely by the proposed increased gasoline tax. No one knows what level of investment may be required to bring our national capital plant back from its present decay. Some estimates run to over $1 trillion. The New York City mass-transit system alone is estimated to require $5 billion over the next five years, and the city as a whole has estimated a need for up to $40 billion during the 1980's. The Federal Government will obviously have to make a much greater effort than is currently being discussed, because local government cannot afford it.

Slowdowns in the growth of Social Security and health-care costs are absolutely essential. At the same time, our defense program cannot be immune from both retrenchment and transfer of funds to domestic nonmilitary investment. If we are serious about defense, we should reinstate the draft and increase our conventional capability. The draft is not an economy measure but a philosophical one: National service cannot be limited to the children of the poor and the minorities; it must include the children of the middle class and the well-to-do. The current target for defense spending over the next five years is about $1.6 trillion. It is hard to believe that $100 billion could not be provided for the R.F.C. and other nonmilitary needs from those funds; in addition, considerable economies could be made in the military programs themselves. . . .

In the industrial field, the R.F.C.'s investments would be limited to those basic industries such as automobiles and steel that could be made competitive. The R.F.C. would provide funds only if there were concessions on the part of labor, management, suppliers and bankers sufficient to make the company competitive with the best foreign producers.

Similarly, in the public-infrastructure field the R.F.C.'s capital would be available only if local support—such as tax changes, union productivity and wage concessions, fare and user fees—assured the viability of the projects. These would include mass-transit systems, sewers, roads, bridges and so on.

The need for political independence for an organization like the R.F.C. is obvious. It would need to husband its resources and to target them. It should require matching investments from the private sector in the case of industrial investments and by local governments in the case of public investments.

The R.F.C. could not be a substitute for an industrial or a regional policy. It would be a useful tool and a needed focus. It would be a small part of a large program, but it could play a critical, *temporary* role. It should self-destruct in 10 years.

Improving life in the inner-city ghetto would be another objective of an R.F.C. Regional development corporations as well as city and state business and labor groups would be created to work with the R.F.C. If the auto industry and Middle Western cities were to get new funds, for example, the program should include inner-city manufacturing facilities tied directly to inner-city school systems, union commitments to minority apprenticeship and possibly two-tier minimum wages during training. The programs should be run by private industry, in facilities financed by the R.F.C. and leased to the companies, in the same manner as the defense plants leased by the R.F.C. during World War II.

Any such program of government-assisted financing obviously would require the input of business and labor as well as government. The board of the R.F.C. would be an obvious focus for this; it would also become a focus for a policy that could relate wage increases to real productivity improvements.

The kind of stimulus our economy needs, both to insure our own future and to avoid a worldwide credit crisis, is much greater than the current forecasts. It will require guarding against a renewal of inflation caused by wage settlements in excess of productivity improvements. Wage and price controls in an advanced industrial society cannot work for long, and a formal, legislated policy, such as a tax-based incomes policy, is probably neither practical nor fair. However, a change in our labor cost structure has to be examined if low inflation is to coexist with high growth. The most practical way to approach this would be for all major labor contracts to expire simultaneously every year, with wage increases related to existing economic conditions and current inflation; significant elements of profit-sharing should reward real productivity improvements. We should take a cue from Japan and Germany and have an annual, national wage negotiation involving business, labor and often the government. The result should be keyed to the performance of the economy. This is the practical equivalent of an incomes policy for most of the economy. . . .

Without an active business–labor–government process of cooperation, coupled with real bipartisanship, none of this can happen. Neither an R.F.C. nor a new approach to labor costs nor a balanced budget with all its implications nor a new and fair Federalism will be politically possible. Such a result will not happen with a hands-off government and a blind faith in the market process.

I believe that we are presently running not only economic risks but risks to our political system. Many of my friends believe that I am seeing ghosts, and I hope they are right. But I did grow up in Europe in the 1930's and I have seen the fragility of democracy when economic events get out of hand. We are now told that basic, permanent unemployment in this country will be close to 6 or 7 percent, but our current, real unemployment would reach 14 percent or more if one were to count unemployment honestly. Not counting those who have given up looking for work is like listing only the walking wounded as casualties in a war. This means that almost every third family in America will be affected. Educational and income disparities are increasing, and even though fairness is a much overused term, too many people question the fairness of the present program to be ignored. A no-growth economy causes the most suffering among those who have the least; it is unfair but inevitable. The recent budget and tax programs, however, have created more instead of less disparity. They will have to be corrected. A democracy, to survive, must at the very least appear to be fair. This is no longer the case in America.

In looking for alternatives to Reaganomics, we therefore need a different philosophy and a different process. We also need a Democratic Party less frightened of its past and more willing to assert its own philosophy and process. There are desirable aspects to Reaganomics and they deservedly enjoy a considerable measure of popular support. Those objectives of Reaganomics that are desirable should be included in an alternative program. An R.F.C., after all, is the liberal version of stimulating the supply side of the economy and a gasoline tax is a perfectly respectable way to tax consumption in order to encourage investment. A balanced budget is a completely reasonable goal as long as everyone pays the price, including Social Security and the military. A viable version of New Federalism should undoubtedly get support among all groups.

All over the world, systems of the right and of the left are trying to find the answers to the same question: how to have a viable economy and a fair and balanced social structure. There may be no viable answers to some of the problems, but there is no alternative to trying, being willing to fail and trying again. There is no alternative to real bipartisanship any more than there is an alternative to real business/labor/government cooperation. . . .

We can no longer deal marginally with a problem that vastly transcends our shores. Whether a Republican or a Democrat is President, bipartisanship at home and statesmanship and cooperation abroad will be required. Franklin Delano Roosevelt's type of leadership in wartime will have to be re-created in the 1980's.

Discussion and Review Questions

1. Summarize Adam Smith's economic and social philosophy. Why is it particularly attractive to a business society?

2. In what ways does modern "mixed capitalism" differ from Smith's "classical" view of the economic system?

3. On what particular grounds does Simon justify his assertion that the "free enterprise system has been a success?"

4. Why does Simon oppose the enlargement of government intervention in the economy?

5. On what grounds does Rohatyn argue for "government intervention in the economy?"

6. How would you describe Rohatyn's view toward the future of the American economic system? Obviously, he sees trouble ahead, but what kinds of trouble in particular?

7. Which philosophy, Rohatyn's or Simon's, do you think represents the majority point of view among American business leaders?

ISSUE 2

Is Business Socially Responsible?

Until comparatively recently, the question of business's social responsibility was mostly a "nonquestion." Simply put, the responsibility of an enterprise was to earn a reasonable profit for its owners. The idea that a firm had broad social obligations—hiring the disadvantaged, paying special attention to environmental considerations, undertaking philanthropic activities, and the like—has come to the front as an important business issue only since the social and political activism of the 1960s. However, while few enterprises in the past dealt directly with social responsibility issues, the somewhat narrower question of business ethics has long been a matter of public and business concern. Before turning to the modern social responsibility debate, it is useful therefore to digress a bit and take up the antecedent question of whether or not business is, or even should be, guided by a clear sense of ethical values. In this way the modern-day social responsibility arguments become more intelligible.

In the introduction, we noted the changed social expectations and political conditions that have produced a "mixed" capitalist economy—a business system that operates within the framework of expanding governmental and legal restraints. Obviously there is a constant tension between the "freedom" expectations of the entrepreneur and the "performance" expectations of an increasingly active and vocal society at large. In surveying the development and application of business law, there is little doubt that the legal restraints on business "freedom" have been drawn a bit tighter.

Apart from the standards of conduct defined and enforced under the law, however, society also is governed by certain generally accepted ethical standards. *Ethics deals with the determination and acting upon what is considered by the society to be morally right.* Ethics may be thought of as either a written or unwritten code of conduct that deals with questions of what is "correct," "fair," "just," or "proper" in a given situation. At the same time the ethical code also spells out what behavior is "incorrect," "unfair," "unjust," and "improper."

Early Ethical Constraints

The maintenance of ethical standards in business affairs has a long and uneven history in Western nations. In the Middle Ages, the Catholic Church prescribed rigorous moral rules to govern business conduct. Under pain of eternal damnation, a producer was compelled to sell at a *just price.* Simply stated, this meant the seller could not take advantage of the buyer's need for the good or the fact that a sudden shortage of the product placed the seller in an advantageous position. From the Church's point of view, there was a higher social good and moral principle to be considered than simply the well-being of the merchant.

Such restraints to earning profits naturally enough discouraged business activity; however, with the Protestant revolt against Catholicism in the sixteenth century, the foundation of a new business morality was laid down, one that made its way quickly to American shores. According to the new Protestant ethic, individual hard work was good, idleness was evil, and individuals had a right to the produce of their labors. The accumulation of wealth became a sign of God's blessings and evidence of living a good and holy life. Nevertheless, the Protestant ethic still prescribed that business affairs be carried on fairly and consistent with the Bible's teachings. The individual capitalist could be a hard, Scrooge-like employer and a shrewd buyer and seller, but he must always be honest. Moreover, the uses of one's wealth could never be for simple gratification of the flesh.

The Decline of Ethical Constraint

The high morality of early capitalism began to fall away in the nineteenth century. John D. Rockefeller did indeed continue to teach his Sunday School class as his Standard Oil Company grew to immense size and wealth. However, any similarity with the Protestant ethic ended there. Old John D. had no reservations about bribing competitor's employees, paying kickbacks to helpful railroads, or lying to congressional investigating committees. The new business ethic of the nineteenth century took its ethical standard from Charles Darwin's theory of evolution. Twisting Darwin's theory of the development of species into a "survival of the fittest" philosophy, it was possible to justify practically any legal (and some very illegal) business activities as being ethical. After all, if the law of the jungle worked for nature, why couldn't it work for the capitalist entrepreneur? The ethic of "survival of the fittest" reduced the moral concerns of business behavior to an all-time low. No one put it any better than Daniel Drew, builder, speculator, and, some would say, "pirate" of the Erie Railroad. Summing up his own business success in the 1880s, Drew observed:

> Sentiment is alright up in the part of the city where your home is. But downtown, no. Down there the dog that snaps the quickest gets the bone. Friendship is very nice for a Sunday afternoon when you're sitting around the dinner table with your relations, talking about the sermon that morning. But 9:00 Monday morning, notions should be brushed aside like cobwebs from a machine. I never took any stock in a man who mixed up business with anything else. He can go into other things outside of business hours, but when he's in the office, he ought not to have a relation in the world—and least of all a poor relation.

Daniel Drew's split view of the world may have maintained his and other business leaders' sanity, but it made many other people angry. The frauds, bribery, stock manipulation, and other schemes of nineteenth-century business produced a growing public reaction. The revolt came from both ordinary citizens and from businesspeople who did not subscribe to the law of the jungle. The public clamor soon led to direct government intervention in business affairs.

The Modern Approach to Business Ethics and Social Responsibility

By the turn of the twentieth century, most business leaders came to realize that the no-ethics, "survival of the fittest" approach was not in business's best interest. Increasingly after 1900, businesses began to organize trade associations to encourage the private and voluntary development of acceptable ethical standards for ordinary business behavior. These associations drew up codes for their members and "enforced" them under threat of expulsion from the association.

Faced with mounting public reaction to business in general after the Depression of the 1930s and again during the Vietnam War and Watergate years, many individual enterprises set about developing their own corporate codes of conduct. The reasons usually given were honest enough: Most Americans believed, rightly or wrongly, that big business had a poor record for honesty and integrity and it was therefore necessary to develop a new public image. Once developed, the corporate code was distributed widely among employees and also given ample advertising space.

The efforts by business to develop voluntary ethical codes doubtless have improved the everyday standards of business performance from the "no-standards" days of the late nineteenth century. However, the comparatively narrow issue of business ethical choices began to blossom into larger concerns in the 1960s. Whereas most earlier ethical matters dealt primarily with two-party situations—a buyer or buyers on the one hand and a seller or sellers on the other—recent responsibility questions have focused upon third-party effects. These third-party responsibilities have been increasingly spelled out in laws affecting employment decisions, the environment, product safety, and much more.

The decision to hire, for instance, is no longer simply a matter between employer (buyer) and worker (seller). Under the Civil Rights Act of 1964 and its later legal interpretations, employment activities of a firm must consider "the pattern of minority and sexual employment" within the firm. In other words, employers must consider the third-party effect of whether their hiring policies reflect discrimination against certain groups.

Probably the most troublesome third-party effects come in the area of environmental protection. Previously, business only had to consider direct costs (labor, materials, equipment, and the like) in producing a good. Now indirect costs, or social costs, must be calculated as well. As the law has expanded to protect third parties, individuals, or whole groups of people from the effects of industrial or product pollution, business production costs have risen. There is no such thing as a free lunch, and there is no such thing as a free emission control system.

While few businesspeople would maintain that business need not be concerned with ethical and social responsibility choices, there is disagreement on the reasonableness of society's expectations in these areas and the ways in which such expectations take on the force of law.

In the first of our readings, Milton Friedman, Nobel Prize winner and featured writer for *Newsweek*, argues that the current concern over business ethical standards and social responsibility has begun to impose legal and moral restraints upon business operations that can lead only to the undoing of business enterprise itself. Countering this rejection of ethical and social responsibility arguments, Richard DeGeorge specifies particular areas of business's moral responsibility. Finally, businessman Albert Carr takes up the mundane but very sensible question of how a businessperson operates morally on a day-to-day basis.

2.1   The Social Responsibility of Business Is to Increase Its Profits

MILTON FRIEDMAN

When I hear businessmen speak eloquently about the "social responsibilities of business in a free-enterprise system," I am reminded of the wonderful line about the Frenchman who discovered at the age of 70 that he had been speaking prose all his life. The businessmen believe that they are defending free enterprise when they declaim that business is not concerned "merely" with profit but also with promoting desirable "social" ends; that business has a "social conscience" and takes seriously its responsibilities for providing employment, eliminating discrimination, avoiding pollution and whatever else may be the catchwords of the contemporary crop of reformers. In fact they are—or would be if they or anyone else took them seriously—preaching pure and unadulterated socialism. Businessmen who talk this way are unwitting puppets of the intellectual forces that have been undermining the basis of a free society these past decades.

The discussions of the "social responsibilities of business" are notable for their analytical looseness and lack of rigor. What does it mean to say that "business" has responsibilities? Only people can have responsibilities. A corporation is an artificial person and in this sense may have artificial responsibilities, but "business" as a whole cannot be said to have responsibilities, even in this vague sense. The first step toward clarity to examining the doctrine of the social responsibility of business is to ask precisely what it implies for whom.

Presumably, the individuals who are to be responsible are businessmen, which means individual proprietors or corporate executives. Most of the discussion of social responsibility is directed at corporations, so in what follows I shall mostly neglect the individual proprietors and speak of corporate executives.

In a free-enterprise, private-property system, a corporate executive is an employee of the owners of the business. He has direct responsibility to his employers. That responsibility is to conduct the business in accordance with their desires, which generally will be to make as much money as possible while conforming to the basic rules of the society, both those embodied in law and those embodied in ethical custom. Of course, in some cases his employers may have a different objective. A group of persons might establish a corporation for an eleemosynary purpose—for example, a hospital or a school. The manager of such a corporation will not have money profit as his objectives but the rendering of certain services.

In either case, the key point is that, in his capacity as a corporate executive, the manager is the agent of the individuals who own the corporation or establish the eleemosynary institution, and his primary responsibility is to them.

Needless to say, this does not mean that it is easy to judge how well he is performing his task. But at least the criterion of performance is straightforward, and the persons among whom a voluntary contractual arrangement exists are clearly defined.

Of course, the corporate executive is also a person in his own right. As a person, he may have many other responsibilities that he recognizes or assumes voluntarily—to his family, his conscience, his feelings of charity, his church, his clubs, his city, his country. He may feel impelled by these responsibilities to devote part of his income to causes he regards as worthy, to refuse to work for particular corporations, even to leave his job, for example, to join his country's armed forces. If we wish, we may refer to some of these responsibilities as "social responsibilities." But in these respects he is acting as a principal, not an agent; he is spending his own money or time or energy, not the money of his employers or the time or energy he has contracted to devote to their purposes. If these are "social responsibilities," they are the social responsibilities of individuals, not of business.

What does it mean to say that the corporate executive has a "social responsibility" in his capacity as businessman? If this statement is not pure rhetoric, it must mean that he is to act in some way that is not in the interest of his employers. For example, that he is to refrain from increasing the price of the product in order to contribute to the social objective of preventing inflation, even though a price increase would be in the best interests of the corporation. Or that he is to make expenditures on reducing pollution beyond the amount that is in the best interests of the corporation or that is required by law in order to contribute to the social objective of improving the environment. Or that, at the expense of corporate profits, he is to hire "hardcore" unemployed instead of better qualified available workmen to contribute to the social objective of reducing poverty.

In each of these cases, the corporate executive would be spending someone else's money for a general social interest. Insofar as his actions in accord with his "social responsibility" reduce returns to stockholders, he is spending their money. Insofar as his actions raise the price to customers, he is spending the customers' money. Insofar as his actions lower the wages of some employees, he is spending their money.

The stockholders or the customers or the employees could separately spend their own money on the particular action if they wished to do so. The executive is exercising a distinct "social responsibility," rather than serving as an agent of the stockholders or the customers or the employees, only if he spends the money in a different way than they would have spent it.

But if he does this, he is in effect imposing taxes, on the one hand, and deciding how the tax proceeds shall be spent, on the other.

This process raises political questions on two levels: principle and consequences. On the level of political principle, the imposition of taxes and the expenditure of tax proceeds are governmental functions. We have established elaborate constitutional, parliamentary and judicial provisions to control these functions, to assure that taxes are imposed so far as possible in accordance with the preferences and desires of the public—after all, "taxation without representation" was one of the battle cries of the American Revolution. We have a system of checks and balances to separate the legislative function of imposing taxes and enacting expenditures from the executive function of collecting taxes and administering expenditure programs and from the judicial function of mediating disputes and interpreting the law.

Here the businessman—self-selected or appointed directly or indirectly by stockholders—is to be simultaneously legislator, executive and jurist. He is to decide whom to tax by how much and for what purpose, and he is to spend the proceeds—all this guided only by general exhortations from on high to restrain inflation, improve the environment, fight poverty and so on and on.

The whole justification for permitting the corporate executive to be selected by the stockholders is that the executive is an agent serving the interests of his principal. This justification disappears when the corporate executive imposes taxes and spends the proceeds for "social" purposes. He becomes in effect a public employee, a civil servant, even though he remains in name an employee of a private enterprise. On grounds of political principle, it is intolerable that such civil servants—insofar as their actions in the name of social responsibility are real and not just window-dressing—should be selected as they are now. If they are to be civil servants, then they must be elected through a political process. If they are to impose taxes and make expenditures to foster "social" objectives, then political machinery must be set up to make the assessment of taxes and to determine through a political process the objectives to be served.

This is the basic reason why the doctrine of "social responsibility" involves the acceptance of the socialist view that political mechanisms, not market mechanisms, are the appropriate way to determine the allocation of scarce resources to alternative uses.

On the grounds of consequences, can the corporate executive in fact discharge his alleged "social responsibilities"? On the one hand, suppose he could get away with spending the stockholders' or customers' or employees' money. How is he to know how to spend it? He is told that he must contribute to fighting inflation. How is he to know what action of his will contribute to that end? He is presumably an expert in running his company—in producing a product or selling it or financing it. But nothing about his selection makes him an expert on inflation. Will his holding down the price of his product reduce inflationary pressure? Or, by leaving more spending power in the hands of his customers, simply divert it elsewhere? Or, by forcing him to produce less because of the lower price, will it simply contribute to shortages? Even if he could answer these questions, how much cost is he justified in imposing on his stockholders, customers and employees for this social purpose? What is his appropriate share and what is the appropriate share of others?

And, whether he wants to or not, can he get away with spending his stockholders', customers' or employees' money? Will not the stockholders fire him? (Either the present ones or those who take over when his actions in the name of social responsibility have reduced the corporation's profits and the price of its stock.) His customers and his employees can desert him for other producers and employers less scrupulous in exercising their social responsibilities.

This facet of "social responsibility" doctrine is brought into sharp relief when the doctrine is used to justify wage restraint by trade unions. The conflict of interest is naked and clear when union officials are asked to subordinate the interest of their members to some more general purpose. If the union officials try to enforce wage restraint, the consequence is likely to be wildcat strikes, rank-and-file revolts and the emergence of strong competitors for their jobs. We thus have the ironic phenomenon that union leaders—at least in the U.S.—have objected to Government interference with the market far more consistently and courageously than have business leaders.

The difficulty of exercising "social responsibility" illustrates, of course, the great virtue of private competitive enterprise—it forces people to be responsible for their own actions and makes it difficult for them to "exploit" other people for either selfish or unselfish purposes. They can do good—but only at their own expense.

Many a reader who has followed the argument this far may be tempted to remonstrate that it is all well and good to speak of Government's having the responsibility to impose taxes and determine expenditures for such "social" purposes as controlling pollution or training the hard-core unemployed, but that the problems are too urgent to wait on the slow course of political processes, that the exercise of social responsibility by businessmen is a quicker and surer way to solve pressing current problems.

Aside from the question of fact—I share Adam Smith's skepticism about the benefits that can be expected from "those who affected to trade for the public good"—this argument must be rejected on grounds of principle. What it amounts to is an assertion that those who favor the taxes and expenditures in question have failed to persuade a majority of their fellow citizens to be of like mind and that they are seeking to attain by undemocratic procedures what they cannot attain by democratic procedures. In a free society, it is hard for "evil" people to do "evil," especially since one man's good is another's evil.

I have, for simplicity, concentrated on the special case of the corporate executive, except only for the brief digression on trade unions. But precisely the same argument applies to the newer phenomenon of calling upon stockholders to require corporations to exercise social responsibility (the recent G.M. crusade for example). In most of these cases, what is in effect involved is some stockholders trying to get other stockholders (or customers or employees) to contribute against their will to "social" causes favored by the activists. Insofar as they succeed, they are again imposing taxes and spending the proceeds.

The situation of the individual proprietor is somewhat different. If he acts to reduce the returns of his enterprise in order to exercise his "social responsibility," he is spending his own money, not someone else's. If he wishes to spend his money on such purposes, that is his right, and I cannot see that there is any objection to his doing so. In the process, he, too, may impose costs on employees and customers. However, because he is far less likely than a large corporation or union to have monopolistic power, any such side effects will tend to be minor.

Of course, in practice the doctrine of social responsibility is frequently a cloak for actions that are justified on other grounds rather than a reason for those actions.

To illustrate, it may well be in the long-run interest of a corporation that is a major employer in a small community to devote resources to providing amenities to that community or to improving its government. That may make it easier to attract desirable employees, it may reduce the wage bill or lessen losses from pilferage and sabotage or have other worthwhile effects. Or it may be that, given the laws about the deductibility of corporate charitable contributions, the stockholders can contribute more to charities they favor by having the corporation make the gift than by doing it themselves, since they can in that way contribute an amount that would otherwise have been paid as corporate taxes.

In each of these—and many similar—cases, there is a strong temptation to rationalize these actions as an exercise of "social responsibility." In the present climate of opinion, with its widespread aversion to "capitalism," "profits," the "soulless corporation" and so on, this is one way for a corporation to generate goodwill as a by-product of expenditures that are entirely justified in its own self-interest.

It would be inconsistent of me to call on corporate executives to refrain from this hypocritical window-dressing because it harms the foundations of a free society. That would be to call on them to exercise a "social responsibility"! If our institutions, and the attitudes of the public make it in their self-interest to cloak their actions in this way, I cannot summon much indignation to denounce them. At the same time, I can express admiration for those individual proprietors or owners of closely held corporations or stockholders of more broadly held corporations who disdain such tactics as approaching fraud.

Whether blameworthy or not, the use of the cloak of social responsibility, and the nonsense spoken in its name by influential and prestigious businessmen, does clearly harm the foundations of a free society. I have been impressed time and again by the schizophrenic character of many businessmen. They are capable of being extremely far-sighted and clear-headed in matters that are internal to their businesses. They are incredibly short-sighted and muddle-headed in matters that are outside their businesses but affect the possible survival of business in general. This short-sightedness is strikingly exemplified in the calls from many businessmen for wage and price guidelines or controls or income policies. There is nothing that could do more in a brief period to destroy a market system and replace it by a centrally controlled system than effective governmental control of prices and wages.

The short-sightedness is also exemplified in speeches by businessmen on social responsibility. This may gain them kudos in the short run. But it helps to strengthen the already too prevalent view that the pursuit of profits is wicked and immoral and must be curbed and controlled by external forces. Once this view is adopted, the external forces that curb the market will not be the social consciences, however highly developed, of the pontificating executives; it will be the iron fist of Government bureaucrats. Here, as with price and wage controls, businessmen seem to me to reveal a suicidal impulse.

The political principle that underlies the market mechanism is unanimity. In an ideal free market resting on private property, no individual can coerce any other, all cooperation is voluntary, all parties to such cooperation benefit or they need not participate. There are no values, no "social" responsibilities in any sense other than the shared values and responsibilities of individuals. Society is a collection of individuals and of the various groups they voluntarily form.

The political principle that underlies the political mechanism is conformity. The individual must serve a more general social interest—whether that be determined by a church or a dictator or a majority. The individual may have a vote and say in what is to be done, but if he is overruled, he must conform. It is appropriate for some to require others to contribute to a general social purpose whether they wish to or not.

Unfortunately, unanimity is not always feasible. There are some respects in which conformity appears unavoidable, so I do not see how one can avoid the use of the political mechanism altogether.

But the doctrine of "social responsibility" taken seriously would extend the scope of the political mechanism to every human activity. It does not differ in philosophy from the most explicitly collectivist doctrine. It differs only by professing to believe that collectivist ends can be attained without collectivist means. That is why, in my book "Capitalism and Freedom," I have called it a "fundamentally subversive doctrine" in a free society, and have said that in such a society, "there is one and only one social responsibility of business—to use its resources and engage in activities designed to increase its profits so long as it stays within the rules of the game, which is to say, engages in open and free competition without deception or fraud."

2.2   Business Has Social Responsibilities

RICHARD T. DeGEORGE

We can outline the kinds of things for which the large, publicly-owned manufacturing corporation is responsible. There may be some things for which the corporation as a whole is responsible. But since the corporation acts only through the agency of those who work for it, we can also identify, at least in many cases, who has responsibility for what. In attempting to outline some of these obligations, we can start by considering the various groups that make up the corporation and the groups with which the corporation interacts. We have . . . the shareholders. They are the owners of the corporation. They are legally represented by the board of directors whose job it is, among other things, to look out for the interests of the shareholders. The board of directors oversees management. Management has the task of organizing the corporation in such a way that it can effect its end—profitably make and market a product. Management is responsible to the board for what it does. In a large firm there are, typically, levels of management. Top management sets policy; middle management implements the broad policies by breaking them down into components and devising a strategy for achieving them; lower management implements the decisions made by middle management by organizing and hiring the workers who actually engage in the production of the goods. Management is responsible for what is produced and for how it is produced. It is responsible to the workers for the conditions under which they work, and to the consumers for the quality of goods produced. The workers are responsible for doing the jobs for which they are paid.

The corporation as a whole is responsible to the other firms with which it deals for fulfilling its contracts—for delivering what was promised when and as promised, for paying the debts it incurs in its operation, and so on. The corporation is responsible to the consumer for the goods it sells. The corporation is also responsible to the general public, or to society, for the actions it takes which affect the public or society in general. All of these obligations can be deduced from the rule that every rational agent is responsible for his actions and is responsible to those whom his actions seriously affect. Each such agent is morally responsible for wrongful injury done to another. To the extent that the corporation acts, it is responsible for its actions, though it is the people within the corporation who must act in order for the corporation to fulfill its obligations. Let us look a little more closely at each level of the corporation and at the kinds of moral responsibility each has.

In a large corporation responsibility falls primarily on the representatives of the owners or shareholders, namely, the board of directors. They are the legal overseers of management. The members of the board are responsible to the shareholders for the selection of honest, effective managers, and especially for the selection of the president of the corporation. They may also be responsible for choosing the executive and other vice presidents. They are also morally responsible for the tone of the corporation and its major policies. They can set a moral tone or condone immoral practices. They can and should see that the company is managed honestly and that the interests of the shareholders are cared for and not ignored by management. They are also responsible for agreeing to major policy decisions and for the general well-being of the corporation. The members are morally responsible for the decisions they make, as well as for the decisions they should but fail to make. To be effective in their role as protectors of the interests of the shareholders and in their role as judges of the performance of management, they should be separate from management. They can hardly be objective in their evaluation of management if the members of the board are also members of management. When the president and the chairman of the board are the same person, for instance, we can hardly expect the board to fulfill its responsibility vis-à-vis management. Nor can we expect impartial evaluation of management if the board is composed of people appointed or recommended by management. We can also not expect a board to be effective if it is not informed by management of what management is doing, if it does not have access to any information about the firm it thinks necessary, and if it does not have the time to investigate what should be investigated.

Management is responsible to the board. It must inform the board of what it does, the decisions it makes or the decisions to be made, the financial condition of the firm, its successes and failures, and so on. Management is also responsible to the workers. It both hires them and provides for the conditions of work. In hiring workers it has the obligation to engage in what have become known as fair employment practices. These include following equitable guidelines and not discriminating on the basis of sex, race, religion or other non-job-related characteristics. Once hired, there is a continuing obligation of fairness in evaluation, promotion, and equitable treatment. There are moral matters which may or may not be specified in contracts but which are implied in the hiring of one person by another. It is not moral for management to ignore the safety of working conditions. It should not endanger the workers by failing to provide screening from dangerous machines where appropriate and available, by not supplying goggles for work where fragments may cause blindness, by not supplying ventilation, and in general by ignoring the needs of workers as human beings.

Employers are not free to set any terms they wish as conditions of employment. They have a moral obligation to employees even if these are not spelled out in contracts or by government regulations. Government regulations, such as those imposed by the Occupational Safety and Health Act (OSHA), make explicit many of the conditions employers are morally as well as legally obliged to fulfill with respect to the safety and health of their employees. The OSHA regulations are sometimes inappropriate for certain firms, or are based on codes inappropriate to particular enterprises. But if employers had lived up to the moral obligation to provide adequate conditions of safety and health for their employees, there would have been no need for OSHA regulations.

The corporation is responsible to the consumer for its products. The goods produced should be reasonably safe when this means that the ordinary user is exposed only to a certain acceptable risk level when using the item in question. People do not expect to get electrocuted when they plug in an electrical appliance. They do not buy such appliances expecting to take that risk. A product which electrocutes them when plugged in is defective and causes harm to the consumer that is not part of the contract involved in the purchase of the product. Goods must be as advertised or labelled, and they should be adequately labelled so that the buyer knows what he is buying. Adequate knowledge is one of the ingredients of a fair transaction, and it is the obligation of the manufacturer to inform the purchaser of those significant qualities which the purchaser cannot observe for himself. For instance, the kind of material a garment is made of is pertinent, as is the horsepower of a vehicle. Goods should be reasonably durable. They should not fall apart on first use. Warranties should be clear and honored. The customer buys a product for a certain price. He should know what he is getting, and he has a moral right to have certain expectations fulfilled. Obviously there are grades of goods. Some are more expensive than others and may be correspondingly safer, more durable, more reliable, and more attractive than cheaper products and made of better quality components. For any transaction to be fair, however, the consumer must have adequate information and his reasonable expectations must be fulfilled by a product, or there must be adequate notice that the ordinary expectation in the given case will not be fulfilled. Damaged goods can be only sold if marked as damaged. ''Seconds'' can be sold as seconds but are not morally sold as ''firsts.'' These few examples do not exhaust the responsibilities of corporations to consumers. We have not questioned the morality of built-in obsolescence, purposeful lack of standardization that ties a consumer into a certain line of products, failure to develop certain products or to prevent the production of items that would benefit the consumer but hurt a particular industry or manufacturer. But we have illustrated enough of the moral responsibilities of a corporation to consumers to indicate where its moral obligations in this area lie.

Finally, the corporation is morally responsible for its actions to the general public or society in general. In particular, it has the moral obligation not to harm those whom its actions affect. We can group these obligations under three major headings. The first can be called its responsibility not to harm the environment which it shares with its neighbors. It has the obligation not to pollute the air and water beyond socially acceptable levels and to control its noise pollution similarly. It is obliged to dispose of toxic and corrosive wastes so as not to endanger others. It must reclaim and restore the environment to a socially acceptable level if its operation despoils and ruins it.

The second group of moral obligations to the general public concerns the general safety of those who live in an area affected by a company's plant. A company has no right to expose those people living near it to a health risk from possible explosion or radiation. Some jobs involve high risk and those who take them are paid accordingly. But a plant has no right to expose its neighbors, even its distant neighbors, to dangers without their consent. Similarly, a corporation has an obligation to the general public for the safety of its products. For instance, substandard tires endanger not only those who purchase them unknowingly but those whom they may kill or injure in the accident the tires may cause.

The third set of responsibilities to the public concerns the location, opening, and closing of plants. These actions affect not only the corporation and its workers but also the communities in which the plants are located. Plant openings can affect a community positively or negatively just as closings can. A corporation must morally consider the impact of its actions in these matters on the community. This is not to say that plants can never morally be closed or opened. In both opening and closing a plant, a corporation has the obligation to minimize the harm and also to consider a variety of strategies to achieve this end.

The opening of a plant may involve a large commitment on the part of the community in which it is located. The community, for example, may have to add sewer lines, increase its fire and police department staff, and add to its social services personnel. Developers build houses for the increased employment the plant makes available. Businesses spring up to provide support services. Schools may be built to educate the children of the workers. The city or county begin to count on the increased tax base the plant represents. All of this may result from the new plant. The corporation does not ask that all this happen; but it expects its workers will be provided housing and services in response to market demand.

The community nonetheless may be said to provide indirect support to the plant. The corporation should, therefore, not ignore the community's contribution to its operation when it considers closing the plant. It may have no legal duty to consider the community with which it has been associated. Morally it has an obligation to consider the effects of its action and to minimize the harm its closing will cause the community.

If we ask who has the obligation to do all this, the answer is the corporation. Management has the major role to play. Yet both the members of the board and individual workers may find on occasion that they have the moral responsibility to take certain actions to satisfy the corporation's responsibility to the general public. . . .

2.3   Can an Executive Afford a Conscience?

ALBERT Z. CARR

Ask a business executive whether his company employs child labor, and he will either think you are joking or be angered by the implied slur on his ethical standards. The employment of children in factories is clearly considered morally wrong as well as illegal.

Yet it was not until comparatively recently (1941) that the U.S. Supreme Court finally sustained the constitutionality of the long-contested Child Labor Act, which Congress had passed four years earlier. During most of the previous eight decades, the fact that children 10 years old worked at manual jobs for an average of 11 hours a day under conditions of virtual slavery had aroused little indignation in business circles.

To be sure, only a few industries found the practice profitable, and the majority of businessmen would doubtless have been glad to see it stopped. But in order to stop it the government had to act, and any interference with business by government was regarded as a crime against God, Nature, and Respectability. If a company sought to hold down production costs by employing children in factories where the work did not demand adult skills or muscle, that was surely a matter to be settled between the employer and the child's parents or the orphanage.

To permit legitimate private enterprise to be balked by unrealistic do-gooders was to open the gate to socialism and anarchy—such was the prevailing sentiment of businessmen, as shown in the business press, from the 1860's to the 1930's.

Every important advance in business ethics has been achieved through a long history of pain and protest.[1] The process of change begins when a previously accepted practice arouses misgivings among sensitive observers. Their efforts at moral suasion are usually ignored, however, until changes in economic conditions or new technology make the practice seem increasingly undesirable.

Businessmen who profit by the practice defend it heatedly, and a long period of public controversy ensues, climaxed at last by the adoption of laws forbidding it. After another 20 or 30 years, the new generation of businessmen regard the practice with retrospective moral indignation and wonder why it was ever tolerated.

A century of increasingly violent debate culminating in civil war had to be lived through before black slavery, long regarded as an excellent business proposition, was declared unlawful in the United States. To achieve laws forbidding racial discrimination in hiring practices required another century. It took 80 years of often bloody labor disputes to win acceptance of the principle of collective bargaining, and the country endured about 110 years of flagrant financial abuses before enactment of effective measures regulating banks and stock exchanges.

In time, all of these forward steps, once bitterly opposed by most businessmen, came to be accepted as part of the ethical foundation of the American private enterprise economy.

Jesse James vs. Nero

In the second half of the twentieth century, with the population, money supply, military power, and industrial technology of the United States expanding rapidly at the same time, serious new ethical issues have arisen for businessmen—notably the pollution of the biosphere, the concentration of economic power in a relatively few vast corporations, increasing military domination of the economy, and the complex interrelationship between business interests and the threat of war. These issues are the more formidable because they demand swift response; they will not wait a century or even a generation for a change in corporate ethics that will stimulate businessmen to act.

The problems they present to business and our society as a whole are immediate, critical, and worsening. If they are not promptly dealt with by farsighted and effective measures, they could even bring down political democracy and the entrepreneurial system together.

In fact, given the close relationship between our domestic economic situation and our military commitments abroad, and the perils implicit in the worldwide armaments buildup, it is not extreme to say that the extent to which businessmen are able to open their minds to new ethical imperatives in the decade ahead may have decisive influence in this century on the future of the human species.

Considering the magnitude of these rapidly developing issues, old standards of ethical judgment seem almost irrelevant. It is of course desirable that a businessman be honest in his accountings and faithful to his contracts—that he should not advertise misleadingly, rig prices, deceive stockholders, deny workers their due, cheat customers, spread false rumors about competitors, or stab associates in the back. Such a person has in the past qualified as "highly ethical," and he could feel morally superior to many of those he saw around him—the chiselers, the connivers, the betrayers of trust.

But standards of personal conduct in themselves are no longer an adequate index of business ethics. Everyone knows that a minority of businessmen commit commercial mayhem on each other and on the public with practices ranging from subtle conflicts of interest to the sale of injurious drugs and unsafe automobiles, but in the moral crisis through which we are living such tales of executive wrongdoing, like nudity in motion pictures, have lost their power to shock.

The public shrugs at the company president who conspires with his peers to fix prices. It grins at the vice president in charge of sales who provides call girls for a customer. After we have heard a few such stories, they become monotonous.

We cannot shrug or grin, however, at the refusal of powerful corporations to take vigorous action against great dangers threatening the society, and to which they contribute. Compared with such a corporation or with the executive who is willing to jeopardize the health and well-being of an entire people in order to add something to current earnings, the man who merely embezzles company funds is as insignificant in the annals of morality as Jesse James is compared with Nero.

The moral position of the executive who works for a company that fails in the ethics of social responsibility is ambiguous. The fact that he does not control company policy cannot entirely exonerate him from blame. He is guilty, so to speak, by employment.

If he is aware that the company's factories pollute the environment or its products injure the consumer and he does not exert himself to change the related company policies, he becomes morally suspect. If he lends himself to devious evasions of laws against racial discrimination in hiring practices, he adds to the probability of destructive racial confrontations and is in some degree an agent of social disruption. If he knows that his company is involved in the bribery of legislators or government officials, or makes under-the-table deals with labor union officials, or uses the services of companies known to be controlled by criminal syndicates, he con-tributes through his work to disrespect for law and the spread of crime.

If his company, in its desire for military contracts, lobbies to oppose justifiable cuts in the government's enormous military budget, he bears some share of responsibility for the constriction of the civilian economy; for price inflation, urban decay, and short-ages of housing, transportation, and schools; and for failure to mit-igate the hardships of the poor.

From this standpoint, the carefully correct executive who never violates a law or fails to observe the canons of gentlemanly behavior may be as open to ethical challenge as the crooks and the cheaters.

"Toxins of Suppressed Guilt"

The practical question arises: If a man in a responsible corpo-rate position finds that certain policies of his company are socially injurious, what can he do about it without jeopardizing his job?

Contrary to common opinion, he is not necessarily without re-course. The nature of that recourse I shall discuss in the final sec-tion of this article. Here, I want to point out that unless the execu-tive's sense of social responsibility is accompanied by a high degree of realism about tactics, then he is likely to end in frustra-tion or cynicism.

One executive of my acquaintance who wrote several memo-randa to his chief, detailing instances of serious environmental contamination for which the company was responsible and which called for early remedy, was sharply rebuked for a "negative atti-tude."

Another, a successful executive of a large corporation, said to me quite seriously in a confidential moment that he did not think a man in a job like his could afford the luxury of a conscience in the office. He was frank to say that he had become unhappy about certain policies of his company. He could no longer deny to himself that the company was not living up to its social responsibilities and was engaged in some political practices that smacked of corruption.

But what were his options? He had only three that he could see, and he told me he disliked them all:

- If he argued for a change in policies that were helping to keep net earnings high, he might be branded by his superiors as "unrealistic" or "idealistic"—adjectives that could check his career and might, if he pushed too hard, compel his resignation.
- Continued silence not only would spoil his enjoyment of his work, but might cause him to lose respect for himself.
- If he moved to one of the other companies in his industry, he would merely be exchanging one set of moral misgivings for another.

He added with a sigh that he envied his associates whose consciences had never developed beyond the Neanderthal stage and who had no difficulty in accepting things as they were. He said he wondered whether he ought not to try to discipline himself to be as indifferent as they to the social implications of policies which, after all, were common in business.

Perhaps he made this effort and succeeded in it, for he remained with the company and forged ahead. He may even have fancied that he had killed his conscience—as the narrator in Mark Twain's symbolic story did when he gradually reached the point where he could blithely murder the tramps who came to his door asking for handouts.

But conscience is never killed; when ignored, it merely goes underground, where it manufactures the toxins of suppressed guilt, often with serious psychological and physical consequences. The hard fact is that the executive who has a well-developed contemporary conscience is at an increasing disadvantage in business unless he is able to find some personal policy by which he can maintain his drive for success without serious moral reservations. . . .

Behind the Boardroom Door

No company that I have ever heard of employs a vice president in charge of ethical standards; and sooner or later the conscientious executive is likely to come up against a stone wall of corporate indifference to private moral values.

When the men who hold the real power in the company come together to decide policy, they may give lip service to the moral element in the issue, but not much more. The decision-making process at top-management levels has little room for social responsibilities not definitely required by law or public opinion.

Proposals that fail to promise an early payoff for the company and that involve substantial expense are accepted only if they represent a means of escaping drastic penalties, such as might be inflicted by a government suit, a labor strike, or a consumer boycott. To invest heavily in antipollution equipment or in programs for hiring and training workers on the fringe of employability, or to accept higher taxation in the interest of better education for the children of a community—for some distant, intangible return in a cloudy future—normally goes against the grain of every profit-minded management.

It could hardly be otherwise. In the prevailing concept of corporate efficiency, a continual lowering of costs relative to sales is cardinal. For low costs are a key not only to higher profits but to corporate manueverability, to advantage in recruiting the best men, and to the ability to at least hold a share of a competitive market.

Of the savings accruing to a company from lowered costs, the fraction that finds its way into the area of social responsibility is usually miniscule. To expend such savings on nonremunerative activities is regarded as weakening the corporate structure.

The late Chester A. Barnard, one of the more enlightened business leaders of the previous generation and a man deeply concerned with ethics, voiced the position of management in the form of a question: ''To what extent is one morally justified in loading a productive undertaking with heavy charges in the attempt to protect against a remote possibility, or even one not so remote?''[2] Speaking of accident prevention in plants, which he favored in principle, he warned that if the outlay for such a purpose weakened the company's finances, ''the community might lose a service and the entrepreneur an opportunity.''

Corporate managers apply the same line of reasoning to proposals for expenditure in the area of social responsibility. ''We can't afford to sink that amount of money in nonproductive uses," they say, and, "We need all our cash for expansion."

The entrepreneur who is willing to accept some reduction of his income—the type is not unknown—may be able to operate his enterprise in a way that satisfies an active conscience; but a company with a competitive team of managers, a board of directors, and a pride of stockholders cannot harbor such an unbusinesslike intention. . . .

What Can the Executive Do?

One can dream of a big-business community that considers it sound economics to sacrifice a portion of short-term profits in order to protect the environment and reduce social tensions.

It is theoretically conceivable that top managers as a class may come to perceive the profound dangers, for the free-enterprise system and for themselves, in the trend toward the militarization of our society, and will press the government to resist the demand for nonessential military orders and overpermissive contracts from sections of industry and elements in the Armed Services. At the same level of wishfulness, we can imagine the federal government making it clear to U.S. companies investing abroad that protection of their investments is not the government's responsibility.

We can even envisage a time when the bonds of a corporation that is responsive to social needs will command a higher rating by Moody's than those of a company that neglects such values, since the latter is more vulnerable to public condemnation; and a time when a powerful Executive League for Social Responsibility will come into being to stimulate and assist top managements in formulating long-range economic policies that embrace social issues. In such a private-enterprise utopia the executive with a social conscience would be able to work without weakening qualms.

In the real world of today's business, however, he is almost sure to be a troubled man. Perhaps there are some executives who are so strongly positioned that they can afford to urge their managements to accept a reduced rate of return on investment for the sake of the society of which they are a part. But for the large majority of corporate employees who want to keep their jobs and win their superiors' approbation, to propose such a thing would be inviting oneself to the corporate guillotine.

He Is Not Powerless

But this does not necessarily mean that the ethically motivated executive can do nothing. In fact, if he does nothing, he may so bleach his conception of himself as a man of conviction as to reduce his personal force and value to the company. His situation calls for sagacity as well as courage. Whatever ideas he advocates to express his sense of social responsibility must be shaped to the company's interests.

Asking management flatly to place social values ahead of profits would be foolhardy, but if he can demonstrate that, on the basis of long-range profitability, the concept of corporate efficiency needs to be broadened to include social values, he may be able to make his point without injury—indeed, with benefit—to his status in the company. A man respected for competence in his job, who knows how to justify ethically based programs in economic terms and to overcome elements of resistance in the psychology of top management, may well be demonstrating his own qualifications for top management.

In essence, any ethically oriented proposal made to a manager is a proposal to take a longer-range view of his problems—to lift his sights. Nonethical practice is shortsighted almost by definition, if for no other reason than that it exposes the company to eventual reprisals.

The longer range a realistic business projection is, the more likely it is to find a sound ethical footing. I would go so far as to say that almost anything an executive does, on whatever level, to extend the range of thinking of his superiors tends to effect an ethical advance.

The hope and the opportunity of the individual executive with a contemporary conscience lies in the constructive connection of the long economic view with the socially aware outlook. He must show convincingly a net advantage for the corporation in accelerating expenditures or accepting other costs in the sphere of social responsibility.

I was recently able to observe an instance in which an executive persuaded his company's management to make a major advance in its antipollution policy. His presentation of the alternatives, on which he had spent weeks of careful preparation, showed in essence that, under his plan, costs which would have to be absorbed over a three-year period would within six years prove to be substantially less than the potential costs of less vigorous action.

When he finished his statement, no man among his listeners, not even his most active rivals, chose to resist him. He had done more than serve his company and satisfy his own ethical urge; he had shown that the gap between the corporate decision and the private conscience is not unbridgeable if a person is strong enough, able enough, and brave enough to do what needs to be done.

It may be that the future of our enterprise system will depend on the emergence of a sufficient number of men of this breed who believe that in order to save itself business will be impelled to help save the society.

Notes

1. For amplifications of this view, see Robert W. Austin, "Responsibility for Social Change," Harvard Business Review July–August 1965, p. 45; and Theodore Levitt, "Why Business Always Loses," Harvard Business Review March–April 1968, p. 81.
2. *Elementary Conditions of Business Morals* (Berkeley, Committee on the Barbara Weinstock Lectures, University of California, 1958).

Discussion and Review Questions

1. How do you react to the point of view expressed by Daniel Drew in the quote on page 46? Do you agree or disagree? Why?

2. Why do you think most large businesses have developed and published "codes of business conduct" in the past twenty-five years?

3. Why does Friedman believe that business does not have the same kinds of responsibilities individuals do? How does he justify this view?

4. What specific kinds of ethical responsibilities does DeGeorge believe the modern corporation has?

5. How much power does an executive really have in developing and operating on a rigid standard of ethical behavior? Is it a personal or a corporate problem at bottom?

6. Assume you are working in an overseas branch of an American corporation. You have an opportunity to make a large sale to the national government of a country you are in but to do so you must pay the procurement officer a sizable bribe. What would you do? Why?

7. For years, your company has dumped its raw materials in a nearby river. A loophole in the Environment Protection laws still allows you and your competition across the river to do this legally, even though it is well known that the waste is killing the river and may endanger people downstream. An earnest young environmental defender who also is a middle manager with the company urges that your company stop its polluting. As an officer of this company, how will you respond to your employee's request?

ISSUE 3

Is Entrepreneurship Still Possible?

The great Austrian economist Joseph Schumpeter concluded that capitalist development had taken place because of the important role of innovation in a production-for-profit society. To Schumpeter, the capitalist search for profit demanded that the society be constantly set in turmoil as individual innovators produced new goods, produced old goods new ways, developed and entered new markets, sought new sources of raw materials, and ever attempted to improve the internal organization of their enterprise. The results of these activities were periodic "gales of creative destruction," as new production ideas replaced old ones and new products destroyed old markets. However, after each economic storm the society was improved—left with better and more efficient productive methods.

The Historical Role of the Entrepreneur

To Schumpeter, the central character in the drama of "creative destruction" was the entrepreneur. The solitary individual (who might on occasion join with a few others) who was driven by the desire for "more" was willing to take the risk and to work hard. While others sat back content, this restless soul turned the world upside down with one phenomenal innovation after another.

In the Introduction we noted the importance of the nineteenth-century entrepreneurs in laying the foundation of modern business enterprise. As we saw, these entrepreneurs were capable of taking a new technological idea (such as the steam engine) and developing a business (a railroad) out of it. Others took an old idea (the general store) and developed a new business (the chain grocery store). To be sure, compared to today, business opportunities in the nineteenth-century were ripe for successful entrepreneurship. Capital requirements for getting under way were smaller. The technology of the time was less complex and therefore cheaper to develop. Entry into a field of business was less difficult than what an individual enterpriser faces at the present time. Moreover, the number of new areas to which an innovative idea could be applied was of course much larger.

The Problems of the Modern Entrepreneur

As a rule, most modern-day small businesses face a common set of problems. First of all *they are small*, which places serious capital and management restraints on how a problem can be dealt with. Because of these restraints, almost *every* problem for a small business becomes a big problem. Second, most small businesses are new and very many are in wholly new areas of goods and services production. As a result the owner–operators of small enterprises are continually breaking new ground in their business decision making. With few models or landmarks on the business horizon to be guided by, it is not uncommon for new enterprisers to make serious and often fatal mistakes in the management of their enterprises. Meanwhile, for the large firm, this is not the case. There is usually a long-standing tried-and-proven technique for dealing with most problems, even brand-new problems that arise.

As a result of the increased demands placed upon the modern entrepreneur, today's small-business owners face a more limited range of business alternatives. They have fewer potential areas to exploit and probably also face greater possibility of failure. We do not have very good data on nineteenth-century business failures, but we know that presently 30 to 35 percent of all new firms fail during their first year. In retailing, less than one-fifth of all new enterprises that survive their first year will last ten years. In manufacturing and wholesaling, about one quarter of the first-year survivors survive their first decade. For a gambling person these are not good odds. In fact, one recently failed businessperson calculated he would have had a better chance if he had taken his money and spent a decade betting on the ponies.

Despite the enormous prospects for failure (almost 70,000 succumbed in 1982), tens of thousands of individuals like the small-businessowner in the first of the following pieces start up their own enterprises each year. As the second of the following articles argues, regardless of the personal hazards, society's gain is very great. However, certainly entrepreneurship is not limited to small businesses. Isn't a sense of entrepreneurial activity essential to the modern multiproduct, multiline, multinational enterprise?

Entrepreneurship and the Giant Corporation

Joseph Schumpeter was so certain that the entrepreneur was the key to capitalism that he concluded that "big business is a half-way house on the road to socialism." To him, big business actually discouraged innovation and discouraged persons to take individual risks for profit. Instead, "going along," "being a company person," replaced individualism. Meanwhile, holding onto what you have rather than taking a chance at more became the corporate psychology. While such ideas may warm the hearts of many who do not hold capitalism in high regard, it poses a problem for others. Does the modern giant corporation really stifle individualism? Can a corporate committee act like an entrepreneur in taking risks and developing new ideas? If one thinks a minute about these queries, they are truly pregnant questions. The implication is obvious: If we have run out of space and time for entrepreneurial activity, then we are also in danger of ceasing to operate a production-for-profit enterprise system.

Alas, it is a question without an answer. Or better, a question with many answers. Some business leaders worry, as Schumpeter did, that big business has lost its risk-taking entrepreneurial style, thus becoming flabby and indifferent to change. Others hold that the entrepreneurial instinct is alive and well in the modern giant firm, although, of course, in an altered form. For big business, the debate on this matter recently has heated up. Among a growing and increasingly vocal group of business leaders and specialists, the argument is offered frequently that big business must return to its own entrepreneurial beginnings. As the editors of *Business Week* maintain in our third selection, American enterprise can be revitalized and productivity increased only if managers drop their self-protective and "organizational" modes of thought and action and again act as innovators and risk takers. Is this really possible, or has entrepreneurship become limited only to the struggling small-businessowner?

3.1   A Case Study in Successful Entrepreneurship

DAVID P. GARINO

Footwear importer Robert Gamm didn't know what to do with his pocket change and keys while he jogged or played tennis. He would tie his valuables in a handkerchief, but then, he says, the problem was "what to do with the handkerchief. I usually stuffed it in a jacket and threw it on the ground."

The inconvenience led to a profitable business. Mr. Gamm was inspired to design KangaRoos, athletic shoes with a zippered pocket on the side and a logo of a bounding kangaroo with baby in pouch. That was five years ago. Sales of KangaRoos for the year ending July 31 should approach $75 million, Mr. Gamm estimates, up from $45 million in fiscal 1982, and just $20 million two years ago. (The men's models range in retail price from $25 to $40 a pair.)

The 62-year-old executive's experience proves once again that a seemingly obvious idea can succeed in a crowded market. It also helped to be tenacious and thick-skinned in the case of Mr. Gamm, who followed his grandfather's and father's footsteps in the shoe business. More than 13 years ago, he left the family's wholesale operation and started Trans World Shoe Import Co., a St. Louis importer of Polish-made dress shoes.

He had some experience in designing dress shoes, but in 1977 he began fashioning an athletic shoe with a pocket. He ordered prototypes from Poland, more than 100 in all. The Polish companies, though, lacked adequate supplies of basic raw materials such as nylon, and the athletic shoes didn't measure up in comfort or aesthetics. Even so, "we did learn things by trial and error," Mr. Gamm says. For instance, the first shoes didn't have zippers—the pockets were covered by a flap. The result: Money, keys and the like often would fall out.

Late in 1979, Mr. Gamm searched for a supplier in South Korea, having been impressed previously with the workmanship and styling of Korean footwear. Several factories turned him down, he says, "probably because our initial order would have been quite small." But a company in Pusan called Samwha "treated us as if we might be important someday."

Samwha turned out more-than-satisfactory samples within a few days. The speed and quality surprised Mr. Gamm, and he committed his company to a monthly run of 44,000 pairs of Kanga-Roos. Total production now is nearly 700,000 pairs a month with Samwha producing about 500,000.

To finance his entry into the athletic footwear market and to establish Envoys U.S.A. Inc., the parent of KangaRoos, Mr. Gamm used profits from his existing business plus personal savings. He was confident his idea would sell. "There were a lot of joggers out there, and there was nothing new in the market." But the general reaction to KangaRoos was ridicule, he says. Even some of his partners in the shoe-import company said the venture was a quick way to go broke. A typical reaction from retailers, he says: "Just what we need, another athletic shoe from the Far East."

But Mr. Gamm's optimism was shared by Mervyn's, a California retailer which stocked more than 10,000 pairs of KangaRoos in the spring of 1980. "They were an instant success," says Alan Beatty, a merchandise manager for Mervyn's. The retailer eventually bought about two-thirds of the initial 44,000-pair production run. "Mervyn's got us off on the right foot," Mr. Gamm says.

Other retailers were more cautious about KangaRoos. "Frankly we were negative. We thought it was a gimmick," says a Wohl Shoe Co. executive in St. Louis. Even so, Wohl test marketed a few hundred pairs. "We decided to let the consumer tell us, and sales have been absolutely phenomenal," the Wohl official says.

KangaRoos introduced Mr. Gamm to the world of marketing. "We never promoted our Polish shoes," he says. "So, from a quiet company we had to become extroverts." To gain visibility for Kan-gaRoos amid masses of athletic shoes, Mr. Gamm set up a $300,000 advertising budget and placed four-color ads in footwear and running publications. This year's advertising budget is $2.5 million, and Mr. Gamm has broadened his pitch to popular magazines such as *People* and *Sports Illustrated*.

Although the initial marketing was aimed at men, the brand also does well with women and children, Mr. Gamm says. "The juvenile market really took off within the past year," he says.

Having found a place in the athletic-shoes field, Mr. Gamm is segmenting the market further. He recently brought out an indoor-soccer shoe with the pocket under the tongue. "That's because you kick the ball with the side of your foot and the pocket shouldn't interfere," he says. Another new entry: basketball shoes. Mr. Gamm also is working on a shoe for aerobic dancing. One difficulty is making the sole slippery enough for easy maneuvering.

Mr. Gamm is learning that success has its price, though, "We took the gamble and carved out the market," he says. "It didn't exist two-and-a-half years ago, and now others are trying to capitalize on our success."

Mr. Gamm has filed more than a dozen patent-infringement suits against distributors and retailers peddling shoes with animals such as greyhounds and lynxes. These shoes have vertical zippers; KangaRoos' zippers are horizontal. Mr. Gamm figures his legal expenses so far exceed $700,000. Perhaps more important, the litigation is taking up valuable time. "Instead of sitting in a courtroom," he says, "I should be in my office designing shoes."

3.2   In Praise of Small Business

ARTHUR LEVITT, JR.

As with most people who buy their own businesses, the odds against Robert Johnson were high. He was confronted at the start with an intimidating list of problems. He had no money, after laying out the purchase price, with which to start building up the business; he had no business experience or training, and he didn't know where to go for advice (beyond the help offered by the local Internal Revenue Service office on how to fill out 10 different Government reporting forms). There were no tax breaks, no Government loans, no expense accounts. Although he purchased the company from his uncle for what he thought was a good price, most everyone else would not have regarded it as a bargain. The Chicago business—Gamecraft of Illinois, which designed and produced board games—had been barely surviving since it was founded in 1968. Sales were declining, and stacks of bills were unpaid.

What Johnson did have was a strong conviction that his energy and imagination would make the business succeed. "My sense of my own worth became tied up in it," he says. "Could I keep it going, make it work?"

With this commitment, Johnson moved the business to his home in suburban Champaign, and began living the double life familiar to many American small-business people. After working full time as a university administrator, he would come home at night and "often put in a second eight-hour day, taking care of every little detail of the business, even boxing the games myself and sending them out."

Now, two years later, the bearded, 37-year-old, soft-spoken Robert Johnson has not precisely been transformed into the popular image of the American businessman at the helm of his company—that dynamic, jet-hopping capitalist in three-piece, pinstripe suit rushing, briefcase in hand, into a Wall Street conference room to swing the deal of deals. But Gamecraft is making money. No immense profits, to be sure. Johnson, still at the university, has turned the business around, revitalizing its marketing effort, expanding its product line (a quarter of its sales are now in computer games) and recruiting a business manager. And, he has been sufficiently bitten by the "business bug" to have begun planning a second company.

Johnson has thus become one of a growing number of Americans who have left the routine of wage earning to try to assert their own vision of making it on their own, of trying to succeed in small businesses—from flower shops to print shops, from pizza parlors to Chinese takeouts, from small manufacturing plants to small service companies. In many ways he is a good deal more representative of the people who run America's 11 million businesses—10.8 million of which are small businesses—than the man with the flying briefcase and pin-stripe suit.

Contrary to the popular notion that American business is concentrating and contracting, with multinationals and conglomerates gobbling up everything in sight, there has been during the last few years an astonishing growth in the United States in the birth rate of small businesses. Since 1976, nearly a million Americans have become their own bosses, bringing the total number of self-employed to an all-time high of more than 6.8 million. For 1980, the Dun & Bradstreet Corporation estimated that 533,500 companies were incorporating annually, and that the number of new incorporations in 1980 was 63 percent greater than in 1975.

To grasp the importance of these entrepreneurs consider that three major economic crises of the 1980's are a lack of jobs, a dearth of industrial innovation and flagging productivity. Then consider that approximately 60 million Americans out of a work force of 97 million find their livelihoods in small businesses. A recent Massachusetts Institute of Technology study found that 66 percent of all new jobs in the private sector were provided by businesses with 20 or fewer employees. In contrast, the National Federation of Independent Business has stated that over the last decade *Fortune* magazine's top 1,000 firms, as measured by revenue, created only 10.6 percent of all jobs. Additionally, I understand that small companies provide more than 80 percent of the jobs for young blacks and other disadvantaged groups.

Consider, too, a recent National Science Foundation study: It found that small firms produce four times as many industrial innovations per research dollar as medium-sized firms do and 24 times as many innovations as the largest firms. Finally, consider, with regard to flagging productivity, that small businesses quite literally can't afford to be unproductive. They have no margin for slack: Productivity is essential to survival.

Indeed, Johnson and other small-business people are beginning to understand their own collective importance. They are realizing that they have interests in common, that they can and should help each other out and that it is to the nation's—and their own— benefit that they do so. They are getting organized in important ways, and developing a sense of unity that I believe will soon make them one of the most potent influences in the economic history of the United States.

It must be said at the start that the small-is-beautiful economic strategy is not as unqualifiedly romantic as it seems to be: Establishing a business is immensely risky. According to a study soon to be published by the Small Business Administration, as many as three out of four new enterprises fail within their first five years, and nine out of 10 fail within 10 years. And the failures are believed to be increasing to a higher rate than at any time during the past decade. It is ironic, therefore, that in the midst of the current recession, small-business people in general continue to back the Reagan Administration's economic policy of tight money and punishing interest rates. They do so out of a belief that inflation is their most pernicious long-term enemy—and so they are willing to try to cope with the short-term tribulations.

The roadblocks are rugged. The biggest is, of course, lack of money. To start a business and to keep it going, the vast majority of entrepreneurs must turn, as Johnson did, to personal savings, or to parents, aunts, uncles, friends. Small companies often cannot get loans when they need them, and when they do, they must often pay significantly higher interest rates than the bigger operations that are granted the prime rate. The National Federation of Independent Business recently asked this question of small-business owners: What was the most important resource for your financing? Forty-five percent answered personal savings, 13 percent said friends, and 4 percent cited private investors. Only 29 percent were financed through banks and other financial institutions, while 1 percent were financed by the Government. Also, less than 1 percent were financed by the unfortunately few venture-capital firms that are in business to make funds available to new enterprises.

If the venture is an entirely new undertaking, the idea behind it must be a good one to begin with or the money to back it won't make much difference. And, especially if the business is new, another major problem with entering afresh into the small-business world is what Leo Wolk, a Minneapolis insurance agent, terms "a severe lack of sound advice." Dun & Bradstreet estimates that a majority of all business failures are due to management inadequacies—from poor long-range planning to errors in accounting. And it is often not that the business owners don't recognize their lack of skills or competence in particular areas; there just appears to be nowhere to turn to for reliable information or counsel.

Then there is the enormous hassle of Government regulation and paper work. Many people believe that any expression of frustration over the level of Federal regulation, for example, is merely big business crying in its beer, or dry martini. But it is truly no exaggeration to say that the labyrinth of horrors of Federal regulations and paper work confronting some small businesses would fire the imagination of a contemporary Kafka.

Yet the renaissance of the entrepreneurial spirit is occurring in spite of these obstacles. Why? How does one explain it? One reason is simply population increase, the baby-boom; another is the nation's shift from a manufacturing economy to a service-oriented one. But there may be a deeper, more compelling reason, having to do with a change in national attitude.

After the Depression, the word "entrepreneur" often conjured up something roughly on the order of a scheming promoter or unscrupulous tycoon. Now, however, "entrepreneurial spirit" seems to suggest at once a more down-to-earth figure and a more romantic one. The phrase invokes independence, self-reliance, risk taking, courage—with overtones, perhaps, of Emerson and Thoreau as much as Adam Smith or 19th-century moguls. And these attitudes can be seen time and time again among these new down-to-earth romantics.

Robert Johnson is a member of what might be called "new wave entrepreneurs," younger people who grew up in a generation that viewed business with contempt, but who now find starting a business a way to gain fulfillment and satisfaction. Although Johnson is uncomfortable with being called a "capitalist," he says that at a certain point he realized that "if you're not involved in the capitalistic system in some way in which you have control, you feel victimized by it."

A similar view is expressed by Kate and Rob Pulleyn of Asheville, N.C. "We were sociology majors in the 1960's and rejected out of hand the thought of 'going into business,' " says Rob Pulleyn. Opportunity presented itself, however, in the form of one of their favorite handicraft shops going up for sale. The Pulleyns used their own private capital for financing and their own guesswork and initiative to build their business. They were becoming moderately successful when Rob had an idea: a newsletter to be distributed free as a promotional device for the handicrafts they sold. At the time they only half realized that they were reaching a small but untapped market of dedicated handicrafts enthusiasts. The newsletter was an immediate success, and it led to another idea which has become *Fiberarts* magazine.

The Pulleyns took a large risk in pursuing their business goal. After moving from New Mexico to North Carolina, Rob recalls that they "proceeded to live the life of the totally desperate. But we were lucky. And young." Both were in their late 20's. "We could live in two rooms and eat beans. That was, in a way, part of the fun. And now people have become interested in us because we owe no money. They asked us how we did it. Well, we broke all the rules because we didn't know what the rules were. If we had known them, we never would have tried the things we did."

Now, along with *Fiberarts*, the Pulleyns publish *Yarn Market News*, have published an elaborate, illustrated coffee-table handicrafts book, organized national handicrafts conferences and, with a large Stockholm publishing firm that sought them out, they have developed a large-circulation magazine—called *Handmade*—on home crafts and restoration.

Harvey and Marcia Cinamon are midlife entrepreneurs—people who, in a sense, have taken even greater risks, quitting successful, secure careers after they were well along in years. "At the time we had five children, one recently merged household, alimony payments, two kids in college. We did it on our reputation and on credit. We didn't care if we didn't make as much money as we had been making as long as we could do things the way we thought they should be done." Today, they are partners in Cinamon Associates, a direct-mail operation in Boston, and are expanding into radio and television, as well as considering entering international marketing.

What does Marcia Cinamon believe are the characteristics successful entrepreneurs need? "Greed. Need. Desire. Probably half the deadly sins. I think most of all it's a person who can't leave something undone. I remember I was sitting with someone, and there was a newspaper in the chair next to me with an undone crossword puzzle. I picked it up, and started doing the puzzle." Has doing the undone been worth it? "Yes. The reward . . . is that you know everything that happens," says Marcia Cinamon. "It is you who has your finger on the pulse of everything."

This desire for action and independence, for some degree of control of one's destiny, is echoed by Sydney Levine, owner of Shipping Intelligence in New York, a company that provides computerized control systems to the shipping industry for use in inventory and record keeping. He believes that to an important extent he makes his own economy. "When people ask me, 'Will the recession affect your business?' I answer, 'It depends on me. If I lose a client, well, then I have a recession. If I get two new clients, it's a much different picture.' "

Self-reliance has its own burdens, however. Stanley Simon, who owns Fitwell Stores for Men in Minnesota, says, "When things take a bad turn, you don't have anyplace else to put the blame. . . ."

That small businesses are filling some pressing national needs as well as filling the needs of the people who run them seems evident.

According to a report by the Panel of Invention and Innovation to the Secretary of Commerce, more than half of the major technological advances of this century were developed by individual inventors and small businesses. Chester Carlson developed the first working model of what became the Xerox machine in a little lab over a bar. Texas Instruments was a tiny company making equipment for finding oil until it paid Bell Labs $25,000 for a license to make transistors. Individual investors and small companies have accounted for insulin, the vacuum tube, Kodachrome, power steering, the self-winding wristwatch, the helicopter, cellophane, ball-point pens, FM radio, shrink-proof knitted wear, the Polaroid camera and the zipper.

Meanwhile, however, some of our largest and most basic industries have been faltering. Chrysler, along with Lockheed, are only two in a series of organizations over the last dozen years that have been kept from bankruptcy by large sums of money in Government support and that indicate that a kind of arthritis is spreading through many of our largest companies. Companies such as Seatrain and Penn Central were bankrupt, but were helped out during reorganization by Federal assistance programs.

Of course, the Government does not bail out small businesses when the going gets rough. Productivity and self-reliance are essential requirements of small businesses, and hence they serve as an invaluable example to the nation. These qualities are really what makes small businesses such an integral part of what might be called "the economic system." . . .

Currently, small business enjoys far fewer tax benefits than big business. I.R.S. figures show that companies with more than $1 billion in sales are claiming various tax credits equal to 61.1 percent of their tax liability, while comparatively small firms—those with $1 million to $5 million in sales—are claiming credits equal only to 6.5 percent. In addition to this, some rules for claiming deductions and credits are so complex that only large companies with vast accounting staffs can take complete advantage of them. . . .

The crippling effect that Government regulation has had on some small businesses must also be considered. To do so requires, first, an understanding that regulations designed for large corporations are often applied inflexibly to smaller enterprises as well. Here are a few of the absurdities that can result:

Robert Bentile runs a small surface-mining coal company in Ohio with 25 employees. He testified before a Washington Congressional hearing that "we have a total of 647 forms per year and a total of 63 different inspectors. When the weather broke a few weeks ago, we had more inspectors here than workers." There should be a way of protecting workers and consumers from the injustices of the past—but do we need 647 forms?

In the summer of 1978, state and local officials descended on Billy Halliwell, an enterprising 11-year-old from Roseland, N.J., who set up shop in his sister's red wagon dispensing coffee and doughnuts to sleepy motorists waiting in gas lines. Billy lacked a peddler's license, failed to collect state sales taxes and neglected to file a quarterly return with state authorities. Only after his father paid nearly $1,000 in legal fees was the boy allowed to resume business—after surrendering 21 cents in tax payments.

Martha Hudson, a housewife from Appomattox, Va., started a business of providing transportation service in her area for sight-seeing trips and shopping expeditions, but she encountered a regulatory dead end. "First," she says,

> I found that my auto-insurance company would not insure a vehicle used for this purpose except through a plan that cost around $2,000 a year. Next, I checked with the Department of Motor Vehicles and found that I would have to obtain a permit from the State Corporation Commission and the Interstate Commerce Commission.
>
> After checking with an attorney, I had to give up the idea completely. He informed me that Greyhound and Trailways bus services had a franchise to provide transportation, and would do everything possible to stop any individual from cutting in on their business. He also said it would cost me up to $100,000 to get the permit from the state. Naturally, I did not have that kind of money.

And it appears that even recent attempts at controlling regulation have simply imposed an additional bureaucratic layer. The owner of a company that manufacturers screws in Chicago explains:

> The Government wants to have a continuing picture of the country's business scene, so it insists that its regulatory agencies develop what they call business and industry "profiles." Now that's a sound enough idea. Government ought to know how things are. But to get this profile, we receive forms from maybe a dozen different agencies, the Bureau of Labor Statistics, the Federal Trade Commission, the Census Bureau and so on. Some of these are 20 pages long. The trouble is they all ask the same questions.

There does, however, appear to be hope on the horizon. Congress enacted the Regulatory Flexibility Act last year requiring that each agency of the Federal Government prepare a report on the impact of proposed regulations on small business. It also requires that the agency consider "two-tiered" regulation if it appears that a particular act would place unfair strictures on smaller businesses in comparison with large corporations. Robert Dotchin of the Senate Small Business Committee appears optimistically ambivalent about what the effects of this new act will be: "It may not have enough teeth in it. But it does insure than an agency be more sensitive to the unique needs of small business, rather than having small business be just an afterthought in the regulatory process. We're keeping our fingers crossed."

Another encouraging sign is that President Reagan has taken partial cognizance of the problem. "Overregulation," he has told Congress, "causes small and independent businessmen and women, as well as large business, to defer or terminate plans for expansion and, since they're responsible for most of the jobs, those new jobs just aren't created." His point is correct and it may well be the first time in a long while that a President has put small business ahead of big business in a sentence.

Whether one talks about the problems of regulation, lack of capital or lack of information, one thing seems clear: small business has found its voice, and its voice is being heard.

From the small-business associations springing up at the grass-roots level across the United States to the major national groups now actively lobbying in Washington, it is apparent that the interests and concerns of millions of American entrepreneurs have begun to crystallize and find expression—much as did the concerns of environmentalists a decade ago. The Council of Smaller Enterprises, the Coalition of Small and Independent Business Associations, the National Small Business Association, the Small Business Legislative Council, the National Association of Women Business Owners—such organizations are thriving and becoming increasingly effective in providing services and representing the concerns of their members to the Government and the public.

Government has begun to hear the small-business community, and to realize that helping this newly unified constituency is now a political imperative. As Gov. Richard D. Lamm of Colorado put it: "There is a tidal wave behind me. Its name is small business. And any politician who does not look over his shoulder at that wave will be a politician out of a job.". . .

Despite all that has been said, it should also be pointed out that small-business people do not want handouts. What they want is a fair opportunity. The free-enterprise system is supposed to allow winners to win and losers to lose. But they should not lose for the wrong reasons. An entrepreneur should have a reasonable chance to see whether his idea—for a product or a service—can fly. Because of what small business gives to this nation, it should be the business of Government, the private sector, labor, and an informed public to see that the coming years bring an increase in the success rate—rather than the failure rate—of new enterprises.

But no matter how much or how little assistance our small-business people are given, the entrepreneurial spirit will stay alive and keep kicking. For though it is true that the nation seems to face intractable economic difficulties, it is also true that there is, living in many Americans, a fiercely individualistic, bullheaded dreamer who, deep down, believes in a kind of magic. It is a magic of effort and ego and obsession that can make happen what other people consider impossible. George Bernard Shaw said: "The reasonable man adapts himself to the world, the unreasonable one persists in trying to adapt the world to himself. Therefore all progress depends on the unreasonable man." Americans can be a mighty unreasonable people when they want to be. And if I am reading my tea leaves correctly, we're starting to become unreasonable again.

3.3   Big Business Has Lost Its Entrepreneurial Instincts

BUSINESS WEEK

Item: Harry J. Gray, 60, chairman and chief executive officer of United Technologies Corp., points with pride to the "Spirit," his company's new commercial helicopter, as a true innovation. Although it drained profits for several years, he insists its potential made the losses worthwhile. Yet he also says that UT will now only make investments with a potential 20% annual return.

Item: H. Jack Meany, 57, president and CEO of Norris Industries Inc., says that over the last decade Norris has spent "more on new facilities than the market value or net worth of the company," even when it has meant settling for 10-year paybacks. Yet Norris managers have their bonuses based on annual financial performance.

Item: Fletcher L. Byrom, 61, chairman of Koppers Co., describes himself as an "enabler"—someone who encourages managers to take risks. Yet Byrom insists on a nonwaivable rule that new investments produce an average 25% return before taxes and interest during the first five years, as well as a maximum five-year payback.

There is a schizophrenia pervading U. S. business today. It is a rare CEO who has not publicly expounded on the need for focusing on the future—usually couched within a speech castigating government or labor unions for their short-term policies. Yet the compensation systems in their companies, the financial requirements for investment projects, the criteria for management-by-objectives goals and for performance appraisal, all point to an exceedingly short-term orientation.

Consultants, academics, and even some politicians have been sounding a red alert for some time. "The measure of achievement and the goals to be reached are as short-term as a politician's next election,'' Senator Lloyd Bentsen (D-Tex.) told businessmen participating in a conference on U.S. competitiveness last April. ''When you want to make this year's annual report look as good as possible, why engage in market-entry pricing in East Asia? Why accept losses for two or three years to build volume and brand recognition?'' he asked.

When pressed, most corporate chiefs will admit that Bentsen's rhetorically scathing questioning is fair. Even Koppers' Byrom wistfully admits that he does not know ''how many potentially good investments never got [presented to me] because they didn't show a 25% return.'' But buck-passing for shortsightedness is rampant. Most corporate leaders blame pressure from Wall Street and from their own boards. ''Stock analysts don't begin to spend the time researching key management structure and ability in the same manner they research the numbers,'' complains Peter G. Scotese, vice-chairman and CEO of Springs Mills Inc. Edson W. Spencer, chairman at Honeywell Inc., adds: ''No matter how much I say about building the company longer-term, short-term performance is the issue that seems to take on most importance.''

To be sure, the complaints are valid. But significantly, they are not universal. Thomas V. Jones, chairman and CEO of Northrop Corp., insists that ''Wall Street can understand [investment in the future]. Investors who are interested only in the short-term shouldn't be our stockholders, and analysts' reports on our company reflect this.'' In fact, the fat profits that Northrop is today booking on its 747 business with Boeing Co. stem from a $62 million investment the company started making in 1966. Although it was a drain on profits for a number of years, Jones states that ''if we hadn't dared [to make] the investment, we wouldn't have the profits today.'' Similarly, James E. Burke, chairman and CEO of Johnson & Johnson, insists that one of J&J's tenets is ''not to be too fearful of failure.'' In the 1950s, he recalls, J&J took a $9 million loss on an abortive attempt to use collagen to replace catgut as a suture material—yet that research has led to a lucrative business in using the collagen for sausage casing. Currently, the company is suffering heavy losses on its acquisition of Technicare Corp., a maker of high-technology diagnostic imaging devices, but Burke is not fearful. ''Diagnostic imaging is going to be important,'' he states simply.

Why are so few business leaders unwilling to buck Wall Street by taking similar risks? The reasons are multifold. Some stem from a society that has stressed immediate gratification to a fault. Many stem from the structure of the typical company. But most stem from the managers themselves.

The tunnel vision pervading executive suites comes from a combination of psychological, cultural, and structural reasons. Corporate chiefs grew up in the same shortsighted culture as their directors and shareholders. And they have shaped the cultures of their companies. Not surprisingly, it is the people who work for companies that have remained entrepreneurial who are most willing to agree with that premise. "The nonentrepreneurial background of top managers attracts similarly minded people whose outlook is to make the fast buck and not plan for the future," says Friedrich W. Schroeder, director of corporate development at Hewlett-Packard Co., which is known for fairly innovative management. The occasional maverick who bucks the system rarely makes it to the top, adds Peter R. Sugges, professor of management at Temple University. "You can only become a manager if you adopt the mores and strictures of managers," he says. "The only way to change any company is to change the way people at the top think about the way business should be operated."

Ironically, the change that is needed probably would involve turning the clock back about 30 years. Before the merger craze of the 1960s, corporate leaders were, for the most part, autocratic, entrepreneurial types who were ready to take risks for ideas they felt in their guts would pan out. David Sarnoff took RCA Corp. into space-age technology. Thomas Watson Sr. and Thomas Watson Jr. plunged International Business Machines Corp. into computers when they were still in the realm of science fiction. Edwin H. Land would have grimaced at the idea of doing a discounted cash flow on research for the Polaroid camera.

But for the most part, today's corporate leaders are "professional managers"—business mercenaries who ply their skills for a salary and bonus but rarely for a vision. And those skills are generally narrow and specialized. Just as the general practitioner who made house calls is a dim memory, so is the hands-on corporate leader who rose through the ranks, learning every aspect of the business before managing it. Today's managers are known as great marketers, savvy lawyers, or hard-nosed financial men. Lacking a gut feeling for the *gestalt* of their businesses, they see managing by the numbers as their only recourse. What is more, they do not seem to generate those numbers through internal growth. All too often they see themselves as managers of a portfolio of companies, much like a portfolio of stocks. They become more concerned with buying and selling companies than with selling improved products to customers. According to Robert H. Hayes, a professor at Harvard Business School, more than $40 billion was spent on acquisitions in 1979 alone—more than was spent on research and development and none of which created new value. James B. Farley, chairman of Booz, Allen & Hamilton Inc., notes that as often as not the acquisitions add nothing to either party. "People used to talk about synergy, but they no longer do," he says. "There really is no synergy in most acquisitions."

Worse, there really is little synergy created between departments and divisions at most companies. And the blame can generally be laid at the top manager's doorstep. Theodore Barry & Associates, a West Coast consulting firm, recently studied 50 companies and, according to James B. Ayers, a company principal, concluded that "most executives have never participated in the line management process, so there is no sensitivity to the problems in this area." Ayers warns that we will "have to see a shift in the background of top executives to technical and operating skills because [now their] attention never goes beyond financial reports."

It does not look as if that switch will happen immediately. Korn/Ferry International, an executive search firm, recently queried more than 1,700 corporate vice-presidents—the group from which future top managers are most likely to be drawn. About 47% began their careers in either marketing or finance, and nearly 64% say that those two areas of responsibility are the fastest track to the top. "Senior-level executives are geared to getting [the] product out the door as opposed to being creative about it," explains John A. Sussman, Korn/Ferry's vice-president for research.

That type of bias filters down to all levels in the organization. Too often, chief executives send mixed signals to their staffs—on the one hand, they demand creativity, and on the other, they reward numbers. Anthony J. Marolda, vice-president of corporate development services at Arthur D. Little Inc., tells about a former client, a U.S. television manufacturer, that lost "bundles of money" by sticking with tube technology while its competitors switched to solid state. "The president, who had a financial background, told his engineering staff, 'If you want the new technology you can have it—but keep in mind that your bonus is based on profits next year,' " Marolda recalls. "He told me later that he wasn't comfortable with the technology so he passed along technical decisions to others."

Not surprisingly, the easiest substitute for comfort with alien technological or marketing concepts is a technique to measure them. Not only has internal rate of return and discounted cash flow replaced educated instincts for deciding on new projects, but quantitative approaches—or, at best, formularized ones—have even pervaded human resource management. Top management has become insulated from its employees. The old days of motivating employees by example and by general day-to-day closeness to the field have given way to consultants' techniques such as behavior modification, climate and attitude surveys, and the like. Salary administration is almost totally depersonalized. Although the term "merit increase" still hangs on in business parlance, most salary programs have degenerated into automatic percentage allocations.

Because the link between payroll and performance has become so fuzzy, corporations have tried to develop incentive compensation systems. But, these too have been formularized into percentages of salary and percentages of profit, so that a manager's bonus is as much tied to the general economy or windfall sales as it is to his performance. Managers are well aware that the people making the bonus compilations often have had little chance to know them personally and that numbers will be their criteria.

For many corporations, the answer seems to be management by objectives or performance-appraisal systems based on goal-setting and review. . . . A few companies have made a point of including nonfinancial criteria in their management-by-objectives goals. But most still couch those goals in terms of increasing sales, profits, or productivity. Even the manager's personal goals are generally stated in quantifiable terms—for example, returning to school for an MBA. If there is a company that encourages managers to set a goal of, say, doing basic research that may or may not lead to an incredible product breakthrough, *Business Week* has certainly not run into it.

It is a frustrating situation for those managers who genuinely believe that basic research or other intangible costs are essential. Walter L. Abel, vice-president of R&D at Emhart Corp., notes that he had a very difficult time getting management to accept development costs for Emhart's microprocessor-controlled shoe-stitching machine, now one of the company's hottest sellers. Yet now management is pestering him to come up with another such success. ''I say, 'Damn you, you won't put up money for three years of building up research knowledge, yet the stitching machine took seven years and that was a fast one,' '' he says.

The problem rests as much in executive mobility as in executive myopia. Harvard's Hayes notes that job tenure is less than five years nowadays, half of what it was in the 1950s. Although a CEO is less likely than a middle manager to leave his job unless pushed, habits built up over a lifetime career are hard to break. Not surprisingly, it is psychologically difficult for the typical CEO, who is nearly 60, to make decisions that may depress current earnings but will prove lucrative for his successor.

And even if he wanted to, chances are excellent that he would have a difficult time within the organizational structure of the typical large corporation. Our major corporations have blossomed into multiproduct, multidivisional, multi-locational hydras. They became far too diverse for any one corporate leader to embrace. So one formerly monolithic company after another decentralized into such things as profit centers, strategic business units, and the like. Every profit center had to have a general manager or a divisional president. Corporate headquarters had to have new staff people to whom the divisional people would report. Layer upon layer of management jobs were added to the structure. This layering created numerous operating-level jobs, making executive job-hopping not only feasible but fashionable, claims Hayes.

And the would-be job-hoppers quickly learned that the best way to get on a fast track in their own companies—or raided by another company—was to turn out good quarterly numbers. That view became reinforced by bonus systems that rewarded those same good numbers. The worst-case example is the recent scandal at H. J. Heinz Co., where management at three subsidiaries allegedly tinkered with accounts payable and receivable in order to smooth out earnings pictures and have an easy crack at meeting each year's financial goals.

No one is saying that the move toward decentralization or incentive compensation or even scientific management techniques were not good ideas at the time. Even the merger movement made sense in that many companies had grown to the point where they needed the benefit of both professional management support and the kind of cash cushion only a larger conglomerate could provide. But resistance to change seems to be endemic in corporate America.

"The greatest danger in turbulent times like ours is not the turbulence, but that you act rationally in terms of yesterday," says Peter Drucker in his new book, *Managing in Turbulent Times.*

No Risk-taking

American B-schools have certainly not helped. Warns Arthur D. Little's Marolda, "Large corporations have been virtually overrun by a proliferation of profit-zealous MBAs who are turning every nut another half-turn to get a payoff." Indeed, MBAs are prepared to apply specific skills to entry-level jobs in specific specialties.

The unabashedly quantitative schools like Carnegie-Mellon University are at least honest about what they are doing—teaching students the mathematical and technique-oriented skills of management. But the qualitative schools do not encourage risk-taking or original thinking any more than do the quantitative schools. The managers steeped in case histories at Harvard rarely think of taking a potentially profitable plunge in a chancy market.

Some business-school deans admit the problem, but they claim their hands are as tied by corporate demands as the CEOs say theirs are by stockholders. "We find that most of the corporations who come to campus to interview our graduates are looking for students with specific skills and characteristics that will be applicable to an initial job," admits David H. Blake, associate dean of the University of Pittsburgh's Graduate School of Business. "My fear is that we've allowed our clientele to determine what it is we do to a great extent."

That clientele, of course, includes the students themselves, and many academics complain that today's youth is quick-buck oriented in a way that would make the flower children of the 1960s cringe. Robert W. Lear, Columbia University's executive in residence, has a set speech that he gives to most graduating classes at the school. "None of you want to be horses," he tells them. "You want to be jockeys, bookies, have the hay concession for the stables, be the jockey's agent, or best of all, the management consultant to the racetrack. That's why none of you will ever be CEO of a major corporation in the U.S."

The danger is that he is wrong, and that it is exactly these dollar-oriented specialists who will be the leaders of tomorrow.

Discussion and Review Questions

1. What did Joseph Schumpeter mean when he described entrepreneurial activity as a process of "creative destruction?"

2. Why does the modern-day would-be entrepreneur face a high probability for failure? What kinds of problems does he/she face?

3. How do you account for the success of the marketing of KangaRoos by a small entrepreneur? Why didn't a big company undertake the venture?

4. How do you react to the argument that bigness in business destroys the "entrepreneurial function" that has historically been the centerpiece of the capitalist system?

5. What strategy would you suggest to keep large enterprises from abandoning their entrepreneurial roots?

PART 3

MANAGEMENT PROBLEMS

ISSUE 4

Has American Management Failed?

As we saw in the Introduction, the earliest American business enterprises were characterized by a single owner–entrepreneur who oversaw virtually all aspects of the firm's operations. Initially, this was not especially difficult since most early- and mid-nineteenth-century businesses were single product or limited product line enterprises. However, with the coming of the 3 Ds—diversification, development, and decentralization—the owner–manager type was replaced gradually by many managerial specialists. Functionally, enterprises were departmentalized into production, financial, and marketing segments, with each functional aspect having its own head. In turn these top managers presided over a hierarchy of lower managerial specialists in their particular field of corporate operations. Gradually, the prerogatives and authority of the owners of the enterprise declined as the real power shifted to the salaried management with its various divisions and layers of responsibility. The presidents and vice-presidents of businesses, not the stockholders, were the effective center of power within the average large firm by the beginning of the twentieth century.

The Emergence of American Management

With the rise and growing authority of the corporate manager, American business leaders began to concentrate their attention on the development of managerial talent and in organizing and defining the diverse responsibilities of the new managerial type. Undergraduate universities began adding business and management subjects to their curricula. Between 1898 and 1914, twenty-five business graduate schools were founded, including the Harvard Business School in 1908. Meanwhile, enterprises began to concentrate their efforts in analyzing and specifying the tasks, responsibilities, and functions of managers. The more ambitious began to talk about management as a "science"—a technique that could be learned rather than being a natural trait or aptitude of an individual. Doubtless the old entrepreneurs, many of whom showed little predilection for the attributes of modern managerial habits and thought—turned over in their graves with these developments. Nevertheless, it all seemed to be working. The American management model of departmentalized and hierarchically ordered business managers was seen by many as the real reason for American business's success in the twentieth century.

At the end of World War II, American management stood as a model for the rest of the world. American corporations had emerged from a long depression to organize the incredible production tasks demanded by the war. Within a matter of months consumer and producer goods industries were transformed into war producers. America became "the arsenal for democracy." By 1943, Henry Kaiser's Portland, Oregon, shipyards were turning out a ship a day (by using prefabricated techniques, Kaiser could assemble a medium-sized freighter in just twenty days). Boeing turned out 80,000 planes, and GM built 100,000 tanks during the war years.

The planning, organizing, directing, and controlling functions of management were so finely tuned that American management methods were quickly appropriated by all industrial nations after the war. The Japanese were particularly attentive students, reconstructing their postwar industrial and corporate operations along the lines of the American model, which, after all, had proved its efficiency by defeating them soundly. Even Communist Russia paid attention to the American model, showing particular interest in the corporate planning and organizing apparatus that had been developed by American industry during the war. As the Soviets knew, "planning" was quite as essential in a socialist society as it was in a capitalist one.

Management in Trouble

By the 1970s, however, American management methods had more critics than copiers. Most of the criticism, however, came not from the traditional liberal and radical critics of business (in fact, they were fairly quiet), but from the most respected business leaders and academic defenders of business. Plainly, American business had failed first to comprehend and second to adapt to the changed economic environment that followed the Arab oil embargo of 1973. As both inflation and foreign competition with American products grew in the 1970s, American management was overwhelmed by a state of inertia. Thomas A. Murphy, retiring chairman of GM, put it well in 1981 as he looked back over the decade: "The seventies were all but a disaster (for management). We seem to have spent most of our time not making decisions."[1]

The generally recessed economic conditions of the 1970s dribbled downward into a deep and, for many firms, chronic business slowdown by the 1980s. The utilization of industrial production capacity (the share of a firm's total facilities actually utilized in producing goods) fell in 1982 to 60 percent, a slowdown not seen since the Great Depression. On top of the bad showing of the 1970s, the recent trends added fuel to the "revisionists" among American business who saw the decline traceable to certain fundamental failures in American management. Dozens of books and articles appeared, arguing that, unless American management methods were radically altered, the American economy—and therefore the American business system—was in serious trouble.

What had happened? How did the American managerial system fall to such a low repute?

Generally, criticism has been leveled in five areas:

1. Corporate management in the United States has developed a short-run bias; that is, short-range goals have become much more important than long-range planning. Firms very frequently continue to squeeze the last pennies of profit from old production facilities and equipment or stay with old "tried and true" business techniques. For instance, although most of the modern steel producing technology used around the world actually was developed in the United States, most U.S. steel producers continue to use equipment and methods that are forty or fifty years old. The reason is that few are willing to undertake the expensive investment necessary now for greater profit in the future.

2. Corporate managers, especially at the top levels, have become very conservative. Unlike the Fords, Carnegies, Rockefellers, and other entrepreneurs of a past era in American business, modern management is not bold. The emphasis instead is on safe investments and certain profitability rather than on new ideas.

3. Many of the top corporate leaders are narrowly trained in financial fields alone, not in marketing, technology, and production. Having

made their way to the top by focusing on the financial side of business operations, they know little or nothing about the day-to-day operation of the firm or the long-run production and marketing problems. More-over, as financial experts, they tend to look for immediate dollar return on any business investment or business strategy. Such an immediate and narrow conception of profitability tends automatically to dismiss any undertaking that may take time to turn a profit. Although profits have indeed been high for most businesses, this short-term profit bias is stealing from the future.

4. With the exception of a few firms such as GE and IBM, American man-agers have not learned the strategy of selling overseas. Despite the growth of multinational firms (see issue twelve), American business has not, like the Japanese and Germans, pursued a vigorous policy of creat-ing overseas markets.

5. American management's approach to labor is outdated. Relying on old union–management strategies and, as we just noted in item one, em-ploying old production methods have encouraged declining produc-tivity.

Let's now proceed to our readings on this issue. The first of the fol-lowing readings expands upon the five points made in the preceding list. It is a strongly worded and powerful attack on contemporary business management practices. The second article takes a more promising view and proposes some cures for American management, largely based upon appropriating Japanese managerial strategy and some distinctly Ameri-can innovations.

Note

1. *New York Times Magazine*, January 1, 1981, p. 40.

4.1   America's Management Crisis

DAVID VOGEL

The creativity of American management has been one of the historic strengths of the American business system. Most of the technological innovations underlying the industrial revolution were developed in England, but it was the United States that pioneered new organizational techniques for improving productivity. Innovations such as standardized parts, introduced by Eli Whitney, the moving assembly line, conceived by Henry Ford, and the principles of scientific management developed by Frederick Taylor were responsible for much of the dramatic gains in America's industrial output during the 19th and early 20th centuries. The modern form of corporate organization now in use throughout the world was developed by railroad executives in the United States before the Civil War. The United States still has the world's most extensive and prestigious system of professional management education.

But American business managers, traditionally an important source of competitive strength, now have become a cause of national decline, even though business executives continue to blame government policies for the poor performance of the American economy. A widely quoted recent article in the *Harvard Business Review* asserted that much of the "competitive listlessness" of the US economy is due to the "attitudes, preoccupations, and practices of American managers." The article charged that preoccupation with "short-term results" and quantitative measurements of performance has led American managers to neglect the kinds of investments and innovations necessary to increase the nation's capacity to generate wealth. The authors, two Harvard Business School professors, conclude that many American managers "have effectively forsworn long-term technological superiority as a competitive weapon." *Business Week*'s special issue on reindustrialization a few months ago featured a similar indictment, specifically criticizing American managers for their lack of technical skills and for their nonentrepreneurial mentality.

Even many corporate executives have become self-critical on this score. In a recent poll, three out of four US executives criticized corporate incentive plans for rewarding short-term performance and thus discouraging risky long-term projects. One out of three believed that senior managers didn't know enough about technology and underemphasized innovation.

There is some hard evidence to support these perceptions. Industry spending for basic research declined 12 percent in real terms between 1966 and 1976. A 1969 survey of manufacturing companies revealed that 20 percent had a policy requiring all capital expenditures for modernization and replacement to pay for themselves within three years. A decade later this policy had been adopted by 25 percent of the companies polled. The change is small, but the trend is significant.

Senior managers have been spending more energy trying to increase their companies' short-term profits through financial manipulation. In 1979 companies spent more than $40 billion in cash on acquiring other companies. This is far more than they spent on research and development. Some of these mergers may have led to improved efficiency, but most of them were little more than private sector transfer payments—money passing from one set of balance sheets to another without producing any net increase in actual wealth. . . .

More and more chief executive officers have only the most casual familiarity with what their companies actually make and how. They are more likely than ever before to have been hired away from another company, often in a completely unrelated line of business. And they are less likely than before to have had any operating or line experience. Since the mid-1950s, the proportion of American chief executives trained in either law or finance has increased by nearly half while the proportion with technical backgrounds has declined by nearly 15 percent. . . .

Critical business decisions too often are made not on the basis of a true understanding of the technology but on elegant formulas learned in business school. Increasingly, executives manage their companies in the detached way that investors manage their portfolios.

The typical chief executive officer now holds office for an average of five years, compared to 10 years a generation ago. Since CEOs tend to be judged and judge themselves by the profits reported while they are in charge, they are understandably reluctant to pursue long-term projects that depress current earnings and won't pay off until after they retire. Executives frequently criticize politicians for making decisions on the basis of short-term considerations in order to ensure their reelection. But the same indictment applies even more to managers in the private sector. Elected officials have a time horizon of at least two years, but executive promotions within companies often are based on earnings calculated on an annual basis. Akio Morita, the chairman of Sony, recently observed: "The annual bonus some American executives receive depends on annual profit, and the executive who knows his firm's production facilities should be modernized isn't likely to make a decision to invest in new equipment if his own income and managerial ability are judged based only on annual profit. . . . I have heard many American managers say, 'Why should I sacrifice my profit for my successor?' "

For many years, a powerful piece of evidence against British management has been that American owned and managed companies in Great Britain have higher productivity than other firms in the British economy. A similar unflattering comparison now may be made between the productivity of native-run and foreign-run companies in the United States. The best known example is a television plant in Illinois. When it was run by Motorola, inspectors found 140 defects for every 100 television sets. Since the plant was bought by Matsushita Electric Industrial Company in 1974, the number of defects declined to less than six per 100 sets. The number of warranty claims dropped by seven-eighths. American managers frequently attribute Japanese efficiency to values peculiar to Japanese culture; but one assembly line at Sony's San Diego plant holds the company's worldwide record for production: 200 days without a serious defect.

The contrast in quality between American and Japanese products has become increasingly obvious over the last decade. American consumers continue to prefer Japanese products (often as not made in Taiwan and South Korea) even as the Japanese price advantage has all but disappeared. According to a recent article in *Fortune*, a new American car is almost twice as likely to have a problem as a Japanese model, and American-made computer chips are three times more likely to fail than Japanese ones.

Both our slow productivity growth and the relatively poor quality of many American goods are connected to the training and incentives of American managers. It is difficult for MBAs—trained to measure discounted cash flow and capital asset pricing models—to work closely with employees in search of ways to improve procedures and equipment. The incentives for managers to make productivity improvements actually declined during the 1970s, as many companies switched from a strategy of expanding sales to one emphasizing immediate return of assets. According to the *Wall Street Journal*, the consequence of rewarding executives by this second measure encouraged them to make small investments that paid off quickly, rather than larger outlays that might greatly improve productivity eventually, but that were riskier and would take longer to show results.

Many large corporations have made the transition from founder–entrepreneur to professional management without suffering any decline of entrepreneurial vigor. Firms such as IBM, DuPont, Boeing, Texas Instruments, and Minnesota Mining and Manufacturing have demonstrated both a willingness and patience in waiting for the pay-off. A company run by a scientist is not guaranteed continued success, as Polaroid's recent experiences indicate. Nor, as the history of the steel industry reveals, does a policy of promoting from within the ranks ensure informed management decisions. Various companies and plants throughout the United States have demonstrated impressive increases in productivity by involving workers in the decision-making process at the plant level. But the overall picture remains discouraging.

Managers are not completely at fault, of course. Just one special problem they face is that American industry is far more dependent on the stock market as a source of capital than our foreign competitors are. Japanese and German firms are financed mostly by borrowing, not selling shares. This frees them to make long-term investments without Wall Street money-managers scrutinizing each quarterly earnings report. It is impossible to determine the precise role played by any one factor in America's economic difficulties. But it is important that public discussion of the economy's poor performance not focus exclusively on the need for changes in government policy.

Under President Reagan the business community may get many of the changes in tax and regulatory policies that it claims it needs. But unless the private sector's own pattern of incentives and training is reformed, US-managed companies are likely to continue to lose market shares to foreign competitors. Instead of hiring more lobbyists, American companies should promote more engineers. We need to reexamine the kind of education that those to whom we entrust our economic future are getting. Has the notion of a professional manager—an individual who learns a set of general analytical, abstract, decision-making skills that can be applied equally well to the problems faced by any institution—become as irrelevant as the British classical Oxbridge education became several generations ago? Why are the nations with the most developed systems of professional management education, the United States and Great Britain, performing so poorly, when two nations that provide almost no professional management training, Germany and Japan, have been the outstanding successes of the postwar period? Virtually none of the nation's major business schools require courses in production or offer adequate training in the management of human resources. Business schools ignore foreign language training and place little emphasis on teaching students to understand foreign cultures. The popularity of finance courses at business schools probably has contributed to the preoccupation of recently graduated MBAs with short-term time horizons.

Corporate critics also need to redirect their thinking. Except in cases of particularly gross blunders, like the recent bloopers of the automobile and steel industries, critics of business tend to take the competence of US management for granted. They most often criticize companies for being *too* successful in their pursuit of profits, and thereby neglecting other legitimate social needs. But Milton Friedman is right in saying that the most important social responsibility of business is in fact to produce wealth. We need to be as critical about the inability of companies to grow and innovate as we are about their failures of social responsibility.

4.2   Overhauling Management

STEVE LOHR

At his desk in New York at 8 A.M., Akio Morita, the small, elegant, slender 59-year-old chairman and co-founder of the Sony
Corporation, is engaged in an overseas telephone call. He is discussing business with a colleague, speaking in rapid, clipped ca-
dence. Upon finishing the call, he rises to greet a visitor and
quickly launches into a highly informed discussion of American
politics. Akio Morita has become a man of two cultures—Japanese
and American—and he also happens at the moment to be the very
symbol of the kind of change in business-management techniques
that has successfully occurred in one culture and, many people believe, must take place in the other.

Indeed, the prevalence in the United States of all manner of
Sony merchandise—televisions, radios, tape recorders, video-cas-
sette recorders and the like—is testimony to the triumph of his approach, and indirect confirmation that American business is in
need of repair.

For years, Morita says, he was one of those who regarded
America as ''a teacher,'' a nation whose management methods
were to be emulated as much as possible. Now, however, he believes that, ''for much of the trouble of the American economy,
American management has to take the responsibility.''

Not that Akio Morita's highly admired achievements—in marketing, product development and quality control, for example—
were arrived at with perfect ease. He was long regarded as something of an outsider in his country, apart from the traditional
Japanese establishment, one of a handful of aggressive entrepreneurs who emerged after World War II and whose brazen style was
considered un-Japanese. Morita, along with his partner, Masaru
Ibuka, started a small electronics business in Tokyo back in 1948.

In the 1950's, when American consumers saw the tag ''Made
in Japan,'' it was a stigma—a code phrase for shoddy merchandise.
Sony, more than any other company, was responsible for revers-

ing that image. The turnabout was so substantial that, by 1972, when Sony opened its first American manufacturing plant in San Diego, Calif., to construct color televisions, its dealers were concerned that its American-made television sets wouldn't match the quality of those made in Japan. The company now has a second factory in the United States, located in Dothan, Ala., which in 1977 began producing magnetic tape, cassettes for the Betamax recorder and audio tape. Today, Sony's American arm is nearly a $1 billion-a-year operation employing 4,500 workers, and the quality seems to have held up fine.

In Morita's view, the trouble with a large segment of American management is attributable to two misguided attitudes: American managers are too worried about short-term profits and too little concerned about their workers. These two mistakes, Morita says, are connected and go a long way toward explaining productivity problems.

"A lot of American companies know they have old machines," he says. "But the manager figures he'll keep the old machines as long as they still run, make a big profit one year, and take that record as an advertisement to get a job elsewhere. So productivity here declines."

Most American managers, according to Morita, take a short-sighted view of their workers. Indeed, it is the antagonism between management and labor in America that Morita thinks is most counterproductive. Here lies one of the greatest contrasts between the United States and Japan, with its tradition of corporate paternalism and lifetime employment. Morita argues that the Japanese approach to labor management is not a cultural eccentricity, applicable only in Japan. He says it can be transplanted, in a slightly watered-down form, into America. As evidence, he points to Sony's plants at San Diego and Dothan, where, he says, productivity has risen steadily so that it now is very close to that of the company's factories in Japan. "The workers in San Diego and Dothan are terrific," says Morita.

It is difficult for an outsider to gauge the success Sony and other Japanese companies have had in bringing their type of management into the United States. But those who have studied the Sony experience here agree for the most part that it has gone fairly well and that American managers should be taking notes. . . .

Though the American horizon has been gloomy, it has also had its bright spots in the past decade—particularly in the computer and semiconducter industry. The rapid pace of technological change in this area is truly difficult to comprehend. Modest folk in the industry are fond of citing the following by way of helpful illustration: If the aircraft industry had progressed as rapidly as the semiconductor or computer business in recent years, the Concorde would now hold 10,000 passengers, travel at 60,000 miles an hour and a ticket would cost 1 cent. Others maintain that what is happening is virtually tantamount to a second industrial revolution.

How did these businessmen triumph when so many others around them were not doing well?

"Unlike steel, autos and some others, this industry has never been an oligopoly," Robert N. Noyce says of the field of semiconductors. "It has always been intensely competitive. And it has always been a brain-intensive industry, rather than a capital-intensive one. It has been an industry where, if your key people don't agree with you, they take off, start their own businesses and become your competitors."

Robert Noyce knows whereof he speaks. In 1968, he and Gordon E. Moore, two scientists working for Fairchild Semiconductor in northern California, split off and, with a grubstake of $2 million in venture capital, founded a fledgling outfit called Intel (for Integrated Electronics). Soon afterward, they were joined by Andrew S. Grove, another former Fairchild scientist. By 1970, Intel, of Santa Clara, Calif., reported sales of $4 million. By 1980, the sales were increased to $900 million, and the work force had reached 15,000. Ironically, though short-term profit has not been its chief goal, Intel has managed to keep its pretax profit margins safely above 20 percent—twice the average of its major competitors—during booms and recessions alike. Accordingly, Intel is probably now the company held in highest esteem in a highly esteemed field.

There's more to Intel's story than a willingness on the part of intelligent employees to disagree with their boss—though that's an important part of it. The whole story tells a good deal about where alert American corporations may be headed in the future, and, by way of contrast, about what many firms have failed to do in the recent past.

First, Noyce, Moore and Grove were not shy about charging ahead with controversial new technologies—initially with the computer memory chip and then with the microprocessor, or computer on a chip. By introducing slight impurities onto a wafer of silicon, used in the manufacture of semiconductors for computers, and etching microscopic patterns on its surface, the Intel manufacturers were able to place many thousands of electronic circuits onto a "chip" smaller than a dime.

The managers have been willing, too, to pour an unusually large share of the proceeds back into the business. They invest roughly 10 percent of yearly revenues in research and development. The company's capital-spending program for new facilities and equipment totaled about $150 million last year.

Intel is not the largest supplier in the industry; it is No. 4— smaller in size than Texas Instruments, National Semiconductor and Motorola. However, the company has not tried to be the biggest, concentrating instead on staying at the technological frontier. Intel has been there first with the most, technologically speaking, and it has done so more consistently than its competitors. Typically, the company will experiment and test-market a new product, then later will have experience in producing it more efficiently and more cheaply than the competition.

All the while, Intel is striving to ferret out the next technological leap needed to renew the cycle. Indeed, the company is now in the midst of another long-range jump in technology, developing devices that will eventually be complex enough to put the computing power of an entire mainframe computer (the nation's largest and most powerful computer) on a handful of silicon chips. Should it slip in this effort, the company would suffer greatly. But based on Intel's track record so far, competitors aren't betting that it will fail.

In combining technological mastery with extraordinary business success, Intel has been a management innovator, both in style and structure. The central management problem for a fast-growing high-technology company is to solve one riddle: how to stay flexible and nimble, in tune with emerging technologies and markets, even as its very growth tends to make the concern sluggish and bureaucratic. The answer may lie both in structure and philosophy.

Intel has a three-man executive office, made up of Noyce, Moore and Grove. Simply put, Noyce is the "outside man," who spends nearly half his time on things not directly connected with Intel, such as speaking to the financial community, Government policy makers and serving as a member of the National Academy of Science. Moore is the company's long-range thinker, charting its product strategy. Grove, a scientist-turned-manager, is the person who runs Intel day-to-day.

Intel is organized to avoid the bureaucratic hierarchy that is characteristic of most corporations. Workers may have several bosses, depending on the problem at hand. Instead of staff specialists for purchasing, quality control and so on, Intel has several dozen committees, or "councils," that make decisions and enforce standards in specialized fields. These groups are overlaid on a grid of about 25 so-called strategic business segments that do product planning.

"What we've tried to do is to put people together in ways so that they make contributions to a wider range of decisions and do things that would be thwarted by a structured, line-type organization," Noyce explains.

But more than structure, it is Intel's "culture," as Drucker puts it, that sets it apart from most American companies. There are no "offices" at Intel, only shoulder-high partitions separating the work space of individual white-collar employees. White collars, for that matter, are scarce as well; there is no dress code and very few of the men wear ties. There are no reserved parking spaces for executives, no limousines, no separate dining rooms. Top managers eat in one of the company cafeterias, along with everyone else, or in lunch-hour meetings with one of the ad hoc problem-solving groups. Everyone is expected to report to the job at 8 A.M. sharp. "I can justify my salary, just as I can justify the salary of a production operator, a technician or an engineer—it's a function of the market," says Grove, the company's 44-year-old president, who wears an open-necked beige shirt with a gold chain underneath. "But I can't justify why I should get a reserved parking space. There's no justification for that at all."

At the council sessions, it is expected that all will participate as equals, with new employees challenging senior executives. Ultimately, the top managers must pass judgment on the projects that will consume the many millions of dollars needed not merely to keep up but, more important, to set the pace of technological development. "But we go through the discussion as equals," says Grove.

Many of the elements of Intel's management approach strike skeptics, especially those familiar with traditional corporate practices, as empty symbolism and affectation. Neither is the case, Grove argues. "It isn't symbolism at all," he says. "It's a necessity, I think, for this company in this industry with the technology shifting so fast, and that rapid change will continue."

He explains: "I can't pretend to know the shape of the next generation of silicon or computer technology anymore. That's why people like me need the knowledge from the people closest to the technology. That's why we can't have the hierarchical barriers to an exchange of ideas and information that you have at so many corporations."

Grove has an example of what is wrong with many companies. He presents a newspaper clipping that described an incident leading to the dismissal of William A. Niskanen Jr., chief economist at Ford. In late 1979, Niskanen had advised his bosses that Government-imposed quotas on Japanese cars would not solve Ford's problems, and this view was not popular among the company higher-ups. "In the meeting in which I was informed that I was released," Niskanen told a reporter, "I was told, 'Bill, in general, people who do well in this company wait until they hear their superiors express their view, and then contribute something in support of that view.' "

"That," says Grove, "is precisely the kind of attitude that we cannot afford here." . . .

If, despite the acknowledgment of serious problems, there seems to be a new optimism in the business community, it may be in part because of the improved political and social milieu in the United States. It is impossible to say with much certainty just what the long-range effect will be of having Ronald Reagan in the Oval Office and more Republicans in Congress. But with the economy a key issue in the election, the results do reflect increasing popular support for the traditional economic goal of conservatives—the creation of wealth—and away from the liberal objective—the distribution of wealth. . . .

The basic optimism comes, however, from the new attitude of management itself. There is a lengthening of corporate sights, now that, as one Japanese executive said privately, "your managers are beginning to recognize many of their industries are engaged in a global fight for survival." He offered the following elaboration: When Japan attacked Pearl Harbor, he said, the United States had the seventh largest navy in the world. By the end of World War II, the American fleet was the biggest. "When forced to," he said, "Americans can respond vigorously. Ultimately, that is what your nation will probably do about its current economic problems, and your corporate managers must lead the response."

Based on talks in recent months with a broad spectrum of representatives and observers of American management, it appears that the response is coming. The past failures and current weaknesses are recognized and accepted, and there is a readiness to try corrective techniques. At present, it is impossible to discern the precise contours of the expected transformation—just how American corporations will be structured and run differently a decade or two from now. Nonetheless, certain harbingers are clear.

Given the ever-quickening pace of change, companies can only benefit from a broader participation in decision making by their increasingly educated workers. To stay attuned to fast-changing markets, technologies and production techniques, it helps to have the information and cooperation of those closest to the operation—the workers. Companies that do this effectively are what Ouchi of U.C.L.A. would call "type Z" concerns (see next issue). However, the label attached to such companies is relatively unimportant; what is significant is that more and more corporations are trying it. And it is not just the Intels or Hewlett-Packards, relatively young companies dwelling in the rarefied realm of futuristic technology. General Motors has completed a project in an assembly plant in Brookhaven, Miss., to increase worker participation in the corporate decision-making process. The company is so pleased with the results—"with trust, anything is possible," the project directors concluded—that it is now undertaking 160 organizational changes at plants throughout the country, with the full support of the United Automobile Workers. And at plants throughout the auto industry, workers have been given the authority to shut down the assembly line if they think that, for whatever reason, quality control standards are not being met—a revolutionary change. The particular corporate milieu, or culture, within which the worker is given greater authority and responsibility will vary from company to company. This changing character in boss–worker relations, becoming more a two-way street, seems one representative example of the shift in traditional management perceptions and practices that is now apparently under way. The changes are, in a sense, a return to elemental American values, to more democratic organizations and away from the hierarchical class structure found in so many large corporations today.

Similarly, the task of corporate management is to fashion solutions to the problems of business that are firmly in the American mold, to borrow perhaps from other cultures but not mimic them. American society is individualistic, pluralistic and entrepreneurial. These are the historic sources of generative energy that largely explain the economic rise in the United States and, most agree, constitute this nation's greatest potential advantage in the unfolding competition for global markets. To renew, encourage and channel these energies is a challenge facing American management today.

Discussion and Review Questions

1. What were the 3 Ds and how did they affect the organization of American business enterprise?

2. What are some of the reasons given by critics to explain the alleged recent deterioration of American management practices?

3. Vogel argues that very frequently chief executive officers of American firms "have only the most casual familiarity with what their companies actually make and how." If this is true, what is the result? How would you deal with this problem?

4. In what important ways does Japanese management differ from current American management style?

5. Do you think managers should start their corporate careers on "the plant floor"? What would be the advantages and disadvantages of such a style?

ISSUE 5

Will Theory Z Replace X and Y *or* What Can Be Learned from the Japanese?

Recently it has become fashionable to be critical of modern workplace activities as boring and unfulfilling. We tend to look back wistfully at work before its domination by machine technology. Yet, for all the idealizing of past work activities and the supposed sense of satisfaction that individual craftsmanship once provided, it is probably true that throughout history the driving force behind most workers was the threat of hunger and privation that resulted from not working. In the preindustrial era, work was defined by and basically limited to the immediate needs of subsistence. In largely agrarian and rural economic settings, these needs were met relatively easily so long as the weather and political conditions collaborated. Most individuals provided for their needs with their own hands. However, with the coming of the industrial–urban era in the nineteenth century, work took on new forms. Individuals in the mills, mines, factories, and counting houses did not produce directly their subsistence but worked for wages, which presumably would buy subsistence needs (and maybe a little more). These individuals also had to adapt to the discipline of machine production with its requirements for regular work attendance, meeting production targets, and laboring in conjunction with others. For the early industrial employers, the problems of maintaining and ever increasing worker output surfaced very early.

The Rise of Scientific Management

At first, the old threat of hunger served fairly well to "regularize and discipline" labor—and to allow for the worst kinds of tyrannical and brutal handling of the workforce. However, by the closing years of the nineteenth century, the complexity and vastness of industrial production required more than driving and brutal bosses to keep labor in line and production up. Studying the problem in the 1880s, Frederick Taylor concluded that the average factory and office worker could be "induced" to increase their labors and thus their output by having employers (1) study and redefine work tasks so as to reduce physical exertion, (2) fit workers to jobs they were particularly skilled at, (3) set up a system of wages that rewarded the better workers who turned out goods at a higher than average rate, and (4) establish "functional foremen" who worked closely with the workers in planning and evaluating labor.

From present-day perspectives, none of Taylor's ideas seem particularly revolutionary. In fact, they seem obvious. However, before Taylor, no one had sat down and systematically studied work, wages, and worker direction and motivation. To Taylor and a generation of personnel experts that followed him, it was assumed that with planning and good management workers naturally would produce more if there were reasonable pay incentives. While the coming of labor unions and collective bargaining eventually reduced management's freedom in setting output goals and wage rates, the Taylor philosophy has stubbornly persisted in personnel management theory (with a few notable corporate exceptions).

Theory X or Theory Y

In 1960, psychologist Douglas McGregor termed the prevailing approach to personnel management "Theory X." According to this managerial view, the average worker had a basic dislike for work and so had to be both coerced and bribed into pursuing specific work tasks. Moreover, according to Theory X, the average worker actually prefers and expects this treatment since he has relatively little ambition and wants security above all. Still, the fear of privation was seen as the underlying motivation to labor.

McGregor, however, felt such a view of labor was both wrong and counterproductive. Instead, he offered "Theory Y," which held that

1. People do not inherently dislike work; in fact, work is "as natural as play or rest."
2. Given some freedom, the average individual will work on his own toward the organization's objectives without need of controls or threats by bosses.
3. How deeply an individual is committed to the organization's objectives depends on "the rewards associated with their achievement." The primary and most important rewards are those that satisfy the worker's ego and provide "self-actualization."
4. The average worker "learns, under proper conditions, not only to accept but to seek responsibility."
5. Many individuals are capable of a high degree of inventiveness and creativity.
6. Nevertheless, under modern work conditions, the intellectual potential of the average human being "is only partly utilized."

McGregor believed that how management treated its workers was a self-fulfilling prophecy: If managers viewed workers as lazy and stupid, that is exactly how workers would behave. On the other hand, if management saw workers as desiring challenge and willing to work on their own, then workers would react accordingly. Obviously, from McGregor's point of view, the enlightened firm would adopt Theory Y, the self-direction approach. In fact, he saw growing problems for firms that continued to follow the old authoritarianism of Theory X.

The Rise of Theory Z

Humane as the Theory Y approach appeared, a number of management specialists proposed going a step further—actually sharing the controls of management and allowing the worker to participate in a portion of the planning and execution of management tasks. In other words, the worker was invited to participate in planning his own labor and perhaps even determining his own reward. Eventually labeled "Theory Z" by William Ouchi in his 1981 bestseller of the same name, the idea was applied and refined early at Hewlett-Packard, Dayton-Hudson, Rockwell International, and dozens of other American firms in the 1970s.

Under a Theory Z plan, management is first encouraged to "bring the employees into the firm." Information about production, marketing, the competition, pricing, and so forth, which usually is held back as part of management's "secrets," is openly provided to the workers. They are brought into the "big picture" of the firm as much as possible so that they can see where the firm is headed and what its strengths and weaknesses are. Having drawn the employee into the "big picture," the next step is to encourage the employee to react openly to production targets and production techniques that directly or indirectly affect his job. Moreover, workers should be encouraged to seek out creative solutions on their own when problems arise. Management should do more listening to the workers and improve its interpersonal relations and communications skills. Orders, when given, should be less like orders and more like group agreements.

Under these conditions management would not fade away but it would fade into the background at the lower levels. It still would carry on most of its overseeing functions, but increasingly the workers themselves would solve problems that in the past had been unilaterally a matter of management prerogative. Production targets, for instance, might eventually be set by the group, not simply by the boss. However, the new worker freedom would not mean the end of all authority. Under Theory Z, management still retains the right to punish or separate nonproductive workers, but, with workers themselves identifying more with the firm's objectives and also with management's objectives, less worker–management friction would exist, even in areas affecting employee dismissals. Workers themselves would support the separation of nonproductive colleagues. This summary of Ouchi's revolutionary argument is expanded in the first of our readings in this section.

As Ouchi and other sympathizers pointed out, the origins for this revolutionary approach to personnel management were to be found in the modern Japanese economy. In the years after World War II, the Japanese, so the argument ran, had produced an economic miracle by increasing worker output by more than 400 percent between 1950 and 1980. At the same time, Japan approached per capita income levels of the United States. The source of this growth was seen as the "special relationship" between Japanese workers and management.

It would be inaccurate, however, to assume that the Theory Z advocates and the Japanese model supporters simply have captured American management thought and practice. Indeed, most companies have not changed their personnel policies, and very many are philosophically opposed to change—not simply because managers might lose their authority but because they do not believe Japanese cultural values would or should be adaptable to the United States. The second article in this section examines the cultural differences that might make it difficult for the American worker and American management to adopt the Japanese style. The concluding article examines as a case study Sharp Corporation, a Japanese-owned, American-based electronics firm.

5.1   The Japanese Management Model

WILLIAM OUCHI

Probably the best known feature of Japanese organizations is their participative approach to decision making. In the typical American organization the department head, division manager, and president typically each feel that "the buck stops here"—that they alone should take the responsibility for making decisions. Recently, some organizations have adopted explicitly participative modes of decision making in which all of the members of a department reach consensus on what decision to adopt. Decision making by consensus has been the subject of a great deal of research in Europe and the United States over the past twenty years, and the evidence strongly suggests that a consensus approach yields more creative decisions and more effective implementation than does individual decision making.

Western style participative decision making is by now a fairly standardized process. Typically, a small group of not more than eight or ten people will gather around a table, discuss the problem and suggest alternative solutions. During this process, the group should have one or more leaders skilled at managing relationships between people so that underlying disagreements can be dealt with constructively. The group can be said to have achieved a consensus when it finally agrees upon a single alternative and each member of the group can honestly say to each other member three things:

1. I believe that you understand my point of view.
2. I believe that I understand your point of view.
3. Whether or not I prefer this decision, I will support it, because it was arrived at in an open and fair manner.

At least a few managers instinctively follow this approach in every company, government office, and church meeting, but the vast majority do not. Some companies have officially instituted this consensual approach throughout, because of its superiority in many cases to individual decision making. However, what occurs in a Japanese organization is a great deal more far reaching and subtle than even this participative approach.

When an important decision needs to be made in a Japanese organization, everyone who will feel its impact is involved in making it. In the case of a decision where to put a new plant, whether to change a production process, or some other major event, that will often mean sixty to eighty people directly involved in making the decision. A team of three will be assigned the duty of talking to all sixty to eighty people and, each time a significant modification arises, contacting all the people involved again. The team will repeat this process until a true consensus has been achieved. Making a decision this way takes a very long time, but once a decision is reached, everyone affected by it will be likely to support it. Understanding and support may supersede the actual content of the decision, since the five or six competing alternatives may be equally good or bad. What is important is not the decision itself but rather how committed and informed people are. The "best" decisions can be bungled just as "worst" decisions can work just fine.

A friend in one of the major Japanese banks described their process.

> When a major decision is to be made, a written proposal lays out one "best" alternative for consideration. The task of writing the proposal goes to the youngest and newest member of the department involved. Of course, the president or vice-president knows the acceptable alternatives, and the young person tries like heck to figure out what those are. He talks to everyone, soliciting their opinions, paying special attention to those who know the top man best. In so doing he is seeking a common ground. Fortunately, the young person cannot completely figure out from others what the boss wants, and must add his own thoughts. This is how variety enters the decision process in a Japanese company. The company relies so heavily on socializing employees with a common set of values and beliefs that all experienced employees would be likely to come up with similar ideas. Too much homogeneity would lead to a loss of vitality and change, so the youngest person gets the assignment.

Frequently, according to my informant, this young person will in the process make a number of errors. He will suggest things that are technically impossible or politically unacceptable, and will leave things out. Experienced managers never over-direct the young man, never sit him down and tell him what the proposal should say. Even though errors consume time, effort, and expense, many will turn out to be good ideas. Letting a young person make one error of his own is believed to be worth more than one hundred lectures in his education as a manager and worker.

Ultimately, a formal proposal is written and then circulated from the bottom of the organization to the top. At each stage, the manager in question signifies his agreement by affixing his seal to the document. At the end of this *ringi* process, the proposal is literally covered with the stamps of approval of sixty to eighty people.

American managers are fond of chiding the Japanese by observing that, "If you're going to Japan to make a sale or close a deal and you think it will take two days, allow two weeks and if you're lucky you'll get a 'maybe.' It takes the Japanese forever to make a decision." True enough, but Japanese businesspeople who have experience dealing in the United States will often say, "Americans are quick to sign a contract or make a decision. But try to get them to implement it—it takes them forever!"

Remember that this apparently cumbersome decision process takes place within the framework of an underlying agreement on philosophy, values, and beliefs. These form the basis for common decision premises that make it possible to include a very large number of people in each decision. If, as in some Western organizations, each of the sixty people had a fundamentally different view of goals and procedures, then the participative process would fail. Because the Japanese only debate the suitability of a particular alternative to reach the agreed-upon values, the process can be broadly participatory yet efficient. In Western-style consensual processes, by comparison, often underlying values and beliefs need to be worked out, and for that reason decision making teams are deliberately kept small.

Another key feature of decision making in Japan is the intentional ambiguity of who is responsible for what decisions. In the United States we have job descriptions and negotiations between employees for the purpose of setting crystal clear boundaries on where my decision authority ends and yours begins. Americans expect others to behave just as we do. Many are the unhappy and frustrated American businessmen or lawyers returning from Japan with the complaint that, "If only they would tell me who is really in charge, we could make some progress." The complaint displays a lack of understanding that, in Japan, no one individual carries responsibility for a particular turf. Rather, a group or team of employees assumes joint responsibility for a set of tasks. While we wonder at their comfortableness in not knowing who is responsible for what, they know quite clearly that each of them is completely responsible for all tasks, and they share that responsibility jointly. Obviously this approach sometimes lets things "fall through the cracks" because everyone may think that someone else has a task under control. When working well, however, this approach leads to a naturally participative decision making and problem solving process. But there is another important reason for the collective assignment of decision responsibility.

Many Americans object to the idea of lifetime employment because they fear the consequences of keeping on an ineffective worker. Won't that create bottlenecks and inefficiency? Clearly the Japanese have somehow solved that problem or they couldn't have achieved their great economic success. A partial answer comes from the collective assignment of decision responsibility. In a typical American firm, Jim is assigned sole responsibility for purchasing decisions for office supplies, Mary has sole responsibility for purchasing maintenance services and Fred is solely responsible for purchasing office machines. If Fred develops serious problems of a personal nature, or if he becomes ill or has some other problem that seriously impedes his ability to function at work, a bottleneck will develop. Office machine orders will not be properly processed or perhaps will not be processed at all. The whole company will suffer, and Fred will have to be let go.

In a Japanese company, by comparison, Mitsuo, Yoshito, and Nori will comprise a team collectively responsible for purchasing office supplies, maintenance services, and office machines. Each of them participates in all significant decisions in purchasing any of those goods or services. If Nori is unable to work, it is perfectly natural and efficient for Mitsuo and Yoshito to take up his share of the load. When Nori returns to work again, he can step right back in and do his share. This does mean that Mitsuo and Yoshito probably will have to work harder than usual for perhaps six months or a year, and they may also have to draw on Masao, who used to work in purchasing but has now been transferred to the computer section. This flow of people can be accomplished only if Mitsuo and Yoshito are confident that the organization has a memory and know that their extra efforts now will be repaid later. Fairness and equity will be achieved over the long run. It also depends upon the practice of job rotation, so that short-run labor needs can be filled internally without having to hire and fire people as such needs come and go. As with all other characteristics of the Japanese management system, decision making is embedded in a complex of parts that hang together and rely upon trust and subtlety developed through intimacy.

5.2 Maybe the Japanese Model Won't Work in America

EDGAR H. SCHEIN

In my experience the effective organization is neither individualistic nor collective; rather, it attempts to create norms and procedures which extol stardom and teamwork equally. The manager's job (just like the good coach's) is to find a way to weld the two forces together. The Japanese solution to this dilemma appears to be aided immensely by the fact that basic traditions and cultural values strongly favor hierarchy and the subordination of the individual to those above him or her. However, this solution has potentially negative consequences, because it reduces the creative talent available to the organization. One might suspect, however, that the effective organization in Japan finds ways of dealing with this dilemma, and that the highly talented individual is not as pressured to conform as the less talented individual.[1]

The Japanese company in the Ouchi model could be expected to be more innovative on those tasks which require group solutions, while the American company could be expected to be more innovative on those tasks that require a high level of individual expertise and creativity. Company effectiveness would then depend on the nature of the tasks which face it, its ability to diagnose accurately what those tasks are, and its flexibility in transforming itself, what I have termed an "adaptive coping cycle."[2] Whatever its human virtues and in spite of its ability to integrate better, a Theory Z organization might have *more* trouble both in seeing changes in its environment and in making the necessary transformations to adapt to those changes. Because of its strong commitment to a given philosophy and the pressure for everyone to conform, it is more likely to produce rigid paradigms for dealing with problems. . . .

But the most important issue to examine before we race into new organizational paradigms is whether or not we even have the right explanation for Japanese success. . . . For example, it may well be that both Japanese productivity and management style are the reflection of some other common historical, economic, and/or sociocultural factor(s) in Japan. . . . [such as] the following important issues:

- The role of postwar reconstruction;
- The opportunity to modernize the industrial base;
- The close collaboration between industry and government;
- The strong sense of nationalism which produces high levels of motivation in all workers;
- That lifetime employment is possible for roughly one-third of the employees in some Japanese organizations because of the system of *temporary* employment for the rest of the employees and the existence of satellite companies which absorb some of the economic fluctuations;
- That all employees retire fairly early by U.S. standards (in their mid- to late fifties);
- That many of the best companies are family dominated and their strong company philosophies may be a reflection of founder values which might be hard to maintain as these companies age;
- That the cultural traditions of duty, obedience, and discipline strongly favor a paternalistic clan form of organization. . . .

Knowing What Is Cultural

If we are to have a theory of organizations or management which is culture free or adaptable within any given culture, we must first know what culture is. This is surprisingly difficult because we are all embedded in our own culture. What can we learn from Japanese managers if we cannot decipher how their behavior is embedded in their culture? Can we attempt to adapt managerial methods developed in other cultures without understanding how they would fit into our own?

The first and perhaps the most important point is that we probably *cannot really understand another culture* at the level of its basic world view. The only one we can really understand is our own. Even understanding our own culture at this level requires intensive analysis and thought. One cannot suddenly become aware of something and understand it if one has taken it completely for granted. The true value of looking at other cultures is, therefore, to gain perspective for studying one's own culture. By seeing how others think about and do things, we become more aware of how we think about and do things, and that awareness is the first step in analyzing our own cultural assumptions and values. We can use analyses of Japanese management methods and their underlying cultural presumptions to learn about the hidden premises of U.S. managerial methods and our own cultural presumptions.

If we can grasp and become aware of our own premises and values, we can then examine analytically and empirically what the strengths and weaknesses of our own paradigm may be. This process of self-analysis is subtle and difficult. . . .

"MAN'S" RELATIONSHIP TO "MAN": INDIVIDUALISTIC EGALITARIANISM

Every society or group must resolve the issue between individualism and collectivism. The underlying U.S. assumption appears to be that the individual always does and should do what is best for himself or herself, and is constrained only by respect for the law and the rights of others. The rule of law implies that there are no philosophical and moral principles which can ultimately determine when another's rights have been violated, and, therefore, the legislative and judicial process must decide this on a case-by-case basis through a confronting, problem-solving process judged by a jury of peers. Buried in these assumptions is a further assumption that the world can only be known through successive confrontations with natural phenomena and other people; that the nature of truth resides in empirical experience, not in some philosophical, moral, or religious system; and that the ultimate "philosophy," therefore, might as well be one of pragmatism. Ambition, maximizing one's opportunities, and fully utilizing one's capacities become the moral imperatives.

These assumptions, in turn, are related to the western rational scientific tradition which emphasizes experimentation; learning from experience; open debate of facts; and a commitment to truth, accuracy, measurement, and other aids to establish what is "real." The openness and pluralism which so many commentators on America emphasize are closely related to the assumption that truth can only be discovered through open confrontation and can come from anyone. The lowest level employee has as good a chance to solve a key problem as the president of the company, and one of the worst sins is *arbitrary* authority ("Do it because I am the boss, even if you think it is wrong" or "If I'm the boss, that makes me right").

Yet teamwork is an important value in U.S. sports and organizational life. It is not clear to me how to reconcile the need for teamwork with the assumptions of individualism. . . . One of the greatest fears that U.S. managers have of groups is that responsibility and accountability will become diffused. We need to be able to identify who is accountable for what even when the realities of the task make shared responsibility more appropriate. According to Ouchi . . . the Japanese deliberately blur individual responsibility and adapt their decision making to such blurring. If that is so, their version of the consensus method may have little to teach us.

Participatory methods can work in the U.S., but they must be based on a different premise: the premise that teamwork and participation are *better* ways to *solve problems*, because knowledge, information, and skills are distributed among a number of people. We must, therefore, involve those people who have relevant information and skills. But the goal in terms of U.S. assumptions is better problem solving and more efficient performance; not teamwork, consensus, or involvement per se. Unless Japanese consensus methods are built on the same premise of effective problem solving, they are in many senses culturally irrelevant.

Similarly, the Japanese concern for the whole person may be based on premises and assumptions which simply do not fit our core assumptions of individualism and self-help. U.S. managers are scared of paternalism and excessive involvement with subordinates, because they see them as "invasions of privacy." If an individual is taken care of by an organization, he or she may lose the ability to fight for himself or herself. Our whole system is based on the assumptions that one must "be one's own best friend" and that the law is there to protect each and every one of us. Dependency, security orientation, and allowing others to solve our problems are viewed as signs of failure and lack of ambition, and are considered to be undeserving of sympathy. On the other hand, if it is necessary to take care of the whole family in an overseas transfer in order to enable the primary employee to function effectively, then we do it. Pragmatism, necessity, and efficiency override issues of what would be more humane, because of the underlying belief that we cannot philosophically agree on basic standards of what is "best" for everyone. What is best for people must be decided on the basis of negotiation and experience (ultimately expressed in laws, safety codes, and quality of work-life standards).

A culture based on such premises sounds harsh and cold, and the things we are told we should do to "humanize" organizations sound friendly and warm. But cultures are neither cold nor warm, because within any given culture both warmth and coldness have their own meaning. We may not like certain facets of our culture once we discover their underlying premises, and we may even set out to change our culture. However, we cannot produce such change simply by pointing to another culture and saying that some of the things they do *there* would be neat *here*. We have not yet begun to understand our own culture and the managerial paradigms which it has created. . . .

Notes

1. See F. R. Kluckhohn and F. L. Stodtbeck, *Variations in Value Orientations* (Evanston, IL: Row, Peterson, 1961).
2. See E. H. Schein, *Organizational Psychology*, 3d. ed. (Englewood Cliffs, NJ: Prentice-Hall, 1980).

5.3   Trying Japanese Management in America

L. ERIK CALONIUS

When word spread that Sharp Corp. of Japan was planning to build an electronics factory here, a lot of people thought the Japanese were making a big mistake.

After all, RCA Corp. had built a TV plant in Memphis in 1966—and shut it down five years later. That facility had suffered just about every labor and management affliction imaginable: wildcat strikes, union-authorized strikes, apparent sabotage of the product and a series of layoffs that took the payroll from a peak of 4,200 workers down to 1,600. At times, so many hundreds of defective TV sets clogged the assembly-line aisles that technicians had difficulty repairing them. Finally, RCA pulled the plug, shipped most of the machinery and work off to Taiwan and left the Memphis labor force with a black eye.

Yet Sharp came here anyway. "People said it was labor problems that caused RCA to close," says Paul Hagusa, the president of Sharp Manufacturing Co. of America, "but we didn't think so. We felt it was RCA's lack of quality in the product."

Success Story

Sharp not only has proved the skeptics wrong but also has vindicated the city's work force. Despite some problems with labor unions, its 500,000-square-foot plant has, in the past four years, rolled out a million color-television sets and a million microwave ovens. It has done so with U.S. labor (all the assembly-line workers and 85 percent of the managers are American) and with mostly American components (U.S. companies supply 70 percent of the TV parts and 75 percent of the microwave parts). Productivity has reached 90 percent of that in Sharp's Japanese plants, and the defect level is low. The plant has toughed out the recession without reducing its output of about 30,000 TV sets and 30,000 ovens a month (except for a slight dip in 1981), without layoffs and without losing its profitability.

Best of all, the Sharp products shipped from Memphis get high marks for quality and durability from consumer groups.

The Japanese company's remarkable success—on the banks of the Mississippi River—can't be attributed to special machinery or automation; American competitors use the same equipment. Nor can it be attributed to employees who sing the company song every morning, dress neatly in company garb, exercise in unison or eat sushi; they don't.

So, what's Sharp's secret?

The assembly-line workers themselves credit the Japanese style of management. At its core, it demands very hard work and an obsession with quality, an obsession with making every seam weld and switch of the product perfect. A Sharp manager agrees, saying: "It's not what we do, but how well we do it. It's the constant striving for excellence."

Twist of Fate

The leader in that drive for excellence, Mr. Hagusa (pronounced huh-GOO-sah), came to his position in Memphis through a full twist of fate. A teen-ager during World War II, he worked in an aircraft plant in Osaka, his hometown, and once, running to work during an air raid, barely escaped death as an American bomb glanced off a trolley-car cable and bounced to a harmless stop just yards away from him. After the war, he became a houseboy to an American Army officer and converted to Catholicism, taking the Christian name Paul. Later, he graduated from engineering school and began his lifelong career with Sharp.

Now, Mr. Hagusa, a small man whose feet just reach the floor as he settles into an American-sized chair, considers his job "a great mission," one that he hopes will ease trade tensions between the U.S. and Japan. And he clearly is presiding at a junction of two cultures.

His office is decorated with a vase of silk cherry blossoms, an ornate samurai helmet and a glowering portrait of Tokuji Hayakawa, the company's founder. But despite his weak English, Mr. Hagusa has learned to live with American customs. ("Shake hand is not so bad, but hug?'' he says, wrinkling his face in distaste.) At the height of last year's Christmas party, Mr. Hagusa raised cheers among the employees by declaring, "There are two things I've learned since coming to America: how to wreck cars and how to drink Jack Daniel's."

Labor Lessons

He also has learned about American labor unions. In October 1980, the National Labor Relations Board charged Sharp with interrogating employees about their union sentiments, threatening to move the plant if employees voted union, suggesting that certain employees quit rather than support a union, telling employees they could be "nailed to the wall" for distributing union literature, and other offenses. In a settlement in August 1981, the company agreed to post in the plant notices promising not to harass employees involved with the union. Last month, Sharp and the International Brotherhood of Electrical Workers, which the employees had voted to represent them, agreed on a contract.

Michael D. Lucas, a union organizer, doesn't place full blame for the contention on the Japanese management. "They aren't any more familiar with American labor law than you or I am familiar with Japanese labor law," he says, adding that the company was led into the litigation by its law firm. "Japanese management is finally getting the idea that we aren't the devils in disguise they were led to believe we were," he remarks.

But the most important lesson learned by Mr. Hagusa has been how little most American companies know about achieving quality. "The most important path to quality," he says through an interpreter, "is that employees feel that they are of one family, playing an important role in the company."

How is a familial feeling instilled? "There must be a change in the way that management in the U.S. treats its employees," he says. "Otherwise, it is difficult for employees to respond" as the Japanese do.

"In America, when sales drop, the first thing American management in general thinks of is laying off employees. In Japan, it is the last resort," he says. Japanese companies cut costs elsewhere, he adds, or temporarily shift production employees into sales even though "they may not be as efficient as experienced sales people."

With their jobs assured, workers—in Japan, at least—feel a responsibility to put the company before all else. "In Japan, an employee tries to work his lifetime with the company he chooses. So he does not put much importance in his personal interests," Mr. Hagusa says. "In Japan, they say, 'Job first, family life comes second.'"

For himself, he says, "I don't work to live; I live to work."

This strong work ethic is apparent at the Sharp plant in Memphis. "The Japanese work much more than we do—telexing home to Japan, checking up on us," says Kevin Hignight, an engineer at the plant. "They work to seven or eight every night and on Saturday mornings. They seem to like it."

And they push the U.S. workers relentlessly. "You won't see people sitting around on the loading docks," says Milton Kee, the company's American manager of quality control. "Everyone here has a job, and they're expected to do it. There are no excuses." He adds:

"I've never worked so hard in my life. It's been hard on me, it's been hard on the other employees, and it probably always will be hard. But I've had 17 years in manufacturing, and the last three have taught me more than all of the previous 14."

"They're Training Me"

Fred Haynes, another engineer, agrees. "It's a tough place to work," he says. "They keep trying to get a little more out of you. They keep going deeper, demanding better quality from you. They're training me. . . . In a way, I'm a Japanese engineer, learning to relate to American companies." Then he concedes, "I think it's real good."

However, not everyone is willing to live under Sharp's ever-tightening standards. When Sharp first asked American suppliers to submit their materials to Sharp engineers in Japan for inspection, almost all failed. Some vendors, exasperated, quit the bidding.

During Sharp's first year here, the Japanese dominance stirred up tension in the plant, too. "They were here to duplicate the plant in Japan," one worker says, "and there was only one way to do things—their way." Especially during that first year, there were some difficult meetings between the Japanese and the Americans.

With American suggestions carrying little weight with Japanese management, "it was sometimes humiliating," one American manager recalls.

Much of that has passed. "They had to learn about us as people first, before they could trust us," one worker says. "Now, I feel they respect us."

The Americans, in turn, express respect for the Japanese, especially for their attention to detail. Although many of the Japanese didn't know English when they arrived four years ago, "they're even starting to correct our grammar and spelling," one American worker boasts.

Going by the Book

In the Spartan concrete-block office of Joe Scott, the production manager for Sharp's microwave ovens, a sign on the wall reads, "Do it right—the first time." But good intentions and hard work alone don't account for Sharp's quality. Another factor is found in a thick book on Mr. Scott's desk. In the book are line graphs that meticulously track the pulse of the assembly lines through information collected from a data sheet attached to each oven. "We let the data tell us what we need to know to correct a problem," he explains. "We don't use personal opinions or emotions."

Although Sharp has been able to track and improve the level of quality in its own plant, it has found it much more difficult to persuade its 70 U.S. suppliers to do so, too. "We're trying to convince vendors that quality actually reduces their costs," Mr. Scott says.

At a recent meeting of vendors, Edward Cox, Sharp's TV-set production manager, explained "Practice Sincerity and Creativity," Sharp's off-repeated business creed. "As for sincerity, we expect you to send us 100 percent quality parts," and precisely on schedule, he said. "As for creativity, we expect you to participate in quality improvements."

"Report Cards"

Suppliers got "report cards" evaluating the quality of their materials, their prices, promptness of delivery and other factors.

Sixteen vendors received a 100 percent quality rating; 15 others also got A's with 95 percent to 99 percent; 18 got B's with 85 percent to 94 percent; nine got C's with 75 percent to 84 percent; and three got D's with 65 percent to 74 percent. There weren't any F's.

"We did about as well as I always did in school, a strong C," says Jeff Talbot, vice president of Talbot Industries Inc., a Neosho, Mo., supplier of wire racks for Sharp's microwave ovens. Mr. Talbot blames his 84 percent rating on a few bad shipments when Talbot Industries started its first run eight months ago. "Sharp does a first-piece inspection with every shipment, and if it doesn't measure out exactly, then the whole shipment is no good," he says. "Other companies would say, 'Well, it doesn't exactly meet our tolerances, but we can use it.' But at Sharp, if it's wrong, it's wrong."

Next year, he says, with a bit of disbelief in his voice, Sharp expects his company to reach 97 percent. "It's not going to be easy," he concedes. "If we can cut our in-house rejection down from a high of 12 percent to 1 percent or 2 percent and then make sure we don't send them over 1 percent defects, that will be the proof of the pudding."

At the head of the class with a 100 percent rating was, not surprisingly, Tabuchi Electric Co. of America, a Japanese supplier of transformers that followed Sharp to America and set up a plant employing 150 persons in Jackson, Tenn. "We are of the same mind," says Itaru Nakagawa, the director of sales and planning. "Not only with Sharp but with our other customers, we have very eager communications. Even if the customer hasn't rejected this time, even if there is but a little possibility of rejection, we will know at the meeting and correct it."

However, Mr. Nakagawa says his performance must be improved. "Their (Sharp's) objective is that they don't need to inspect our product at all," he says. "It's an objective that is very hard to approach."

Being tough is only half the formula for getting quality. The other half is making suppliers also feel a part of the family, Mr. Hagusa says. Indeed, once a supplier begins working with Sharp and shows willingness to improve, the relationship can last a long time.

"We'd really have to step all over our toes to get thrown out of here," says Mr. Talbot, the maker of microwave wire racks.

"They'd give us every consideration under the sun because we have done a good job." Adds Mr. Hignight, the Sharp engineer, "If the company has a problem, we can telex Japan to see if they've solved that problem in the past. Our job actually is to help the vendors get their rejection rates down so they can make some money."

Richard Hollington, vice president of Bryan Custom Plastics Inc., which sells about half a million plastic pieces for Sharp TVs each year, says, "They demand jewelry. There just is not any comparison between the quality Sharp demands and that demanded by RCA and Zenith."

But at the same time, "they helped us with our quality-control layout and training," Mr. Hollington says. "They developed hourly audits of our assembly line to isolate problems sooner."

Like a score of other vendors, Mr. Hollington has been called before Sharp's quality-improvement committee, a body formed two years ago to help vendors. "It's not a hell-raising session at all," he says. "They are providing us with the expertise of their top management. At American companies, if they find a problem in your product, it's your problem. At Sharp, we work it out together."

On a recent day, one of Sharp's "quality circles" is meeting. Led by a trained leader, Sharp's quality circles "brainstorm" ideas, select a problem to be solved and then collect data on the problem. Later, the problem and possibly a solution are presented to Mr. Hagusa and other members of management.

Two Innovations

At one table, five microwave assembly workers are discussing one worker's innovation: a metal dowel that fits into the center hole of a five-hole microwave-oven bracket. "I saw that people were having trouble lining up the holes," says Randy Howie, "but if someone before them had put in the center screw, the person didn't have a problem." So Mr. Howie developed the metal dowel, which, when slipped into the middle hole, aligns the bracket while the other four holes are screwed down.

At another table, a group of employees are discussing a second innovation: a plastic table top with countersunk holes in which to stand screws. The device makes the screws simple to pick up and keeps them from rolling off the table and onto the floor. As a result, productivity has improved by seven units a day, the circle leader says.

However, Sharp doesn't expect a dollar payback from the circles, which meet on company time. Instead, a manager explains, the circles are a "human-relations program."

That comment harks back to a remark by Mr. Hagusa:

"Once there was a time when the Americans had very efficient machines and equipment, and Japan did not. At that time—regardless of the workers—those with the most modern machines had the competitive advantage." But now, he says, one country soon has the same machinery as another. "So, what makes the difference today," he says, is "the quality of the people."

Discussion and Review Questions

1. How does Theory Z differ from Theories X and Y? Which of the three views of workers do you subscribe to? Why?

2. William Ouchi argues for "team" decisions by management. What benefits and what problems may result from such an approach?

3. Do you think the Japanese model is adaptable to American management and work conditions? Why or why not?

4. What is your reaction to the article on Sharp Corporation? Would you like to work there? Why or why not?

5. Are there certain "special conditions" which explain the Japanese success? If so, what are these special circumstances?

ISSUE 6

Who Needs Unions?

High on many business leaders' lists of causes of the nation's recent economic difficulties is unions. In fact, during recent years labor–management relations have deteriorated from what was a more-or-less harmonious accommodation only about a decade ago into outright labor–management conflict. As the economy has contracted, bargaining has become more bitter, bringing back memories of an earlier unpleasant era in labor–management relations.

Labor's Early Struggles

The earliest American efforts at unionism were *craft unions*, composed of skilled artisans engaged in the same profession or craft. In the eighteenth century, shoemakers, carpenters, printers, tailors, and artisans of similar skilled trades began to organize in secret societies. Their objectives were to agree jointly to acceptable wages and hours and to pledge not to work for employers who would not meet these demands. They also set high standards for entrance into their trade in an attempt to keep the demand for their services high and to keep their wages up. Secrecy was of the greatest importance since employers, who founded their own associations, quickly dismissed workers suspected of affiliation with any labor society. Meanwhile, strikes were routinely held by the courts to be illegal conspiracies. Under the law of the time, workers could be fined or jailed for combining to strike against their employers.

Stalled by the courts, employer associations, and considerable public opposition to worker organization, the craft unions remained small and limited to individual cities. Not until 1869, with the formation of the Knights of Labor, was a truly national trade union organized. The Knights of Labor sought to get beyond narrow craft lines. Their approach was to organize both *skilled and unskilled workers* of an entire firm or industry into one union. At first, progress was slow. By 1884, only 70,000 members had been signed up. However, after winning a long strike against Jay Gould's Wabash railroad in 1885, membership grew to over 700,000.

The Knights' fall from power was about as swift as their rise. Most of the skilled workers opposed being included with the unskilled. Increasing friction also developed between the national office and the local leaders, many of whom considered the national office to be too radical. Meanwhile, the Haymarket riot of 1886—during which a bomb was hurled into the ranks of Chicago policemen who were attempting to halt a labor rally—produced a wave of public reaction against labor unionism of all types. To make matters worse, national economic conditions had turned sour. Many workers were either out of work or unwilling to take the chance of losing their jobs because of labor union affiliation. By 1890, the union had fewer than 100,000 members, and within another few years it had passed out of existence.

The Rise of the AFL

The same year the Haymarket bomb blasted the hopes of the Knights of Labor (1886), a number of national craft unions joined to form the American Federation of Labor (AFL). Despite the generally unfavorable public and government attitudes toward unions and the increasingly violent struggle between workers and management during the 1890s, the AFL under Samuel Gompers steered a steady course. There were losses: Andrew Carnegie broke the AFL strike at Homestead, Pennsylvania, in 1892 by sending in an army of strike breakers and the National Guard. And, there were no-contests: Gompers refused to support the American Railway Union during the Pullman Strike in 1894. Nevertheless, AFL membership grew, reaching 500,000 by 1893 and more than 2 million by 1917.

Despite the growth of the AFL, many workers saw the union as too timid. Businesspeople, encouraged by their strike-breaking efforts at Homestead and Pullman, undertook an all-out effort to eliminate unionism among the workers. Strike breakers, company police, wholesale firings, and cruel judges, not paternalism, were management's tools in the growing conflict between worker and owner. Large numbers of workers responded by turning to radical and clearly revolutionary workers' groups. Probably the best known of these was the Industrial Workers of the World (founded in 1905). The IWW, or "Wobblies" as they were called, had a simple revolutionary philosophy: Organize one big union for all workers; never compromise with employers; employ direct action such as sabotage (destroying company property and machines), mass picketing, and violence if necessary; and *finally*, overthrow the capitalist system. Although rarely winning any of the dozens of strikes they organized, the Wobblies thoroughly frightened the business community. The IWW seemed to be the first stirring of outright class war in the United States.

Shocked by the excesses of the IWW, many businesspeople began to reconsider their views on unions: The "red" IWW, of course, was totally unacceptable; on the other hand, perhaps the AFL was a union that could be dealt with. Its leader, Samuel Gompers, had pledged the union to support the existing economic order and to keep out of politics. Ever so slowly business leaders recognized that limited compromise with labor was much better business than continued warfare. The modern business attitude toward labor unions was developing.

Labor Unions Accepted

The union movement gathered momentum in the 1930s. The administration of Franklin Roosevelt promised a "New Deal" for American labor. With the passage of the National Labor Relations Act in 1935, the promise became a reality. Under this landmark act, management could no longer ignore the desires of its workers to unionize. An employer had to recognize and negotiate with any union chosen by a majority of its workers. Also employers could suffer heavy fines if they attempted to fire or punish workers who attempted to organize unions.

A few large firms fought the inevitable; however, protected by law, the power of the federal government, and a new public attitude toward unions, union membership swelled to 6 million by 1940 and almost 12 million by the close of World War II (1945).

Most of this growth was accounted for by a new union, the Congress of Industrial Organizations (CIO). The CIO, an offshoot of the AFL, was in fact a union of unions. The CIO brought together autoworkers, sheet metal workers, steel workers, and others into industry-wide unions. The CIO saw in industry-wide organization the possibility of developing enormous power. In dealing with an employer, they could call out all of their members on strike, whereas the AFL's craft organization meant it had control of only a few skilled workers in any firm. As machines replaced skilled workers, the AFL was losing its power.

During World War II, union power grew enormously. Firm after firm and industry after industry turned to unionization. However, many employers and ordinary citizens believed that unions had grown too large. Despite promises not to strike during the war, unions had carried out a number of work stoppages that affected the flow of critical war supplies. In the reconversion period just after the war, practically all major industries had been hit with strikes as workers battled for higher wages. As a reaction to these alleged union excesses, the Taft-Hartley Act was passed in 1947. The new act took away from the unions some of the power they had obtained in the "New Deal" 1930s and attempted to rebalance the power between labor and management.

Even though the right to compel union membership as a condition of employment in a unionized firm was lost, the union movement continued to grow. In 1955, when the AFL and the CIO formally merged their 16 million members, there were almost 18 million union members of all kinds in the United States. However, unionism was changing its direction. Industrial employment, the backbone of American unions, had ceased to grow in the United States and unions began to move on new fronts—service workers, government workers, the white-collar workers in business, and even professional athletes. Unions enjoyed some successes, but, by 1981, their membership stood at slightly less than 20 million, no more than 22 percent of all American workers. Moreover, many nonunion workers, especially in the growing service sector, showed little interest in the union movement. The graphs of union membership in Figure 1 reflect this recent decline in interest.

Labor-Management Era

In the growing national economic crisis after 1975, unions lost ground. In Washington, the mood of presidential and congressional leaders changed and a number of important pieces of "union" legislation were defeated. At the bargaining table, as national unemployment grew and prices rose, unions were confronted by increasingly hostile management negotiators. In the early 1980s unions had to accept the unthinkable—approve temporary "givebacks" in union wage rates and benefits in such endangered industries as steel or autos.

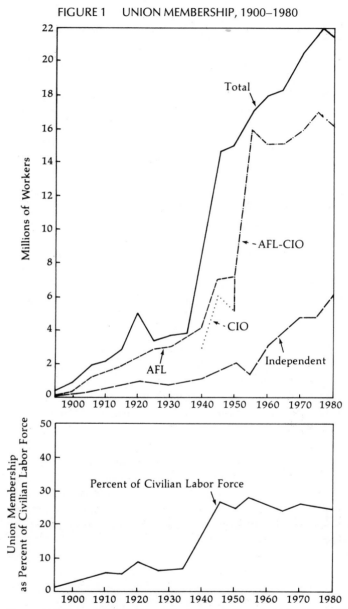

FIGURE 1   UNION MEMBERSHIP, 1900–1980

Source: U.S. Bureau of the Census, *Historical Statistics of the United States*, 1976, p. 389, and the U.S. Bureau of Labor Statistics.

Despite the long history of union–management conflict in the United States, it would be inaccurate to characterize all management as antiunion. Unions' long battle for improving the lot of the ordinary worker is accepted today, at least in a general way, as a noble objective by most corporate leaders. Moreover, few modern business leaders would be comfortable playing the role of "union buster" that Henry Ford, George Pullman, and others did in the past. Quite simply, that is just not the corporate style today, except in some very rare cases. The experts in the public relations department are quick to point out that a corporate image of being antilabor actually can hurt the company. Most consumers, after all, are workers (although perhaps not union workers). As workers, they can identify very easily with many of labor's complaints against management. If these complaints seem to be supported by strong antiunion activities by management, the firm may indeed lose some of its customers.

Although the old-time antagonism has therefore been toned down by most managers, there remains considerable business opposition to the goals of unions. The opposition is rarely the simple matter of ideological principle it was to Henry Ford, who saw unions as a first step down the road to communism; it is an economic question. The objective of any private firm is to earn profits, and practically any union goal can be measured in higher production costs, which usually mean lower profits.

The first of the following articles, by an embittered and disappointed corporation president who saw his workers vote for unionization, reflects a strong antiunion position. The second is a defense by the AFL–CIO of the right *and* necessity of unionization. While the first position may seem to be attractive to business leaders, it is doubtful that such a view dominates in many corporate boardrooms, partly because broad decertification of unions is an unrealistic strategy and partly because an unfamiliar but promising type of labor–management collaboration is now emerging. As the third article shows, this collaboration is an outgrowth of recent technological and economic developments. It examines how this new collaboration promises to rejuvenate both unions *and* corporate profits.

6.1 "I Said We'd Never Have a Union"

JOSEPH E. RICHARDSON, JR.

For 131 years the Richardson Brothers Co. has been cutting lumber and making furniture in Sheboygan Falls, Wis. I'm the fifth generation of Richardsons in the family-owned business, and we've always declared we'd never have a union. I felt strongly about that when I became president and chief executive officer in 1975 after 16 years as sales manager. I still felt strongly about it in 1977 when the United Furniture Workers of America, AFL–CIO (UFW), finally succeeded in organizing our furniture plant. And I was determined then that even if we had to have a union contract we'd never have a union shop—i.e., required membership.

Now, a year later, we have even that. Every new employee has to join the union. It hurts me like hell, but it was the only way to get back to the business of making furniture.

Union organizers, I've learned, are astute businessmen. They're concerned about just one thing—getting those dues—and they're good at it. In our battle with the union I finally came down to a hard choice: either indulge in the personal philosophy of Joe Richardson and the Richardson family or be a businessman and run the business. We really had no other choice.

And although we're running smoothly and profitably now that I've accepted the union shop I said we would never tolerate, I'm still opposed to the union for the same basic reasons as always.

First, roughly half of our employees don't want a union. I feel that I've let them down, especially when a new, young worker asks me, "Do I really have to join?" All I can say is, "Sorry, we're here to make furniture and we need peace and quiet to do it. It was the only way to end the hassle."

Second, the union does nothing for our employees. The unemployment rate in this area is only 3.3%, so we have to offer a competitive wage and benefit package or good employees will leave us. Neither they nor we need a union to tell us that. Wages and benefits have never been an issue at Richardson Brothers. The chief issue has been union security, which means income for union officials. Our workers might as well throw their nine bucks a month union dues into the Sheboygan River.

The events that led to where we are now began in 1956—two years before I came into the company. The UFW was soundly beaten then in an organizing election. I guess that since then, getting us has been a matter of pride to them. Some 80% of the furniture business in Wisconsin is organized, and we were the largest nonunion wood furniture manufacturer in the state.

The UFW was back again in 1959, for what proved to be a tough and acrimonious fight. Dealing with an organizing attempt is something like planning and running a political campaign, but our 1959 campaign strategy was more by the seat of the pants than planned.

We did emphasize three points—that we've always offered annual wage increases; that our employment package is as good or better than that of other furniture manufacturers in the area, union or nonunion; and that we have a record of treating people fairly. We passed out handbills inside the plant gate at quitting time, and that made the union organizers furious, because they had to stay outside the gate.

The 1959 election was a tie—meaning that the union lost. They filed objections to the election, attempting to have it held again, but the objections were rejected by the National Labor Relations Board (NLRB) and the election was certified in 1960.

Meanwhile, one of our employees suggested that we form an employee action committee to meet regularly with management, express gripes, and find mutually acceptable solutions. A representative from each department would serve on the committee. Previously, we had followed an open-door policy. Any employee with a gripe had free access to my office at any time.

We thought the committee was a great idea and encouraged the employees to go ahead with it. Because of the pending NLRB action, management was prohibited by law from direct involvement in setting the committee up. But the employees worked out the details despite discouragement from union supporters. The committee set rules and compiled an employee handbook. And we began meeting on a monthly basis, or more often if there was a specific complaint. It worked beautifully.

The NLRB hearing in Milwaukee on the vote eligibility finally came in May 1976. It took two days. Then we had to wait for the examiner's ruling. That didn't come until September 1976. The examiner allowed four votes to be counted, but threw out the votes of the two part-time workers. That should have made the election a tie at 61–61, giving the victory to us.

But before the votes were counted, the union appealed the examiner's ruling, taking it to NLRB headquarters in Washington. Our attorney assured us that the chance of overturning the district office was very remote. It would happen only if there was an obvious mistake, he said. He was wrong. The NLRB threw out the vote of the leadman, accepting the union's assertion that he had authority to reprimand employees and therefore was part of management. In fact, he did not have such authority. His role was simply that of a utility player, filling in as required to keep production going. The ruling knocked out the potentially tying vote, making the union the winner.

I was stunned by the decision. After 130 years, Richardson Brothers Co. was going to go union—on a technicality over one vote. We appealed and lost. And so it was final. We had no other recourse. We had to accept the union and negotiate a contract. I was determined that if we had to have a contract we were not going to have a union shop. No one was going to be forced to join a union that they didn't want or need.

The contract negotiations got under way in May of 1977. There was no dispute over salary and benefits. We offered what we would ordinarily have given, and the union accepted it. The union didn't even insist on a union shop. But they did insist on a two-year contract and maintenance of membership. That means that everyone who joins the union must remain a member for the duration of the contract. We insisted on a one-year contract with no maintenance of membership. We felt that no one should be required to remain a member against his will.

The negotiations came to a stalemate in September. The union was telling our employees they were fighting for working conditions and wages—not their real demand of union security. They accused us of stalling.

So at the end of September, I decided to meet with the employees and let them know exactly what the sticking points were. I felt they were entitled to know the truth—that the hang-ups did not relate to their own jobs but rather to the aggrandizement of the UFW. That's precisely what the local's president and its business agent didn't want the workers to hear.

We delivered our final offer to the union on October 5, 1977. It was a one-year contract with no maintenance of membership. To make sure our employees weren't misled about what was in the package, we passed out copies of it that day.

The union was furious. They accused us of revealing secret negotiations and insisted on putting the proposed contract to a vote in an employee meeting that night. "Either they accept the package as is and we'll go along with it, or we're going to strike," warned the union. They permitted all employees to attend, union members or not. Well, it was a long evening, but our employees accepted the contract by two votes. So on the morning of October 6, the union capitulated.

"If that's what the employees want, they can have it," the union leaders said. "But you're going to have problems."

They were right. The contract took effect on January 1, 1978, and we soon found that the union strategy was to harass us at every opportunity by pouncing on every petty grievance they could find. I guess that given their objective—getting those dues—they had no choice. The contract gave them little power in the plant. So they had to put on a good show to try to convince the workers that the union was representing them.

The incidents were petty indeed. Our new personnel manager, for example, made an error on the seniority list, placing one worker higher than she should have been. When we discovered the mistake and corrected it the union insisted that the error stand. They took that to arbitration and lost, but it cost us over $500 in direct expense alone.

At one period we were dealing with a couple of such matters a week. The lost time, the lost production, and the energy spent in frustration was incalculable.

In that first year of unionization it appeared that the disruptions were getting to the employees, too. The union started the contract year with about 90 members out of our total work force of 185, and membership dropped to about 40 by year's end.

And in June 1978—six months into unionization—our anti-union employees collected enough signatures to petition the NLRB for a decertification election. We were off on another campaign, but this time management had to watch from the sidelines.

Legally, a decertification contest is strictly between the employees—the prounion ones on one side and the antiunion ones on the other—and management is not involved. Although we were intensely interested in the outcome, we had to be careful what we said. It's touchy because if the union loses, they'll really jump in and pick apart everything you said to challenge the election.

The decertification vote came on September 15, and our antiunion employees lost, 60 to 69. Ironically, I'm convinced that they lost because we *didn't* have a union shop and because we *didn't* have maintenance of membership. A typical employee view seemed to be, ''What have I got to lose with the union here? I can always join or quit, but I've got it if I want it.'' If there had been forced membership, I believe, there would have been at least five workers sick of paying $9 a month. Five changed votes is all it would have taken to put the union out.

With the sobering thought that the lack of union security had made the union secure, we had to turn our attention quickly to negotiating a new contract to become effective January 1, 1979.

The union indicated that if we'd give them acceptable security, they'd be reasonable and leave us alone. And after all the unrest and disruption we'd been through, there was no question that we had to find a way to establish peace and stop the aggravating grievances.

We decided that the time had come to get back to work at the business of making furniture. If some of our people want a union, then we'll have to accept that as fact and work with it, I reasoned.

This time, what the UFW meant by acceptable security was a union shop. I recalled my promise to our employees at the time of the vote on the first contract that they would never have to join a union if they didn't want to. And my own convictions of principle against a union shop were still strong. But I could see no alternative.

So, effective January 1, 1979, the UFW has a three-year contract and a union shop. I did keep my word to my old employees. The contract specified that they could join or not, as they chose. Eighty-eight of 148, or 60% of them, chose not to join, but people hired after January 1 have no choice.

I will say that the union has kept its word, too. We've even solved the problem of the incentive program in the sanding department. The terms for changing the piece rates were negotiated into the contract, and since January we've reset many rates in that department. One of the sanders—the most prounion guy in the shop—raised the roof, and the union filed a grievance. We had only to point to the contract.

The union hired its own time-study consultant, who agreed with us. "Boys," he pointed out, "it's right there in the contract. You negotiated it." That settled the grievance. Ironically, the very issue that brought the union in has been resolved to our total satisfaction.

Now we're going through the plant resetting many piece rates and putting our house in order. Previously, we might not have, fearing disruption in the form of another organizing campaign.

We have very few grievances now. The union won't waste time on foolish complaints. We're running smoothly, making good furniture and making it efficiently.

True, we lost the union fight and I had to swallow my convictions. But I think the real loss is suffered by our employees. They're not getting anything for their nine bucks a month that they wouldn't have gotten otherwise. It's the United Furniture Workers of America who have gained.

Perhaps down the pike in three years, if the same antiunion crew is here, they'll launch another decertification campaign and vote the union out. If the situation is to change, they'll have to change it themselves. But I'll do everything in the world legally to help them.

6.2   Labor in Defense of Unions

AFL–CIO FEDERATIONIST

What is clearly evident . . . is that the working people of
America have had to unite in struggle to achieve the gains that they
have accumulated during this century. Improvements did not
come easily. Organizing unions, winning the right to representation, using the collective bargaining process as the core of their activities, struggling against bias and discrimination, the working
men and women of America have built a trade union movement of
formidable proportions.

Labor in America has correctly been described as a stabilizing
force in the national economy and a bulwark of our democratic society. Furthermore, the gains that unions have been able to achieve
have brought benefits, direct and indirect, to the public as a whole.
It was labor, for example, that spearheaded the drive for public education for every child. The labor movement, indeed, has served as
a force for American progress.

Now, in the 1980s, as the American trade union movement
looks toward its second century, it takes pride in its first "century
of achievement" as it recognizes a substantial list of goals yet to be
achieved.

In this past century, American labor has played a central role
in the elevation of the American standard of living. The benefits
which unions have negotiated for their members are, in most
cases, widespread in the economy and enjoyed by millions of our
fellow citizens outside the labor movement. It is often hard to remember that what we take for granted—vacations with pay, pensions, health and welfare protection, grievance and arbitration procedures, holidays—never existed on any meaningful scale until
unions fought and won them for working people.

Through these decades, the labor movement has constantly
reached out to groups in the American society striving for their
share of opportunity and rewards . . . to the blacks, the Hispanics

and other minorities . . . to women striving for jobs and equal or comparable pay . . . to those who work for better schools, for the freedom of speech, press and assembly guaranteed by the Bill of Rights . . . to those seeking to make our cities more livable or our rural recreation areas more available . . . to those seeking better health for infants and more secure status for the elderly.

Through these decades, in addition, the unions of America have functioned in an economy and a technology marked by awesome change. When the Federation of Organized Trades and Labor Unions gathered in convention in 1881, Edison had two years earlier invented the electric light, and the first telephone conversation had taken place just five years before. There were no autos, no airplanes, no radio, no television, no air conditioning, no computers or calculators, no electronic games. For our modest energy needs—coal, kerosene and candles—we were independently self-sufficient.

The labor movement has seen old industries die (horse-shoeing was once a major occupation) and new industries mature. The American workforce, once predominantly "blue collar," now finds "white collar" employees and the "grey collar" people of the service industries in a substantial majority.

The workforce in big mass production industries has contracted, and the new industries have required employees with different skills in different locations. Work once performed in the United States has been moved to other countries, often at wage levels far below the American standards. Multinational, conglomerate corporations have moved operations around the globe as if it were a mammoth chessboard. The once thriving U.S. merchant marine has shriveled.

A new kind of "growth industry"—consultants to management skilled in the use of every legal loophole that can frustrate union organizing, the winning of representation elections, or the negotiation of a fair and equitable collective bargaining agreement—has mushroomed in recent years, and threatens the stability of labor–management relationships. A group of organizations generally described as the "new right" enlist their followers in retrogressive crusades to develop an anti-union atmosphere in the nation, and to repeal or mutilate various social and economic programs that have brought a greater degree of security and peace of mind to the millions of American wage earners in the middle and lower economic brackets.

Resistance to modest proposals like the labor law reform bill of 1977, and the use of lie detectors and electronic surveillance in probing the attitudes and actions of employees are a reminder that opposition to unions, while changing in style from the practices of a few decades ago, is still alive and flourishing—often financed by corporate groups, trade associations and extremist ideologues.

Yet through this dizzying process of change, one need remains constant—the need for individual employees to enjoy their human rights and dignity, and to have the power to band together to achieve equal collective status in dealing with multi-million and multi-billion dollar corporations. In other words, there is no substitute for the labor union.

American labor's responsibility in its second century is to adjust to the new conditions, so that it may achieve optimum ability to represent its members and contribute to the evolutionary progress of the American democratic society.

AFL-CIO President Lane Kirkland expressed that concept in his formal statement on labor's centennial in 1981:

"Labor has a unique role in strengthening contemporary American society and dealing adequately and forcefully with the challenge of the future.

"We shall rededicate ourselves to the sound principle of harnessing democratic tradition and trade union heritage with the necessity of reaching out for new and better ways to serve all working people and the entire nation. . . ."

6.3 What's in It for the Unions

CHARLES G. BURCK

American labor leaders have by and large had little use for well-intentioned schemes to make them partners with management. In the words of Thomas R. Donahue, secretary-treasurer of the AFL-CIO, most have been "the worst kind of nonsense," perpetrated either by "pied pipers who promised 'no supervisors, no assembly lines' or romantic academics espousing European-style codetermination." Either way, says Donahue, "they set everyone's teeth on edge."

But a remarkable turnabout is under way. Unions are becoming almost as interested as companies in innovative efforts to give employees more say about how they work—schemes like quality circles and quality-of-worklife systems that solicit their ideas and accord them a status akin to partnership. . . . Union leaders who used to worry that their members would accuse them of selling out to management have been surprised to find that this new kind of cooperation has raised their standing with the rank and file.

The United Auto Workers, the United Steelworkers of America, the Communications Workers of America, the International Brotherhood of Electrical Workers, and the Telecommunications International Union—together representing a fifth of the nation's organized workers—have signed national labor agreements committing themselves to plans for bettering worklife. The United Rubber Workers, the Bakery, Confectionery, and Tobacco Workers International, the United Food and Commercial Workers, and others have quietly supported locals that try new ways of cooperating with management. Still others are watching cautiously, and nowhere are national union leaders speaking out against the concept. Even William Winpisinger, the International Association of Machinists president whose militant rhetoric about the folly of cooperating with management brings to mind the firebrands of the British labor movement, considers quality of worklife an issue apart—an improvement, he says, that he's been fighting for all along.

A good deal has changed since those days when the pied pipers came tootling through. Managers increasingly see that workers want to take their jobs seriously, and to be taken seriously by their supervisors. Today's quality-of-worklife concepts are far different from discredited schemes of the past: they offer clear benefits to both workers and management.

Adversity has helped make labor leaders readier to examine old orthodoxies. Unionized labor's share of the total work force has been declining for years, and its leaders are beginning to suspect that labor–management cooperation holds interesting possibilities for reversing the decline. Trapped nonetheless by their past adversarial posturing, many leaders remain uncomfortable about collaboration—particularly since experience has taught that management-inspired programs usually result in work speedups or manpower reductions.

During the early 1970s, for example, the major steel companies and the United Steelworkers agreed upon a bold plan to fight the growing threat of imported steel: joint labor–management committees would sit down together to reason out ways of raising productivity. Lloyd McBride, now the Steelworkers' president, remembers well the first of those meetings he attended as a staff representative at the Granite City Steel Co.

"The management guys came in and said, 'Well, we want to talk about the productivity of this operation,' " McBride recalls. " 'Down in this department we could eliminate this job and that job, and over here we can have so-and-so double up because it's not very busy.' Our committee sat there for a minute, and then one of our guys got up and said, 'Well, that would create some problems for us. But the problems would not be so great if we could get rid of your brother-in-law down there who's not doing much, and Smith's cousin who's just sitting around and hasn't done a goddamned thing for years. If we could get rid of those problems, it's *really* going to improve our productivity.' " The nepotism McBride remembers in that plant wasn't a way of life in most steel mills, but the confrontational attitudes were: the entire productivity program was soon abandoned.

At about the same time, the United Auto Workers was trying to develop a plan jointly with General Motors to deal with roughly similar problems. But the approach was entirely different. GM had become increasingly concerned about the restiveness of its work force and aware that traditional ways of boosting productivity were of only limited use when workers came in late or failed to report at all. Its organizational-development staff, headed by a thoughtful psychologist named Delmar L. "Dutch" Landen, was determined to find ways to get workers more involved in their work. Irving Bluestone, then director of the UAW's GM department, saw an opportunity to advance his own long-held belief that unions could co-operate with management to advance the workers' responsibilities and stature.

Bluestone was a maverick within his union—his fellow officers thought he was making an enormous mistake—but he pressed on with his views. The company and the union began to talk about the possibilities in 1972, and in the 1973 contract negotiations they signed the first national quality-of-worklife agreement in the U.S.

The Word Not Mentioned

That agreement has become the model for just about all the others undertaken since. Nowhere in it did the word productivity appear; the underlying premise was that management would seek its rewards from such improvements as higher product quality and lower absenteeism, which might be expected to spring naturally from a more satisfied work force. All the quality-of-worklife under-takings were to be strictly voluntary, and none would be used uni-laterally to raise production rates or reduce manpower require-ments. The systems that evolved have been almost as diverse as the plants that practice them. But all have given workers more con-trol, and opened up communications with supervisors.

The UAW's years of experience have done much to persuade others in the labor movement that joint programs with manage-ment can serve the interests of both sides. "They're a strong union and nobody's patsies," says John W. Shaughnessy Jr., president of the Telecommunications International Union, whose 60,000 members are mainly Bell Telephone workers. "They've given qual-ity of worklife a lot of credibility."

Like managers, labor leaders cannot always quantify the gains from such changes, but local disputes and grievances—a sure ba-rometer of labor relations—are down dramatically. Just about every national settlement in the auto industry has produced protracted guerrilla warfare as local units struggle—sometimes for many weeks—to resolve disputes. The 1979 settlement broke with tradition. At GM, a half dozen locals settled their problems even before the national contract was concluded—astounding, say bargainers on both sides of the table—and 63 others wrapped up matters simultaneously with the national agreement or a few days afterward. Virtually all were at plants with active quality-of-worklife efforts.

Labor leaders have been no less surprised than managers by the benefits of employee participation. Like the foreman who cannot believe that workers have useful ideas, the old-line militant shop steward cannot imagine how cooperating with management will advance his own career. But like the foreman, the union representative can become much more effective in his job once he learns how to take advantage of the new system. "Participation creates a new role for him," says Donald F. Ephlin, who is director of the UAW's Ford department. "The committeeman becomes more than a committeeman; he becomes a co-leader with management of a program that is bringing new status to the employees."

The typical shop-floor leader has to spend most of his time on grievances—answering members' calls, writing up complaints, and nagging foremen for weeks or months to get responses. In some plants, grievance backlogs run into the thousands. "I tell people they should weigh them rather than count them," jokes UAW President Douglas A. Fraser. Most are generated by a misanthropic minority and are often inconsequential—a burned-out light bulb or an overflowing trash can—but they vent deeper discontents. Union representatives are often frustrated by such pointless exercises, but are nonetheless compelled to fight for their constituents.

Where employees become participants, the grievance load invariably goes down. The general atmosphere of the plant improves, and many of the issues that might become grievances can be resolved informally. A broken toilet might not be repaired for a week when the union representative has to bring it to management's attention in writing. But if he can drop a word in the foreman's ear, and the foreman can dial plant maintenance on the spot, the plumbing gets fixed in a hurry.

The floor representative's own quality of worklife goes up under such circumstances—as does his rapport with the people he represents. "If I'm part of a process where we're talking things out, I'm spending more time getting acquainted with the members and building personal relationships," says William Horner, who retired from the UAW last year after serving most recently as Bluestone's administrative assistant for developing quality-of-worklife programs.

The practical results have done much to allay unionists' fears that employee participation would make the local leader superfluous. Quite the opposite: leaders in quality-of-worklife plants find themselves politically more popular than ever. To date, according to UAW leaders, virtually every slate of the union's officers who campaigned by supporting an established quality-of-worklife effort has won.

Honoring the Compact

Many union leaders feared that labor–management cooperation would undermine the collective-bargaining system, the very foundation of the U.S. labor movement. After all, nothing could be further from the spirit of the bargaining table than a process in which both sides wrestle with mutual problems by putting their best ideas forward at the *start* of a discussion. Some unionists worried that management would use quality-of-worklife programs to chip away at benefits won through bargaining. Others took precisely the opposite view: they saw participation as a way to squeeze out gains they failed to get during negotiations.

In practice, the lines between combat and cooperation have remained remarkably clear. Few managers or labor leaders in the auto industry have tried to abuse the compact, and none has succeeded. Yet neither side feels constrained to shelve issues that cannot be resolved cooperatively. GM and Ford are relentlessly pressing the UAW for wage concessions—and the UAW is mincing no words in telling the companies where to go. "When we get an issue where both sides feel they're right, we get our mad on," says Bill Horner. "At the extreme, we prepare for a strike or even go out. But someday it's resolved. Then the union and the company have to ask each other whether they want to continue the warfare or go back to cooperation. Invariably, we agree it's a better life to go back."

A Cautious Beginning

Old suspicions do not die easily, however, and unions that have recently committed themselves to pursuing shop-floor collaboration are proceeding with care. The agreement the United Steelworkers signed with the industry's nine major producers as part of last year's contract set up so-called labor–management participation teams that will function at the department level (rolling mill, shipping department, and so forth). These teams will have a charter to discuss practically any issue that might come up—with the important exclusion of grievances or matters negotiated in the contract.

Cooperation is an especially alien notion in the rough-and-tumble, highly authoritarian atmosphere of the steel mills. Here only a few teams are functioning so far, and they are still regarded as experimental even though workers in nearby departments who have seen the results are clamoring to be included. As McBride says, "It takes careful planning and training to prepare both sides for these new roles." Neither the industry nor the union wants to risk a reprise of the earlier fiasco.

Cooperative efforts in autos and steel were unquestionably spurred by the crises those industries have faced. No comparable threat from foreign competition has confronted the communications industry, but labor and management have found themselves in extraordinary agreement about their long-term needs. When the Communications Workers of America presented its quality-of-worklife proposal at the 1980 contract negotiations, says President Glenn E. Watts, "AT&T's counterproposal was so close to ours that we were quite surprised." Union members were increasingly frustrated by what they call job pressure. In its efforts to raise productivity, the company was scrutinizing performance through a microscope. Some techniques were extreme indeed—listening in on operators to judge their efficiency or ringing absentee workers at home to confirm that they were sick when they claimed to be.

AT&T was no less eager to break with such procedures; it believed that making jobs more satisfying would yield productivity gains over the long run. "The company has made a decision to accept the union as a limited partner," says Michael Maccoby, director of the Project on Technology, Work, and Character in Washington and a guru to both sides. "But in return it is getting a much higher level of cooperation, more flexibility as far as technological change is concerned, and the potential for huge savings by increasing managers' spans of control—because fewer of them will be needed to supervise the workers."

Figuring Out the Realities

Thoughtful labor leaders are tantalized by the idea that participation may help them resolve some profoundly troubling union problems. No major labor leader in the U.S. today has illusions about the relationship between corporate profits and the well-being of his constituents. But down in the ranks, it's usually a different story: the myth remains widespread that corporate resources are somehow limitless, and labor's claim on them consequently open-ended. Labor leaders may have felt they could afford to encourage this nonsense for their own political ends during times of rising prosperity, but many are now faced with the unpalatable job of telling their members why demanding less will be good for them. They find it hard to explain the facts of life to the membership until—as with Chrysler—an afflicted enterprise is on the brink of collapse. Even then, leaders cannot do much to break the momentum of the old party line; writers of the UAW newsletter *Solidarity* still churn out broadsides telling auto workers they are impoverished, despite what they hear from the "big-business-controlled media."

Many labor leaders now hope—though they do not like to say so explicitly—that members who become participants will figure out the economic realities for themselves. As McBride puts it, "Workers with more information will be able to make better decisions about union policies."

This indeed seems to happen where management has shared financial information with the workers, as at many auto plants, and where local leaders overcome their own fears about being accused of selling out to the company. "It's not getting in bed with management—that's the clarification you need to make," says William "Red" Hutchins, president of United Rubber Workers Local 87 at GM's Inland Division in Dayton. "We have to stop looking at whether we're afraid somebody will think we're taking a wrong position just because we want to see the company make money. If the company doesn't, it's hard for us to go back and negotiate increased benefits or wages." While Inland is not operating in the crisis atmosphere typical of many automotive operations these days, the union leaders are looking warily to the future. Dayton has lost its share of employers in recent years, and as Hutchins says: "We don't want to become another Frigidaire, NCR, or Dayton Press"—all of which have cut back or closed their plants in the city. "We're starting early to keep that from happening." The division's worker-participation effort began just over a year ago.

Opinions are still divided about whether employee participation is a threat or an aid to new organizing efforts. In some non-union plants, management has used it to resolve discontents that might have brought in a union. Yet some leaders believe it can give unionism new leverage in attracting the unorganized. "Where you run into a 'no union' attitude, it's because the union is seen as a belligerent and aggressive outfit coming in to upset the established work relationship," says Shaughnessy of the Telecommunications International Union. The TIU's California local has won 13 elections over the past two years in Pacific Telephone Co. offices by eschewing the classically confrontational rhetoric offered up by its rival, the CWA local. (Like AT&T operating companies, the union locals have considerable discretion over their own operating styles.) Pushing joint labor–management committees that will head off problems before they turn into grievances, the TIU organizers have won over workers who previously resisted representation.

Counsel from the Bridge-builders

For most union leaders, worker participation is still too unfamiliar to embrace. But many who want to learn more about it are seeking counsel from specialists in labor–management bridge-building like Maccoby, Ted Mills of the American Center for the Quality of Work Life in Washington, and Jerome M. Rosow, president of the Work in America Institute in Scarsdale, New York. Rosow's institute last year organized the Productivity Forum to provide a neutral ground for corporate executives, labor leaders, and government and educational managers to meet and discuss measures for improving working relationships and productivity. The AFL-CIO and five unions are now regular members of the forum.

Even two years ago, only a rare labor leader would let himself be seen joining executives in an organization with "productivity" in its name. But given the current climate, unionists—like managers—cannot afford to overlook any possibility for strengthening their institutions for combat in the marketplace. As Glenn Watts of the CWA observes, cooperating with management may appear to expose a union to high risks, but some form of cooperation is essential for the long-run survival of both parties. "The only real risk," he says, "is if the union does *not* participate."

Discussion and Review Questions

1. The growth of unionism in the United States has seemed to parallel the development of basic industries—railroads, coal, steel, autos, and so on. These industries, of course, have been in decline in recent years. What impact do you think the gradual decline of these industries will have on the union movement?

2. Why did most large corporations "come to accept the inevitable" and stop fighting unionization efforts in the late 1930s?

3. How do you react to the strategy employed by the union in its efforts to organize Joseph Richardson's company? How about Richardson's strategy? Was it well chosen?

4. The AFL-CIO seems to argue that, without unions, virtually no improvements in jobs and wages would have taken place for American workers. Do you agree with this view? Why or why not?

5. "Worker participation" and "cooperation between workers and management" are newly emerging concepts in labor–management relations. How do you view this development? Is it a good idea, or do you see problems down the road?

PART 4

MARKETING PROBLEMS

ISSUE 7

How Is the American Consumer Changing?

For a very long time, most firms doing marketing research for new products, or even for old standbys, started from pretty much the same basic assumptions: The market for virtually all goods would continue to expand as both the population and the buying power of Americans continued to grow. In other words, practically every seller of goods and services, industrial as well as consumer, subscribed to the cheery view that the long expansion that began after World War II would go on and on. With the exception of three or four relatively brief recessions, the American economy hummed along for more than two and a half decades until, in the early 1970s, economic and business activity began to slow down.

The long expansion, of course, had not meant that simply *any* product would find its desired place in the market—after all, even Henry Ford's company had failed to sell its Edsel—but it certainly produced a persistent belief that "market growth" was a comparatively small and in some cases irrelevant issue in product development considerations. Recently, however, marketers have been brought up short by a number of developments, both economic and demographic, that have compelled a reassessment of just who the average American consumer of the future will be and what he or she will be buying. With both economic and population growth slowed, marketing specialists face a mixed bag of opportunities. Some markets have simply ceased to grow and, therefore, invite special caution in developing and marketing new products. Others, meanwhile, have developed simply because general economic and population growth has ceased. As a result, the basic market strategies affecting product development, pricing, promotion, and product placement have become much more complex.

The Changing Demographic and Economic Foundations

While it is impossible to examine all of the demographic shifts of the past couple of decades, a number of salient changes can be generalized very quickly. First, the nation's population growth rate has fallen to about half of what it was during the soaring 1960s. Second, as a result, the average age of the population, while still comparatively young (about thirty), is rising and will continue to rise quite swiftly over the next few decades. Third, the old nuclear family of Mom, Pop, and the kids is changing in favor of either households headed by women or single-person households. Fourth, while the locational shift of Americans toward the suburbs continues, it is a dribble compared to the flood of the 1950s and 1960s. Fifth, population movement away from the northeastern parts of the nation to the southern and western parts continues, although not at the rate of a decade ago.

Matching, and of course deeply interconnected with many of these demographic trends, has been a decade and a half of disappointing economic performance. Characteristic of this economic change of fortune has been a near stagnation of disposable (after-tax) income. However, while overall income averages have shown little improvement, this masks income shifts among different groups. Relatively speaking, incomes have risen in the South and the West and fallen in the Northeast. Meanwhile, the disparity between blacks and whites, which not so long ago seemed to be closing, has increased. The raw numbers of Americans who fall into the economic category of "poor" (average family of four; annual income of under $10,000) is growing, but the incomes of the upper 20 percent of the population are growing faster than in the recent past. While women have made some economic gains (mostly in those segments of the population with higher levels of education), most remain well behind their male counterparts in earnings. For many American families, the decade and a half of economic contraction and high interest rates has meant an abandonment of "the home in the suburbs" dream. Yet even with the average price of a new home reaching $80,000 in 1982, some other Americans were still able to buy new houses and outfit them handsomely. Table 1 graphically presents some of the more important changes.

Developing New Marketing Strategies

For the marketing expert, the shifting and sometimes contradictory economic and demographic trends require more thoughtful approaches to targeting and segmenting markets than existed in the not-too-distant past. In particular, they demand rethinking the "middle-class bias," which for so long was prominent in the development and marketing of consumer goods. This middle-class emphasis focused upon a large, and for many years growing, segment of the population that was composed of predominantly suburban nuclear families with a male head of household and steadily rising real income. Women in this group were mostly homemakers, and, as the advertising for floor waxes and detergents stressed, they presumably were personally concerned about "waxy build-up" and "ring around the collar." Children were similarly stereotyped as upward bound through elementary and secondary school, with

Table 1.   The Changing Profile of the American Consumer

Characteristics	1960	1970	1980
Population (in millions)	180	204	227
Percent aged 55 & over	17.8	18.9	22
Percent young adult (18–34)	21.6	24.4	29.5
Children (17 and under)	11.3	8.4	6.5
Median family income (1980 $)	$15,637	$20,926	$21,023
Median white family income (1980 $)	$16,235	$21,722	$21,904
Median black family income (1980 $)	$ 8,987	$13.325	$12,674
Average annual unemployment (percentage)	5.5	4.9	7.1
Consumer Price Index (1967 equals 100)	88.7	116.3	272.4
Number of families (in millions)	45.5	52.2	60.3
Number of people living alone (in millions)	11.1	15.5	27.1

Source: Economic Report of the President, 1982.

a high probability for college attendance, and apparently leading onward to lives just like their parents'. This average middle-class American family apparently consumed appliances, furniture, cars, vacation paraphernalia, razors, pens, clothes, aspirin (especially children's aspirin), cosmetics, housewares, and prepared foods in ever-increasing quantities and improving qualities. The consumer dreams of this middle-class family were the stuff that American marketing was made of.

Now, however, there is abundant evidence that "middle-class America" no longer aptly describes the majority of American consumers. Rising divorces and separations have reduced greatly the number of male-headed households. With more than half of all women over the age of sixteen working full or part time, the full-time American housewife has become a vanishing species. At the same time, more men and women are living as singles, nearly three times as many as in 1960. Meanwhile, the under-sixteen population has declined by 15 percent over the past fifteen years. Over the same period, the over-sixty-five population has grown by 40 percent. Median real income, which doubled between 1952 and 1972, has grown scarcely at all over the past decade, indicating that the growth of "discretionary spending" for all those "middle class" commodities has about stopped. Markets for autos, appliances, and other big-ticket items are now mostly replacement markets.

The combination of these age, family, and income shifts has produced in a startlingly short period of time a new "average American"— or at least most marketers believe that to be the case. The resulting changes in developing market targets and segments have appeared in both subtle and obvious ways, from the single-serving soup can and one-serving frozen gourmet meals to plain-label packaging.

The dissolving of the traditional American middle class has forced modern marketers to redesign products, abandon certain lines, and develop entirely new products. The first two articles in this section examine two important trends among American consumers: (1) they are getting older and (2) both husband and wife are working. For marketers, these are important trends that must be taken into consideration in the designing, pricing, and selling of products. The third article examines the marketing research problems faced by marketing managers. The final article examines the efforts of one entrepreneur to meet these wide-ranging needs through an innovative retail outlet.

7.1   Over 55: Growth Market of the 1980s

CAROLE B. ALLAN

The American marketing community for years has been obsessed with the cult of the young. "Age 49 and out" has governed the advertising and marketing decisions made along Madison Avenue. Only the young in this country—or so the TV commercials would lead one to believe—wore clothes, cleaned their homes, ate in restaurants or traveled to ports unknown. The "old," on the other hand, were at home polishing their dentures and worrying about their arthritis.

So when a grandfatherly face suddenly beams out of the crowd in a recent Pepsi Generation commercial, nothing short of a revolutionary phenomenon is under way. While the traditional obsession with youth has not been totally abandoned—as the current infatuation with teen-age models as the arbiters of taste and fashion vividly reveals—the tide is clearly beginning to turn. Older consumers—the gray market, the maturity market, the older market, whatever the name currently in vogue—are fast becoming a major force in the U.S. marketplace. Long thought to possess limited economic potential, persons 55 and older are emerging as one of the most conspicuous spending groups in the country today—representing more than $400 billion in annual personal income and one quarter of all U.S. consumer expenditures.

And marketers—ranging from such giants of the cosmetics industry as Estée Lauder and Elizabeth Arden to travel companies such as American Express, Eastern Air Lines, Amtrak and Greyhound, from food manufacturers such as General Foods to manufacturers of sporting goods such as Wilson and a myriad of other companies, including Procter & Gamble, Colgate-Palmolive, Bristol-Myers and the like—are jettisoning their preconceived notions and taking a fresh look at this long ignored market and liking what they see. For many, the "maturity market" has become the growth market of the '80s.

Why the sudden interest in the older market? Sheer numbers alone are a partial explanation. Here is a consumer force of 45 million, one of five Americans, growing at a rate twice that of the overall population. In size it is greater than the combined population of 20 of our 50 states and the entire population of Canada. In terms of U.S. consumer households, one of three, or more than 28 million, is headed by a person 55 or older. And, contrary to popular belief, most persons 65 and older continue to head up their own households. Few live in institutions—little more than 5 percent—and only a small percentage live with their children. The number of older persons heading up their own consumer household has grown dramatically in recent years, and the trend is expected to continue.

But one must look further than demographics to explain the sudden turnaround in perception of the older market. The full answer is probably threefold—a heightened awareness of that market's size and characteristics, the discovery of its true economics and the dramatic diminishing of other markets and the profits therefrom.

The fact that the youth market is no longer expanding at its once unprecedented pace, that children of the postwar baby boom have all come of age, has been the precipitating force in the awakening to the older market. During the '50s and '60s, growth of the youth population far outpaced that of other population groups, and marketers saw little reason to explore new horizons. During the '70s, however, the population under 18 actually decreased by some 8 million, a direct reflection of the postwar baby bust.

And in the current decade the age group 18–24—the primary years when new households are formed—will experience a drop of some 4 million. Reflecting the changing U.S. age structure, the median age of Americans will rise by some five years in the next two decades. And by the year 2000, half the U.S. population will be over 35. The "graying of America" is clearly upon us.

At the forefront of the companies discovering the older market are those whose profits have been dependent on catering to the needs of an expanding youth population. Thus, Gerber Products, which for years prided itself on the slogan "Babies are our business, our only business," has abandoned the motto and introduced a product line that now includes insurance and health care products for older people. Levi Strauss & Company, which built its fortune clothing generations of teen-agers in blue jeans, is changing with the times and is now marketing a profitable line of clothing for the more "mature" figure. And McDonald's, the fast-food giant, while not abandoning the youth market as prime consumers, has recently implemented marketing plans designed to attract more adult customers.

Not unexpectedly, it is on the more youthful segments of the "older market" that the initial attention has been focused. Many in the cosmetics industry still define the older woman as someone over 30; a well-known commercial speaks to the "older woman" by stating its product "actually makes skin over 25 look younger." But signs of change are on the horizon.

Leisure-time industries in particular have turned to the retiree market to take up some of the slack caused by the diminishing of other markets. The bowling industry, faced with a severe drop in daytime bowlers—due to both a decline in the youth market and an increasing number of women entering the work force—is cashing in on the retirees' availability to bowl during "off" daytime hours. A Washington-based sports membership organization, the National Senior Sports Association, offering sports-oriented vacations, competitive opportunities and other events to the senior sports enthusiast, has attracted nearly 15,000 members in its first year of operation. And educational institutions nationwide are aggressively, and successfully, seeking out older students to combat slackening enrollment.

If changing demographics have been the impetus compelling business to seek out new markets, discovery of the true economics of the maturity market has been the cement that sealed the deal. Historically, the marketing community has turned its back on the older consumer for one basic reason—a belief that the age group has limited spending power. Add to this the belief that the group had limited consumer needs (with the exception of health care products), had less inclination to spend and lacked distinctive mar-

keting characteristics, and only one conclusion seemed possible—
targeted marketing strategies, whether in terms of new product development, promotion or advertising efforts, would not justify the
costs involved.

Nothing could be further from the truth. The real economic
power of the 55-plus market—by any standard—is of compelling
proportions. In fact, households headed by a person 55 or older account for:

- Thirty percent of total U.S. personal income.
- Nearly 80 percent of all money in savings and loan institutions.
- An estimated 28 percent of all discretionary money in the U.S. consumer marketplace—nearly double that in households headed by persons 34 or under (households headed by a person age 25 or under—the much sought-after youth market—represent a mere 1 percent of all discretionary money).

''Yes, but even if older people have money, they don't spend
it,'' or so the prevailing wisdom has always been. Marketing data
beginning to emerge on the spending patterns of the 55-plus consumer again belies that stereotype. As noted, households headed
by a person 55 or older account for more than one quarter of total
consumer expenditures in the country. In fact, a comprehensive
consumer expenditure survey conducted by the U.S. Bureau of Labor Statistics in 1973 revealed that older households contributed
$160 billion worth of consumer purchases to the U.S. economy at
the time—and all indications are the figure has increased substantially since then. (These are the latest government data available
but the general trends are corroborated by more recent market research studies done by private sources.) . . .

Health care spending habits of the 55-plus consumer household have long been known, accounting for nearly $4 of $10 spent
in the marketplace; less reported is this group's consumption of
other products. For example, households headed by 55-plus consumers account for:

- $1 of every $4 spent for cosmetics and bath products.
- $4 of every $10 spent on women's hair care services in beauty par-lors.
- $3 of every $10 spent for food consumed in the home (40 percent of all coffee purchases alone).

- $1 of every $4 spent on alcoholic beverages, including one third of all purchases of hard liquor.

In addition, these households own one quarter of all cars and make up the bulk of all stockholders on major and over-the-counter exchanges.

When one looks at the per capita expenditure figures, the picture becomes even more striking. In fact, in terms of per capita expenditures, the 55-to-64-year-old household becomes the single most important consumer market in the country today. It is a time of life when, freed from the constraints and financial responsibility of child-raising, spending on self becomes the order of the day.

It is also a time when household income and earning power are at a peak, with money for new clothes, travel, the theater, dining out and new furnishings for the home. Per capita expenditures for travel by the 55–64 group are the highest of any age group. And, despite inflation, these people are prime buyers of luxury goods such as top-of-the-line cars, vacation homes, expensive jewelry, gourmet food and wine, microwave ovens and high-priced stereo and video recorder systems—a fact that has taken the exploding consumer electronics industry by surprise. . . .

The potential and diversity of travel needs of the older traveler are just beginning to be grasped. Persons 55 and older are the major customers for round-the-world cruises where fares may range between $15,000 and $150,000, and, at the same time, are the bread-and-butter market for low-cost motor coach excursions—accounting for nearly one third of all bus charter trips in the country. A Chicago travel agency, catering exclusively to the 55-plus market, reports landslide business.

The maturity market offers the three ingredients of a travel marketer's dream—time, money and desire. All three are expected to increase in the current decade, partly because more people are choosing early retirement.

Capitalizing on the retirees' flexibility to travel during non-peak vacation periods, major carriers, hotels and tourist attractions are successfully wooing this market with off-season discounts and other promotions—filling up passenger seats and hotel space that would otherwise go vacant. Disney World, hardly a name linked to the "older set," considers its senior promotion, "Young-at-Heart

Days,'' offered for two weeks in May and September, so successful it is now planning an extended promotion in cooperation with Eastern Air Lines.

City and state departments of tourism also have discovered the older traveler as a major market source for stimulating local tourism. Tennessee this year organized a statewide promotion, Senior Season, during the month of September—a slow time for tourism but a prime time for travel by retirees. Hotels, restaurants, sightseeing attractions and merchants organized special ''senior'' events; Greyhound offered a discount bus fare, as did Ozark Airlines, to travelers 55 and over on selected routes to Tennessee. The Tennessee experience prompted other tourism offices to launch similar promotions. Many participating merchants plan to continue their offerings throughout the year.

Financial institutions—brokerage houses, insurance companies and banks—also are zeroing in on the senior market by offering specialized investment counseling for widows, retirement planning seminars, even ''senior savers'' clubs that not only provide specialized financial services but a range of social activities as well. Bank surveys reveal that persons 55 and over keep more and larger checking and saving accounts than other age groups. Banks offering such specialized services report healthy increases in new depositors and profits.

The founder of one such program states the matter succinctly in a recent article in *American Banker*. ''Senior citizens offer the greatest profit potential there is.''

The U.S. beauty industry, too, is beginning to view the older market with new interest and respect. Cosmetics houses are launching new product lines and advertising campaigns aimed at meeting the beauty care of the ''mature woman.'' These houses now are recognizing that concern about appearance and looking one's best does not stop at any given age, that women 50 and older are not necessarily looking for guidance on how to look younger but on selecting products that will best suit the makeup needs unique to the changes in skin type, coloring and facial contours that accompany the aging process.

Major cosmetics companies such as Estée Lauder and Elizabeth Arden recently have come out with product lines specifically designed for the older woman; Helena Rubenstein, an early entry in targeting the mature woman with its "Madame Rubenstein" line, reports that sales of the line have doubled every year for the past three years—and are expected to double again during the current year. The Arden "Millennium" line, on the market little more than a year, has experienced sales "far beyond projections," according to marketing executives.

Similarly, retailers and merchants—from major drug chains to the Fred Astaire dance studios and Vic Tanny health clubs, from major league baseball teams to department stores and grocery chains—report great expansion in sales through targeting the 55-plus market. For the most part, retailers pursue the market with various discount offerings and off-hour specials, but other approaches have proved equally successful.

Yet, many questions remain unanswered. Having ignored everyone over 49 for so long, many marketers now find a lack of research on the needs and consumer characteristics of the middle-age and senior population. Little is known, for example, about how life-style patterns, psychological and attitudinal sets, and environmental and physical considerations affect purchasing decisions of the 55-plus population. Thus, in conversations with marketing executives today, a frequently raised question is "We know the statistics—but what are older people like?"

A wrong answer can be costly, as witness several years ago when the Heinz company introduced a product line labeled "senior foods." The Heinz experiment failed—the majority of older persons do not need an easily digestible food akin to baby food, and the small number who might do not want to be labeled as such.

In truth, there may be no specific answers to "What are older people like?" or "What are the key characteristics of the older market that need to be considered in making marketing decisions?" Members of the older population, a diverse group, do not become more alike with age but more dissimilar. Thus, it could be argued there really is no such thing as the older market. In fact, age per se is not the best predictor of consumer behavior or personality characteristics. Many persons age 80 have more vitality and *joie de vivre* than 40-year-olds. Lumping them together in one consumer group called the older market results in pairings ranging in age from 50 to the centenarian, those still in the labor force full-time and the retired, the middle-age housewife living with spouse and the newly widowed or elderly widow living alone, the physically active and those with varying physical limitations.

A definitive market survey of such a conglomerate is impossible. So, successful marketing must depend on successful segmentation of this vast consumer group, plus carefully researched marketing strategies.

Meeting the needs of the maturity market will require the development of new products, or a modification in design of existing products, creating an ease of access to the marketplace and a change in advertising and promotional approach.

The latter must counter the stereotyped depiction of older persons in ad copy. Interviews with older persons reveal that it is not only where they are seen in ads that is the problem, but also where they are not seen. People do not stop wearing clothes in middle or old age, but you would never know it from today's fashion magazines. Members of the maturity market want to look as fashionable as anyone else—and they want to see these fashions on models with whom they can identify.

The time for targeting the maturity market has been long overdue—marketers who miss the boat will have only themselves to blame. Not only has the business sector failed to fulfill real and essential needs of this population group, but has forgone a major opportunity for its own economic expansion.

The older population's importance and power will continue to grow in the years to come, as their numbers and economic and political strength continue to increase. It is a reality that the business sector can no longer afford to ignore.

7.2 The Big Clout of Two Incomes

ARLENE HERSHMAN, WITH MARK LEVENSON

With the median price of a new house soaring past $60,000 and mortgage rates at 10% plus, who can afford one these days? For that matter, who can afford those $450 microwave ovens, $250 food processors, $7,700 Ford Thunderbirds and multithousand-dollar vacation trips to sun-blessed Acapulco?

Sales of these delightful and expensive products and services continue to climb even though inflation is pinching everyone's real income, consumer debt is at record highs and savings are down. Someone has to pass the credit tests and make the monthly payments on all these wonderful goodies. Who can?

The two-income family can.

Obviously, two-income families alone don't buy all these items. But they account for a whopping share, and they are dramatically changing the demographics of the consumer market. Yet economists, manufacturers and retailers—with a vital stake in this group—have done very little research into exactly who the two-income families are, whether they are a permanent part of the American scene and whether their buying habits differ from other family units.

To gain some insight into these areas, *Dun's Review* combed the latest Census Bureau and Labor Department data and interviewed economists, pollsters, consumer marketing experts and manufacturers. The profile of the two-income family that emerges is of a group that is vast in numbers, young, well educated and well off. . . .

Of course, there have always been two-income families. But today's group differs both quantitatively and qualitatively from those of yesteryear. To begin with, there are far more of them. Latest figures, for March 1977, reveal that there are 24 million families in which both partners hold jobs. In fact, there are now more families with two wage earners than there are with only a single worker. The lines crossed only recently, in 1976. . . .

The big increase comes, of course, from the steady influx of wives into the job market. Some observers suggest that this is a result of the virulent inflation of the past few years, driving women to work so that a family can make ends meet. But while this certainly is a factor, the evidence suggests that it is not the basic reason. The practice seems to stem much more from a change in attitudes, in life-styles—a conclusion bolstered by the fact that the trend has been going on for decades. Back in 1958, for example, only 30.7% of all married women worked. That rose to 38.6% in 1968 and to 47.6% in 1978.

Other data indicate that today's working wives are a permanent part of the labor market, and that's another important difference. Traditionally, working wives fell into a pattern that formed what American Express economist John Casson calls ''the double hump on the age curve.'' The first bulge came in the 20-through-24 age bracket. Then the participation of wives dropped off as large numbers left the market to raise children. The curves rose again in the 45–54 bracket as large numbers of women returned to work after their children had grown up. But that double hump has been eliminated recently.

While wives in the 20–24 group still participate most heavily in the job market, the subsequent decline in the 25–34 bracket is now much smaller—and this group also participates more heavily than the 45-through-54-year-olds, who used to form the second peak. ''The interesting shift over the past few years is not the growth in the number of working women per se, but the great bulge of working women with young children,'' comments economist Sandra Shaber of Chase Econometrics.

Surveys support the statistical evidence that larger numbers of wives are a permanent fixture in the job market. According to director Richard Curtin of the University of Michigan's Survey Research Center, wives who are asked about their working plans no longer talk in terms of transitory income goals such as ''until we can afford the down payment on a house,'' or ''until we have children'' or ''to pay for the children's education.'' Instead, they take a job with the idea that they will be working all their lives.

Job = Car & Loan

Their spending habits reflect this idea of permanence. "In the 1950s, working wives making transportation arrangements bought used cars or used public transportation or a car pool for the two or three years they planned to work," says Curtin. Now they expect to have a career, so they buy a new car and take on the commitment of paying off a three- or four-year installment loan. The obligation "makes sense to them" because they intend to stay in the work force, Curtin adds.

Another prevalent belief is that the poorer families are the ones with working wives, but the evidence indicates that two-income families come from the more affluent groups. The most recent Census Bureau data on the matter, covering 1976, show that the median income for families in which only the husband worked was $14,543 a year. But in families with two working spouses, the average income was $17,570 a year, despite the fact that in half of such households the wife worked only parttime. Assuming the basic cost of living is fairly equivalent for both types of families, the $3,000 difference represents substantial extra buying power for the two-income family. And the numbers are even more dramatic when both partners work full time. In that case, median income jumps to $19,750. . . .

Just what two-income families buy and how and why they make their spending decisions is just beginning to be revealed in sales reports and surveys of buying patterns. But analyzing the motives and other factors behind various purchases is difficult because they usually overlap and interact with one another. Dual-income families seem to prefer some products and services because they are young, others because they are well educated, still others because they are affluent or because they have little time or because they have different ideas about sex roles than earlier generations did. They are also influenced by the prevailing "me" generation philosophy and feel they deserve whatever they can afford because they work for it. Whatever the combination of motives, the fact that there are two incomes is of central importance.

And they are eager consumers. "They seem to want to have immediately everything their parents worked twenty years to acquire," comments Larry Thurston of Dayton, Ohio's Heritage Real

Estate. Very often, the young couples he sells houses to have saved the wife's income for a year to accumulate the down payment, and then they buy the house, two cars and all the appliances in the next year, he reports.

Buying Time

Time, or the lack of it, is a major consideration. In buying big-ticket items such as appliances and TV sets, for example, they willingly pay extra for time-saving devices. The sensational sales increases of microwave ovens are closely identified with working couples. A survey of 1,000 microwave oven buyers two years ago showed that 48% were bought by two-income families, says Amana product manager Rose Rennecamp. "I would estimate that they now account for 52% of the market," she adds. She also reports that they are heavy buyers of a premium-cost item that programs the oven to go on at a specific time.

The higher priced items are also perceived as being of better quality, likely to last longer and need less servicing—a vital consideration when no one is home to deal with service calls. Remote-control TV tuning devices made with solid state components are easy to sell to working couples because they are considered less likely to break down, reports executive editor Fred Gottesman of *Merchandising* magazine, a leading journal in the appliance and housewares field.

Studies made by marketing professor Roger Blackwell of Ohio State University offer "tentative evidence that people will spend about a third of what they earn per hour to save an hour of time." For instance, working couples will buy a high-powered lawnmower that does in one hour what others do in three even though it costs five times as much. Similarly, when they buy high-priced frozen dinners or eat out, they pay more per ounce or pound than for comparable unprepared food. But considering the "time value" of the people who buy them, he says, "they are bargains."

Two-income families are also affecting store hours. Retailers now find that the big surge of business comes at noon and 5 p.m., says Professor Blackwell, so many of them don't open until late morning. The shopping centers in Columbus, Ohio, for example, open at 10:30 a.m. . . .

When it comes to making buying decisions, male–female sex roles seem to be eroded in the two-income family, and this could be one of the most significant long-term marketing impacts of such household units. Traditionally, men buy certain products, such as cars and stereo equipment, and women buy things like food and housewares. This is less and less the case with two-income families; there is more crossing over and more joint decisions. Ohio State's Blackwell observes: "We used to talk about behavior being different between males and females, whether the females worked or not. Not true anymore. Data indicates now that the groups most alike in buying patterns are males and females with jobs—not females with and without jobs."

They Save Less

Similarly, the two-income family is associated with lower savings rates, but market analyst Hoyt of Whirlpool maintains that this is not the result of being frivolous. "They simply don't need as much savings as one-wage families," he insists. For one thing, they have no children or have fewer children. For another, there isn't only one money stream that could be cut off in the event of illness or death.

What will happen to the two-income family in the event of a recession is very hard to determine. It could be that these families will weather a downturn easily, suffering less hardship than they would if they had only one income. But pessimists worry about the debt load they have taken on—which often requires two incomes to support. In that instance, a takeoff on an old joke seems applicable: When you lose your job, it's a recession; when I lose my job it's a depression; but when my wife loses her job, it's a panic.

7.3 New Trials in Test Marketing

SANDRA SALMANS

The brand managers at XYZ multibillion-dollar packaged-goods company are convinced that the company's new product is the best thing since sliced bread. The hotshots on Madison Avenue think they've created an unforgettable advertising campaign. Everybody is keen on sending his particular banner up the proverbial flagpole. But will anyone salute?

To answer that all-important question, companies engage in an often expensive, lengthy and frequently inconclusive exercise known as test marketing, in which they try out their new product or marketing program in a handful of towns that mirror, as nearly as possible, the demographics and buying patterns of the nation.

It is an effort to determine not merely how a product or marketing strategy will play in Peoria—itself a popular test-market town—but, based on Peoria, how it will be received nationwide. Because a national introduction may involve outlays of millions of dollars, test markets are a safety net under mass-marketers' slender high-wire.

But nothing is constant in marketing and, as demographics and technology have changed, so has test marketing. Currently, the recession is taking its toll. Although the number of new product introductions appears to be rising after a couple of sluggish years, it is far smaller than in marketing's go-go days of the early 1970's.

In this tight economy, that means two things. First, companies are doing more fine tuning of their marketing plans, increasing test-market usage with such promotional tinkering as new coupon issues and advertising. ''The package grocery business is growing at 1 percent, and we want to grow faster,'' said Robert Sansone, general manager of General Foods' beverage division. ''So we're experimenting more with different commercials, levels of advertising, prices." But in addition, they are honing their use of test marketing.

There are no firm figures, or even generally accepted estimates, of what is spent nationwide on test marketing each year. Packaged-goods companies tend to be closed-mouthed about their business, and especially about new products and marketing plans. For one thing, they don't like to publicize their failures. For another, they live in fear—which, given the amount of spying and sabotage known to have taken place, seems justified—that a competitor will become aware of their new product or plan while it is in test, and beat them into the national marketplace.

What is known is that a single, classic test marketing exercise, including research, media costs, production and packaging, can cost upwards of $1 million. And in its last two major tests, Quaker Oats, for one, spent that sum on research alone, according to Dudley Ruch, the company's research director.

Partly as a result, many companies are seeking faster answers at lower costs by stepping up their pretesting—submitting their products and advertising to small groups of consumers. When they do get to the test market itself, it is often in smaller markets and through limited distribution, according to marketing research firms.

"Interest rates have created the need to shorten the pipeline," said Harlan Janes, manager of health, beauty aid and drug industry services at the A.C. Nielsen Company, the nation's largest market research firm. "This is the era of marketing productivity."

That sort of precision of concept fits somewhat ill with the inescapably imprecise nature of the test-market exercise. Some marketing experts even question whether any data generated under the current economic cloud can safely project sales in the presumed fairer climate of a year or two hence. "A budget-priced item, such as a pet food, that is a success now might not sell well in more affluent times," said Donald Kanter, chairman of Boston University's marketing department.

Even in the best of times, test markets are imperfect barometers. Marketers often cite the case of Procter & Gamble's Pringles, the potato chip that passed its tests with flying colors but crumbled when it was sold nationally. More tragically, Rely tampons, another P.&G. product, never indicated any connection to toxic shock syndrome during its test, which lasted three years; the product was fully national for less than a year before it was recalled, in September 1980.

And while the biggest and best marketers, such as Procter & Gamble, General Foods and General Mills, weed out approximately half of their new products in test market, as many as 30 percent of those that survive to be introduced nationwide fail to meet expectations.

To project the national performance of a product from a test, the choice of test market is crucial. It is also, due to the multiplicity of criteria, an almost impossible task. "Test-market selection may be one of the most arbitrary or haphazard decisions made in marketing," said Edward Tauber, a professor of marketing at the University of Southern California.

The goal is a "magic town," in the vocabulary of market researchers. (The term is borrowed from a 1947 James Stewart movie about a pollster who arrives to take the pulse of a small town, hailed as the "mathematical miracle" of the United States, that is typical in every way.)

"The objective is to reproduce the typical American city," said Martin Friedman, editor of the monthly, New Product News. "As the Northeast gets tired, old and poor," he added, the test marketers head increasingly for the Sun Belt, abandoning Buffalo for Phoenix and Sacramento.

Like, the Seven-Up Company's new caffeine-free cola, for example, was introduced last month in Albuquerque, Phoenix and San Diego, as well as three Middle Western and two East Coast markets. But some companies, notably Procter & Gamble, still favor the Middle West. And the so-called Quad Cities—Rock Island and Moline in Illinois, and Davenport and Bettendorf in Iowa—are perennial favorites of many marketers.

Occasionally, the choice may be inspired by less scientific measures. "Some markets are popular because they are places people like to visit," said Ira Weinblatt, director of media planning for Dancer Fitzgerald Sample, a New York advertising agency. "Very few companies test market in Fargo, N.D."

But generally, some sort of science prevails, and demographics are only part of the equation. Ideally, the town's per capita consumption of a product category or a brand should equal the nation's. There is no point in peddling pasta, for example, in a town where everyone eats grits. Nor should a test market be overused, or "interviewed out," in the words of Mr. Kanter of Boston University. In Fort Wayne, Ind., at one time, "the manufacturers created a group of citizens who did nothing but try new products," said Mr. Friedman. Test markets are occasionally dropped from researchers' lists, giving the population a chance to recover before being tested again.

Market researchers also seek towns that, in terms of media influence—and thus of advertising—are self-contained. In advertisers' jargon, a target town is an "area of dominant influence," defined by the television stations that serve it. Does the town receive substantial broadcasting and advertising from outside its boundaries? Alternatively, does the local television station serve an area significantly larger than the town? If so, advertising dollars are being wasted. "We look at how cost-effective the town is," said Mr. Weinblatt, noting that he has dropped Seattle from his list for that reason.

Another important criterion is distribution—the company's local sales force or brokers, and the retailers whom they must persuade to stock the wares. "Some chains take an antiresearch view," said Fitzhugh Corr, chief executive of Burgoyne Inc., a Cincinnati marketing research firm that has run tests for such clients as Procter & Gamble, Pillsbury, Campbell Soup and Colgate-Palmolive.

At some divisions of Winn-Dixie, a leading supermarket chain, he complained, "They say they don't want to clutter their stores with products that won't make it."

To insure that their products reach the supermarkets, and reach them faster, a growing number of manufacturers are using forced distribution. Unlike the classic method of test marketing, where the product goes through conventional distribution channels, in forced distribution a market research firm ushers the product into supermarkets and even onto the most desirable shelf.

For his cooperation, the grocer may be paid as much as $50 to $100 for each weekly visit, according to Mr. Corr. The forced distribution method, which may still get the product to most of the retailers, is used mainly in cities with populations of 100,000 or so—minimarkets, to the researchers.

Critics of forced distribution complain that it is not a genuine test, because it circumvents the often unwieldy distribution system. But it is hard to argue with the price, which may be half or a quarter of the million-dollar price of conventional test marketing.

And some marketers even balk at spending that much. If a test carries a six-digit price tag, "you'd better have a darn good idea, with enough profit margin to justify the expense," said Robert Slocum, marketing research director for International Multifoods of Minneapolis. "If it's a little idea—and most ideas are—it doesn't warrant all that money."

The most economical route—apart from a short cut directly to national selling, a gamble taken with repeated success by the Gillette Company—is the simulated test market, a method that is also gaining currency during the recession.

In a simulated test, a company may put its new product into a handful of stores for a period as brief as a weekend, and woo shoppers with gaudy displays, coupons and aggressive salespeople. Two weeks later, consumers are telephoned for their reaction to the product. Obviously, the system is badly lacking, especially in opportunities to determine whether the customer will come back for more. Still, "if you do it over and over, you begin to develop some data," said Mr. Slocum. "At $30,000 to $50,000 a shot, you've saved yourself a million dollars—if you believe in it."

Apart from the price tag, such simulations offer one main advantage: They are too brief to attract the attention of a company's competitors. "Once you introduce a product to a test market, you announce to the world what you're doing," said Jeffrey Pope, a partner of Custom Research, a Minneapolis consulting firm, and author of "Practical Marketing Research."

In a test market, noted Mr. Sansone of General Foods, "the competition can read the results almost as well as you can." The major test markets "develop their informants, who live in the town and pay off the supermarket managers to be allowed to hang around," said Mr. Kanter. "You see these mysterious characters, watching how fast the Mighty Dog is moving, and in what sizes."

Nor does the competition stop at espionage. "Sabotage is one of the risks of test marketing," said Mr. Pope. Companies with rival products may suddenly slash their prices, double their couponing or even give samples away, stealing potential customers from the test marketer. For example, when General Mills test marketed Speak, an ill-fated, premium-priced dog food, General Foods cut the price of its Gainesburgers.

Or, the competitor may buy up cases of the new product, to ship back to headquarters for analysis. In either event, the effect is to distort the test results, sometimes beyond use.

Sometimes, however, the marketers are themselves guilty of skewing test results. According to research firms, a company may be so eager for a hit that it spends more heavily, proportionately, than it would at the national level. "A brand manager is very ambitious to have his new product take off," said Mr. Kanter. "He becomes 'the man who . . .' and can virtually double his salary." By the time the product flops nationally, the brand manager will probably have moved on to a new job. And with the wave of mergers and acquisitions by food companies, senior executives are equally "desperate to make a record," he added.

As the technology of marketing research improves and becomes more available, it may be harder to manipulate tests and results. The advent of supermarket scanners, which read each product's Universal Price Code by means of a laser, will yield more precise records of all products sold, by price, size and even the extent of coupon redemption.

In a handful of towns, research firms are using scanners in conjunction with cable television, permitting intricate testing and quick reliable results. "Ten years from now we will be able to do large-scale cable scanner testing," said Rick Tanler, vice president of Information Resources Inc., which runs four such markets. "That will give us more flexibility, as we can put products in only certain parts of a market."

In the final analysis, however, the only real measure of the validity of a test market is how the product performs when it is introduced into the real world. "Life is not always perfect," said Mr. Weinblatt, "Neither are test markets."

7.4   Future Shop

CURTIS HARTMAN

It is, for Sandy Zimmerman, the perfect summer's day. The air is chill, and torrents of rain cascade from a leaden sky. The doors of Cohoes Specialty Stores Ltd., his store in Cohoes, N.Y., opened just half an hour ago, but already Zimmerman's parking lot is awash in Volvos and Hondas, Cadillacs and Chevettes, cars from the Albany area and beyond, day trippers and summer tourists from nearby Massachusetts and Vermont and from distant Florida and Texas, flooding the store.

Zimmerman can feel the energy inside, the pre-August adrenaline. August—his biggest month in a $30 million selling year, equivalent to other retailers' Christmas rush—is just three days away, with its Sunday hours and late nights, art shows, professional models, and furs shipped up from Manhattan. Mostly, it is the crowds, throngs of people at nearby Saratoga Springs for the racing season: Angel Cordero and Martha Raye, assorted Whitneys and a gaggle of Du Ponts, celebrities, socialites, and big spenders walking out with 26 pairs of shoes or $30,000 worth of fur.

Zimmerman stands by the wide staircase leading up to the second floor, tan suit pressed, blue polo shirt crisp, Italian loafers polished, a proprietary half-smile playing across his round face. At 52, for all his years in retailing, he is still impressed by how many motivated people it takes to make a store hum. Three times today he has cruised the floor, trying to get a seat-of-the-pants feel for what the figures tell and rallying the staff, remembering not just their names, but that the new painter up on the third floor this morning is the son of Ted in maintenance, that John the operations manager has just painted the company station wagon, and where Sylvia in furs plans to go for her vacation. "Hello, Mark," he says, patting a salesman's shoulder. "I hear you sold someone seven pairs of slacks this morning." His brown eyes catch a scrap of paper on the carpet—he picks it up. A stray packing case stands by the techni-color sweater bar—he will have it moved. "My Dad says you're a pretty good shoe salesman," he compliments a hidden figure cart-ing a pillar of boxes through the 90,000-pair stockroom. The outfits above the shoe display are still summer goods—he will have them changed for fall. And wouldn't the cosmetic section look better if the light were a little closer?

His sales staff of more than 300 people, nearly four times that of a comparably sized suburban department store, is on the floor. Ads are running in the local papers, the *Saratoga Racing Form*, the program for the Saratoga Performing Arts Center, and on AM/FM radio—all designed to stress the concepts that make Cohoes unique: quality fashion goods in the latest style, presented with flair, sold with full service, and priced for less. Many discount houses resemble dingy barns crammed with junk, low quality for low price, no amenities, no displays, and no service. Off-price stores like Loehmann's Inc. in New York or Melville Corp.'s Mar-shalls chain, the current darlings of the retail analysts, may carry brand names for less, but their goods are seconds, overcut mer-chandise, or last season's styles.

Cohoes has nothing but the latest—and the best. The mer-chandise has been pouring in, moved from the loading dock to the marking room to the floor: Calvin Klein jackets and Fila tennis wear, Dean sweaters and Albert Nippon dresses, each with its price tag proclaiming the value that draws shoppers from miles away. A Trigère coat, manufacturer's suggested price, $400; Co-hoes price, $270. A $440 Ralph Lauren men's suit, $340; a $1,700 Judith Leiber handbag, $1,270; $40 Opium perfume, $32. An $11,900 Piaget Polo watch, $8,900. Everything is discounted.

A discount operation, even one as extraordinary as Cohoes, was hardly what Zimmerman had in mind when he decided to leave the corporate world. He had built a 27-year career in depart-ment stores by stressing customer service and staff satisfaction. But as he climbed the career ladder, retailing was changing; staffs and service were being cut to meet rising costs. And once he got near the top, as chief executive officer of Abraham & Straus, of Feder-ated Department Stores Inc., he no longer had time for contact with the day-to-day business on the floor; instead he was en-meshed in corporate politics.

In 1979, in what *The New York Times* politely called "a policy disagreement," Zimmerman left Federated. Along with Ben E. Ames, a fellow Federated malcontent, he invested "several million dollars" to buy Cohoes Manufacturing Co., a small 43-year-old discount/retail business with a strong local reputation. He bet against the crowd—for service and against markups—and the business boomed. Sales grew more than 20% each year, and volume doubled to more than $30 million, with an aftertax profit of 6%, twice the industry average. With the opening this past July of his first branch store, halfway between Hartford, Conn., and Springfield, Mass., sales growth its expected to continue.

Let other retailers rely on sales, he thinks. They're just cutting their own throats. At Cohoes the excitement is with the merchandise; profit comes with productivity. Cohoes is the store of the future, he says proudly, "and, damn, it's exciting."

His eyes catch a woman flipping through packaged Danskin leotards, a Fendi bag strung across a bony shoulder. "Excuse me," he says, his voice so soft she has to lean forward to hear him. "Did you notice that we have Fendi bags in the store? We just got them in."

"Oh, you don't want to tell me that," she answers happily. "I've already spent all my money." . . .

Zimmerman and Ames took control on August 1, 1979, then spent the first year just watching and listening. "It's human nature to want to bring in your own tricks," Zimmerman says. "But there were people here who had been with a very successful business, who were watching to see how we were going to change the place. And when you don't do anything you fool them; you have time to win them over."

Since that first year, however, change has been constant. The old Cohoes stressed dresses, handbags, and shoes; Zimmerman emphasized sportwear and menswear. The old Cohoes had been clean and neat, but hardly dramatic. Zimmerman remodeled the interior, adding floor space and easing access between merchandise groups. Then he painted the ceilings dark and the walls bright, put in an oatmeal carpet, display cases, and wall groupings, and began building additions. The old Cohoes had spread its reputation by word of mouth; Zimmerman began a modest advertising campaign. The store had once been run like a small family operation; Zimmerman added planning and systems, a common order form to keep track of purchases, an automated checking and marking division, and regular six-month employee review. Inventory accounting was changed from FIFO to LIFO.

The strategy he had developed for A&S "fit like a glove," as did his management style. Although he added staff, luring such career professionals as a former merchandise manager from Bloomingdale's and the mens buyer from Bergdorf Goodman Inc., in his three-year tenure no one, buyer or executive, has left the company.

"I just want people with a good batting average," Zimmerman explains. "No one is going to bat .600 or .700; we want people who will hit .400 and will learn from their mistakes. That's how you win.

"We can turn on a dime. We're not muscle-bound by red tape and administration. The average department store buyer is a glorified clerical who reports to a merchandise manager who reports to a vice-president who reports to an executive vice-president who reports to the president. Our buyers really buy. They go into the market confident and strong, knowing that we'll never try to second-guess them." . . .

"Our salespeople are motivated because they like the business, they like the management, and they want us to win," Zimmerman explains. "Commissions don't lead to good service. Salespeople begin to say, 'I don't want to get tied up with customers who don't look like they'll spend a lot of money.' But there are other things than money to motivate people.

"There is a lot of psychic income from selling. The fact that Michael Maloney sells 26 pairs of shoes and we tell him to get a babysitter and take his wife out on the town, we'll pay, or that I rush down and congratulate Mark for selling seven pairs of slacks, that's psychic income."

Shopping in Cohoes can surprise a customer. It is not just the sheer number of salespeople, or even their relentless enthusiasm, but it's also their dedication to the shopper. Salespeople have just one responsibility at the store: service. Cashiers total the bill, and wrappers wrap the packages; managers make exchanges, and there is a credit applications lady at the front door. No salesperson says, "That's not my department." They can travel anywhere, selling you everything from hats to shoes. There are even salespeople in the dressing rooms.

Everything is designed for the customer. Free men's alterations, layaway and easy credit, free shopping bags, and couches with *The New York Times* by the sportswear department for weary husbands. Zimmerman's return policy is legendary in the business; once, at Famous Barr, he let a customer return a rug five years after the original purchase.

The problem, Zimmerman admits, is getting customers in the door: "It's damn difficult to communicate what this store is." The store's advertising budget, nonexistent four years ago, is now 1% of sales, about one-third of the industry average. Word of mouth has been supplemented with radio, billboards, print, and a small amount of local TV, always stressing the nature of Cohoes.

Sensitivity to vendors precludes the use of specific brand names in advertising. Although it is illegal for a manufacturer to refuse to sell to a discounter, few quality vendors are anxious to attract a discount image. And their main customers, the regular department and specialty stores, are not eager to try to sell a product that is available for 20% less a few miles away from the mall.

"When I talk to new vendors they are reluctant to sell to us," Zimmerman says, "until they see the store. Then they see that they'll be next to quality merchandise in a full-service atmosphere and that they'll do a lot of business with us."

Vendors may do a good business with Zimmerman, but they are reluctant to talk about it. They avoid discounters, but Cohoes is a special case. "We will not sell in a discounted atmosphere," the East Coast sales manager for Fila sportswear says. "That's all my attorney will allow me to say." Cohoes is excepted on two grounds. "It's out in the middle of nowhere," the national sales manager for Calvin Klein points out, and "it's a specialty store."

Location has an advantage beyond calming nervous vendors. Zimmerman owns the building in Cohoes and charges himself a scant $4 a square foot rent. One reason for not locating his branch store in a mall was that he wanted rock-bottom costs there, too. Advertising represents another significant saving. But the most impressive measure of Cohoes is productivity—Cohoes has a yearly sales average of $600 a square foot, five times the industry norm.

Zimmerman rejects many of the profit strategies of competing retailers, arguing that they shortchange the consumer. He keeps inventory high and, consequently, has a turnover below the industry average, "because I don't want to disappoint the customer who comes a long distance. When a customer comes from Rochester or Montreal they may come once a year; they should be able to find the goods. And then if they like a shoe they may want it in four colors, or a pair of pants in size seven." Many retailers have turned to house brands, sewing their labels into unnamed goods to increase margins. Zimmerman rejects the idea, believing it weakens the store's reputation for "having name merchandise at the right place and the right time." For the same reason he rarely buys off price, goods sold for less at the end of the season for a significant markdown. He uses store "extras" as selling tools: vinyl bags instead of paper because people reuse them, advertising the store's name; the sandwiches in the hospitality lounge—"If we let them go out to a restaurant they'll spend two or three hours. Here they can eat in 20 minutes and be back buying."

Both volume and profit are expected to increase with the establishment of his 25,000-square foot branch, set in a renovated building in East Windsor, Conn. The location was chosen in order to build on a strong base of customers who had been traveling to the mother store and so that executives who needed to supervise the opening would not be burdened with a long trip. East Windsor, already thriving, was meant to be a model "to chart a course for other stores." Zimmerman hopes to open a branch a year but would like to stay private, generating cash for expansion, as he did with the first branch, from his healthy sales volume.

There is, he knows, an irony in an executive who left a corporate situation because it was getting too big turning around and pushing to expand his new small business." But I came to the conclusion that I was built that way," he says. "It's in my nature to want to see the business grow." . . .

"We can provide quality merchandise that is timely, in depth, and at the right price, so people will travel that extra mile," Zimmerman says. "We have arrived at a moment in time when it is accepted that it is good to save money; people no longer look down on you for that.

"Most department stores are wrong; they overpromote. They're training their customers to buy on sale only.

"Department stores and specialty stores, sooner or later, are going to have to address themselves to the day-to-day business again. They'll have to address themselves to store proliferation, and to paying rent on places where productivity is as low as $70 a square foot. And they'll have to find new ways to be profitable—if they keep resorting to higher markups and higher gross margins they aren't going to be competitive.

"This is nothing new, it is just now being applied to soft goods. I remember at Famous Barr we thought the world would end when the hard-line people decided to sell to discounters. A lot of department stores threw Sony out because of that. But all that means is that a lot of Sonys are being sold, just not in department stores.

"I think it will be fascinating to watch the future. Eventually everyone will have to do what we're doing."

Discussion and Review Questions

1. Examine Table 1 on page 167. What important population, income, and social trends have developed over the past thirty years? How might these trends be analyzed and interpreted by such representative firms as (a) a household furnishings company, (b) an automaker, (c) a children's apparel manufacturer, and (d) a quick-food chain?

2. How does the present-day "average American consumer" differ from the "average American consumer" of two or three decades ago? Consider the changes for both men and women.

3. What are the implications, to marketers, of an aging workforce?

4. Why do marketers test-market products? What are some of the problems test-marketing encounters?

5. In terms of marketing strategy, what is the key to Sandy Zimmerman's approach? Do you think it is a durable strategy or will it only be a passing fad?

6. Recently, rising unemployment with accompanied falling income has been an important economic fact of life in tens of millions of American households. How might such a fact affect marketing strategies in consumer goods?

7. Looking down the road twenty years—about the time you will be at the peak of your business career—what important shifts in consumer behavior do you anticipate?

ISSUE 8

What Are the New Products for the 1980s and Beyond?

Before a product can be sold, if indeed it can be sold at all, it must be developed. Although critics of American advertising, and even some overeager defenders, argue that virtually any item can be sold as long as the sell is hard enough, such a view is incorrect. Some products catch on and others do not, and virtually all products eventually saturate their market and pass into decline.

Types of New Products

A new product appearing on the market may be classified in a number of ways. A brand-new commodity totally unlike any product on the market is an example of *product innovation*. Such products are fairly easy to identify. The telephone, the radio, the gasoline-powered automobile, the electric lightbulb, the record player, and the computer are examples of important historical products totally unlike anything that had preceded them in their fields. These new products, or inventions, as we are inclined to call them, opened up new areas for sales while at the same time changing the lives of ordinary people. They produced whole new companies, industries, and investment opportunities. As a result, product innovations stand out when the process of product development is discussed; however, product innovation amounts to only a very small fraction of all new products introduced each year.

Most new products are either imitations or adaptations of existing products. A *product imitation* is designed and sold as a commodity that is similar or identical to already existing products. A new brand of detergent, a new ballpoint pen, or a new designer jean label are obviously imitations of other products that already have established a market.

195

For instance, in 1915, when the adventurer–inventor Clarence Birdseye discovered that Eskimos froze their caribou meat and then thawed it and cooked it months later, a product innovation began to take shape. Nine years later, with his founding of General Foods Company, frozen food products were introduced. Very soon General Foods sold or leased their patents for frozen food products and within a decade there were dozens of product imitations of the Birdseye invention.

Meanwhile, *product adaptations* are already-established products, redesigned or newly packaged to meet new consumer needs or requirements. Birdseye and its imitators may have pioneered the freezing of corn, peas, carrots, and meats, but it remained for Swansons, Mortons, and others to package meat and vegetable combinations in that uniquely American meal called the TV dinner. Frozen complete meals were an attractive adaptation to a generation in which more women were working outside the home, organized sports and other activities pulled the young from the house, and everybody became increasingly addicted to watching "the tube." Most adaptations, however, are less noteworthy than the TV dinner development. For the most part the adaptations amount to "new and improved" claims for soap, cereal, and certain other products, or the steady proliferation of new engineering variations on the shaving instrument, the pen, the toothbrush, the vacuum cleaner, and practically any product that has been on the market for a long period of time. Nevertheless, product adaptation is important. For consumers, it does improve the quality of life. Vacuuming a shag rug with a 1928 vintage upright Hoover or shaving with a straight razor are experiences that happily may be avoided. For firms, product adaptation means longer life for older products, the development of new markets, and, naturally enough, improved profits.

The Product Life Cycle

Virtually every product, meanwhile, goes through a "life cycle." This cycle includes the stages of *introduction, growth, maturity,* and *decline.* While the product life cycle appears as a symmetrical bell-shaped curve (see Figure 2), it is well to note that different products have different time frames for the various stages. Some products catch on quickly and others take a long period of introduction to the market. Some die quickly and others linger a long time. In large part, this reflects the nature of the product. Pet rocks, for instance, were an instant hit and an almost equally instant failure. Home radios, although catching on fairly quickly, have been in a long stage of maturity and decline.

During the introduction stage, the product attracts growing public attention. This demands considerable and expensive promotional and selling efforts by the firm. Generally, a firm accepts very low profits and often loses money during this period; in fact, sales may be too low for the firm to utilize its production capacity fully or to recapture its research and development costs. Such losses are considered as investments that will pay off in greater sales as the public learns of and accepts the product.

FIGURE 2   PRODUCT LIFE CYCLE (WITH REPRESENTATIVE GOODS)

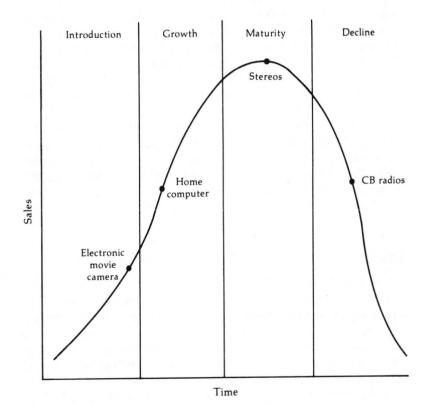

The growth stage begins when the product "catches on." The introduction and growth stages of the computer, for instance, were fairly lengthy, as both the technology of the product and consumer acceptance moved along slowly. Other products, especially specialized consumer goods, often catch on quickly. In the 1920s, the automobile, the electric refrigerator, and the telephone caught on; and more recently such items as video games, radar ranges, and frozen prepared foods are good examples of items that quickly achieved growth by capturing the public's interest. For producers of such items, sales and profits suddenly take off. With the edge over their imitators in product development and promotion, firms introducing the product follow an aggressive sales policy to assure their continued market domination.

With more firms producing imitations or even adaptations of the original product, the product life cycle now enters a maturity stage. Quite simply, the market becomes saturated and the number of potential buyers dwindles. Industry sales grow for awhile and then begin to soften. The initiating firm, moreover, usually has lost a large part of its share of the market. Often supply exceeds demand and prices are forced downward. Although economies in mass production and mass selling actually may lower producer costs, falling prices begin to squeeze per-unit profits.

Finally, the product tumbles over into the decline stage. Profits become greatly reduced and finally perhaps disappear altogether. Many of the product's producers, perhaps even its originators, drop out altogether. Very often a new product or commodity comes along to replace the original product, just as the electric light replaced gas illumination and automatic washers replaced the old agitator–wringer washing machine.

Troubling Trends in the Product Life Cycle

Students of the life cycle process have become increasingly aware that many of the goods that propelled American industrial growth in the recent past are reaching the terminal stages of their cycle. The automobile, for instance, was once the single most successful product in the American market. Year in and year out, domestic production moved upward, topping out at 10 million in 1973. Since the "oil crisis" year of 1973, sales of American-produced automobiles have declined to about 6 million in 1982. Part of this decline reflected the rise of foreign imports, but mostly it reflected a general decline in the demand for automobiles. For years, American businesspeople had believed that as automobile sales went, so went all sales, and so went the nation; which of course brings us to the issue under consideration.

If the automobile—as well as a number of other products such as TV, the telephone, washers and dryers, and the refrigerator—are on the downside of their product cycle, what products are on the rise or look promising for the 1980s and beyond? Our readings examine two promising new products, the home–office computer and an electronic camera. Both stories reveal some of the problems faced by modern marketers in developing and gaining public acceptance for new products. The third article, however, attacks the new-product discussion from an entirely different perspective by offering the decidedly unsettling suggestion that possibly there are no "great new products" for the immediate future. Its pessimism stands in sharp contrast with the hopefulness of the first two articles.

8.1   The Computer Comes to Main Street

PETER NULTY

Visitors to Chicago's huge Merchandise Mart these days can see impressive evidence that the time of the small-business computer has come. Along a corridor just inside the main entrance, no fewer than six glittering new computer showrooms stand side by side, all featuring the data processing industry's hottest-selling product, desktop microcomputers. At the low end of the price range, that category takes in personal computers costing less than $2,000, but the industry expects much larger revenues from more capable microcomputers that currently retail for $5,000 to around $20,000. Some upscale consumers buy them as personal computers, and big businesses use quite a few as supplements to their main data processing systems. Something like 60% of all microcomputers sold in stores, however, are purchased for business use by small enterprises or professionals.

Until recently, microcomputers could do little more around the office than store customer lists or the boss's correspondence. But the newer models perform accounting, budgeting, and inventory management tasks in a fraction of the time it takes stubby pencils to do the job. And sales to small enterprises are increasing briskly. Elliott Greene, who owns two Computerland franchises on New York's Long Island, figures he's selling three times as many small business machines this year as last. Industry seers are guessing that microcomputer sales will grow from about $2 billion last year to as much as $10 billion in 1985. Says Greene: "I hear the cannons' roar."

How loudly they roar will largely depend on how effectively the industry deals with a tough marketing problem. Big rewards await the contenders who solve it. Oblivion awaits those who don't. And if progress toward solving it isn't made before long, disappointment with microcomputers may quiet Greene's cannons and keep those new showrooms at the Merchandise Mart depressingly empty.

The quandary is this: computers require meticulous care and service, and their operators need a good deal of training—"hand holding" in industry parlance—but makers and sellers of small computers can't afford to provide much of that. In the market for larger computers, the cost of hand holding is easily rolled into the high price of the hardware. According to Bill Meserve, a management consultant with Arthur D. Little Inc., the price of a $100,000 minicomputer includes about $7,000 in sales calls, installation, training, and so forth.

"Computer Illiterates"

With microcomputers, the leeway is squeezed drastically. Yet small businesses acquiring small computers need as much coaching as large businesses with large computers, and sometimes more. Most small enterprises that buy a computer are doing so for the first time. The industry describes these customers as "computer illiterates." The small-business computer market is analogous to the automobile market in the first months after Ford's Model T started rolling off the assembly line. The machine was a marvel, but there were few gas stations, few paved roads, and hardly anyone had ever changed a tire.

Plenty of competitors are eager to get a piece of this risky market. Retail computer stores with names like Computerland and MicroAge are popping up like fast-food franchises at shopping malls these days. And these are only the vanguard. Coming along in force are newcomers to retailing like IBM and Xerox, and newcomers to business computers like Sears Roebuck. Less visible are vendors called "systems houses," which package computers with programs tailored to specific types of users, such as dentists or accountants. Jumping in with the systems approach are companies like Victor, Monroe, Moore, and Safeguard, which have been selling business equipment and office forms for years. . . .

In the industry lingo, each approach is a "channel to market." Most computer makers are exploring several at once, because each channel has different strengths and weaknesses.

Retail computer stores have the advantage of offering a variety of products and, at present, the disadvantage of not knowing much about them. The stores provide a bare minimum of support and service with the price of the hardware—they don't install equipment, customize software, or spend more than a few hours instructing customers. Most of them, however, do provide additional instruction for a fee. According to Future Computing Inc., a market research firm in Richardson, Texas, 80% of the stores offer training courses, often in little computer-equipped rooms in the stores. Service contracts, which usually add 10% to 15% to a computer's cost, are available from the stores or from third parties like TRW, RCA, or General Electric.

Since retail computer stores first started appearing in the mid-1970s, over 1,800 have opened, including 275 of Tandy Corp.'s Radio Shack Computer Centers and 240 Computerlands. According to Future Computing, the average retailer's annual revenue has reached $1 million. Computerland, which acts as a central purchaser for its franchises, is opening ten new shops a month. Its revenues are expected to top $350 million this year, up from about $200 million in 1981.

What Exploded the Market

Computerland's robust growth may account, in part, for IBM's decision to plunge into retailing. And a strange entry it is. IBM has opened 18 Product Centers selling only IBM hardware, including typewriters and the company's first personal computer, called simply the IBM Personal Computer. Competitors scoff at the single-brand approach to retailing, saying the stores are nothing more than company showrooms. But with a reputation like IBM's to ride on, it just might work.

IBM won't discuss financial results, but by all outsider accounts the Personal Computers (if not yet the stores) are a smashing success. IBM Personal Computers "have given microcomputers credibility and exploded the market," says Portia Isaacson, a founder of Future Computing. They cost about $4,500 and are also sold by Computerland, Sears Business Systems Centers, and some smaller independents. David Crockett, a senior vice president of Dataquest, a market research firm, estimates that IBM is selling all it can make—about 20,000 a month—and that sales reached $70 million in 1981, the year the machine was introduced.

Starting with a Captive Audience

Some other big-time manufacturers have also gone into computer retailing, notably Control Data, Digital Equipment, and Xerox, which plans to open 200 to 300 stores. Control Data and Xerox offer two or three brands at their outlets. A salesman at a Xerox store in Massachusetts cheerfully volunteers that his best seller is not the Xerox 820-II, at $3,295, but the portable Osborne, at $1,795.

Control Data started with the advantage of a captive audience. As a natural extension of its computer services division, which processes data for small companies on Control Data computers, the company has established 55 Business Centers since 1980. These offer—along with microcomputers—insurance, management consulting, training, and loans (for general purposes, not just for equipment purchases). "We're opening service centers, not hardware stores," says J. P. Wilson, vice president of strategy and product management. Wilson estimates that 80% of the customers who buy computers previously took out loans or used the Control Data computer services. Manufacturer-owned outlets like Control Data's offer the advantage of nationwide service networks expert at repairing company hardware.

One innovative idea for retailing microcomputers is being promoted by real estate developers—computer malls containing many computer hardware and software vendors. The computer alley in Chicago's Merchandise Mart is a forerunner. A mart that Transcontinental Development Inc. plans to build in Cincinnati will include a team of consultants paid for by the mall's tenants. New customers will be directed to the consultants, who will advise them without charge on the type and size of computer to buy. Transcontinental also has plans for computer malls in Denver, Philadelphia, San Francisco, and Tampa. Other developers have announced malls-to-be in Dallas and Boston.

Though their numbers are increasing rapidly, retail stores won't work everywhere. Generally speaking, they do well in communities of 250,000 or larger, according to Portia Isaacson. The strongest competitors in smaller communities and towns are local office-supply dealers and systems houses. There are scores of systems houses, reaching out through phone, mail, and ad campaigns.

The business supply and equipment companies now pushing into the microcomputer market already have extensive sales networks. Their special strengths are that they know their customers personally and they know a lot about their customers' businesses. Moore Business Systems, a division of Moore Business Forms, is going after dentists, accountants, trucking companies, and gas stations. The company has been in the computer business three years and expects computer-related revenues to reach $22 million this year.

When it started out, Moore discovered that computers were too sophisticated to add to the list of goods the forms salesmen were carrying. So the company has trained a sales force of 75 dedicated to computers and knowledgeable enough about the business procedures of their customers to be able to explain how a computer can help them. Moore salesmen know that for dentists a big selling point—called a "hot button" in the trade—is that computers can easily be programmed to keep track of checkup notices to dental patients. Most checkups result only in a cleaning by a dental hygienist, and that's a high-margin activity. A big selling point for gas stations is that the system keeps a close check on sales, thus plugging the leakage of the station owner's money into the pump attendant's pocket.

Extra Bites for Dentists

Several companies have marketing approaches that defy categories. Texas Instruments, which experimented unsuccessfully with retail stores for consumer products, has decided to let others sell its microcomputers. To support them, however, TI is opening small-computer schools, called Learning Centers, to teach salesmen and customers to use TI equipment. There is a fee for the courses, but TI says it will be happy just to cover costs (and, presumably, win some customers). K-Comp Inc., based in Los Angeles, sells computers with specialized programs for dentists through a network of part-time distributors. Most of the distributors are themselves dentists, using professional contacts and credibility as a marketing tool. Each distributor tries to enlist new distributors and gets a cut of the new recruits' sales.

Wilson Jones Co., a subsidiary of American Brands, has come up with something it calls the "shop in a box." Wilson Jones sells about $100 million a year of forms and office products through 12,000 independent office-products stores, some in towns as small as Mason City, Iowa (pop. 30,000). Many of these dealers fear that computers will make the forms they sell obsolete. So Wilson Jones offers them portable, free-standing display rooms for their stores. The package, which costs $45,600, includes software and models of Wilson Jones computers. So far, Wilson Jones has sold 27 shops in boxes.

Competition in the small-computer market has been getting tougher lately, and will undoubtedly get more so. Until last year, demand for microcomputers exceeded production, and almost any company that could assemble a small computer could find a vendor to sell it. Now, with heavyweights like IBM muscling into the market, a tumultuous struggle for channels is raging among smaller computer makers. Many are finding it hard to get on the shelves because vendors, in an effort to limit customer confusion, are holding down the number of brands they carry.

The customer's confusion, though, is likely to linger even after he decides what brand to buy. Equipment failure is all too frequent when users are inexperienced and undertrained. Operator failure is even more frequent. Instruction manuals are available for computer purchasers, of course, and some run on for hundreds of pages. But vendors of computers—like vendors of many other things—complain that customers don't read. Says an executive of one computer manufacturer: "If the book says there are two disk drives, A and B, the guy is already lost, and he reaches for the phone." Elliott Greene reports that the record for calls from one customer in one day at his stores is 14.

On the other hand, customers complain the manuals aren't fit for reading. A year ago James Baehler, a management consultant based in New York, bought a microcomputer to help him with his business. After he began to feel handy with it, he tried modifying some of the programs he was using. To do that he had to understand the operating program, called CP/M, which coordinates the functioning of the machine. Says Baehler, an eager learner who once took an IBM computer course: "I defy any amateur to get through the CP/M manual—*anyone*." Professional help, moreover, is expensive. Getting even the simplest software modified can cost hundreds, even thousands, of dollars.

The nitty-gritty is that connections between the microcomputer and the user—training, instruction manuals, programs—are underdeveloped by comparison with the marvelous machines themselves. The inexperienced purchaser with perfunctory training can tap only a portion of the machine's capabilities. He is lucky, indeed, if he can just get it operating satisfactorily without unanticipated hassles and delays. As Baehler puts it, with exasperation: "The engineers who designed microcomputers performed a miracle, and there are plenty of people game to try them out. But the link between the two is missing."

Extinctions Ahead

Over the next few years more adequate links will gradually evolve. In the meantime, though, some manufacturers and a lot of vendors will become extinct, leaving customers with obsolete equipment and worthless service contracts.

Development of better connections between machines and users will proceed along three paths. To begin with, more and more users will get good at making the machines do their things. Literacy on small computers, after all, is more easily attained than, say, literacy in Latin.

What's more, engineers and program writers are making each generation of computers easier to use than the last. "Industry says it will soon have really friendly machines," says Bill Meserve of Arthur D. Little, "but I call it idiot-proof." Gradually, the industry is replacing instruction manuals with instruction programs that enable new owners to learn how to use computers by using them. And more machines are being designed with self-diagnostic features. When you turn on the IBM Personal Computer, it runs a ten second check of all its parts. If some part isn't functioning, the computer tells which one. In other words, the computer and what comes with it will supply more and more of the support and service now provided—or not provided—by vendors.

Finally, as vendors build up experienced staffs, they'll give better support and service. Small-computer retailing is so new and growing so fast that salespeople are often only a few weeks ahead of customers shopping for their first computers. As time goes by, customers will be dealing with clerks who know more about their wares. The salespeople most likely to stick at it are those who find computers fascinating and enjoy using them. And use them they do. A customer who goes into a computer store these days is likely to see clerks at the machines, tapping away. Sometimes they're working, sometimes they're playing, but either way they're learning.

The Missing Recruit

A story told by the owner of a Computerland store in Vienna, Virginia, holds a hint for the future. The store requires new salesmen to take a computer home for practice. One day a recruit who had done that failed to show up for work. Rich Doud, the owner, repeatedly called the young man's home but got no answer. The police checked reports of accidents and emergencies. "I thought he might have died," says Doud. Then, three days late, the recruit returned, alive, well, and raring to sell. He had become so entranced by the computer, he explained, that he shut himself in and unplugged the phone.

8.2   Kodak's Quest For a Camera

BARNABY J. FEDER

When the Sony Corporation announced in October that it would introduce an all-electronic camera in 1983 designed to display still photographs on the home television screen, no one here at the headquarters of the Eastman Kodak Company said it couldn't be done.

The world's largest photography company, with earnings last year of $1.15 billion on revenues of $9.73 billion, knows a great deal about electronic, or filmless, cameras. It recently began selling a $110,000 high-speed electronic movie camera system known as the SP-2000 for motion analysis of fast-moving mechanical components and manufacturing processes.

And shortly after Sony's announcement, Colby H. Chandler, Kodak's president, stressed that Kodak had an electronic still camera for amateurs that was similar to Sony's.

But Kodak says it won't follow Sony's lead. In fact, it is hinting that it will introduce a technological alternative—a system that will capture images with traditional cameras using chemically-based films and then process them into electronic signals for television display.

The possibility of a technology shootout, pitting Japan's most successful consumer electronics company against the respected photography giant, is downplayed by photography experts and analysts. For one thing, a number of other companies have the skills and, analysts believe, the intent to get involved.

More important, the technologies might well coexist. Sony's all-electronic approach could attract those who want to take large numbers of pictures that can be viewed instantly and erased, while Kodak might focus on consumers who cannot afford the $600 to $900 investment that the Sony system will require, according to analysts' estimates, and on those who want negatives capable of producing high-quality prints.

Nevertheless, the divergent perspectives represented by the two companies have fueled a great deal of speculation about the future of amateur photography and the companies that have dominated it. If Sony is correct that its system—dubbed Mavica—will appeal to a large group of consumers, film sales could suffer, along with such film giants as Kodak, Polaroid, Agfa-Gevaert of West Germany, a subsidiary of Bayer A.G., and Fuji Photo of Japan.

"Developments in the younger field of electronic imaging technology will come at a more rapid clip," William Relyea, a photography analyst at Paine Webber Mitchell Hutchins, wrote in a recent study. The result: Conventional and instant photography companies will fare poorly when investors compare growth potential, direction of costs, and risks.

In addition, even Kodak might find itself strategically stymied by new alternate technologies nibbling away at its domain. It could make electronic cameras, but analysts doubt that it could match the dominance, and profits, it has achieved in traditional photography. "There's not much you can do if technology is headed away from you," Mr. Relyea said.

So far, Kodak has described its video photo strategy in theoretical terms, suggesting in speeches by company officials that all-electronic cameras will cost too much and perform too poorly to satisfy consumers.

Theory could well be fleshed out into practice in February when Kodak is expected to announce its new, long-awaited amateur camera line.

Most of the talk has focused on the likelihood that the film roll will be replaced by a round disk resembling the slides used by children in View Masters. But Gene Tremblay, an industry analyst for Wellington Management in Boston, said he believed that a system to display pictures from the camera on television would be announced. An attachment allowing the disk impressions to be displayed on television could cost $150 to $200, according to educated guesses—an unusually expensive consumer device for Kodak, which prices all of its amateur cameras between $20 and $100.

A wide range of companies possess the skill to develop competing products. On the electronic side, these include RCA, Fairchild, Hitachi, and Matsushita and among leading 35-millimeter camera makers, Canon, Nikon, and Olympus.

Still, Kodak's plans deserve the most attention, in the view of photography analysts, because no company has been more involved in mastering the linkage of the two powerful technologies—photochemistry and electronics—converging on the new photo-television link. "There is a friendly internal competition going between the electronics experts and the photochemists," said Jack Thomas, senior vice president and director of Kodak Research Laboratories.

Traditionally, making a photograph was almost pure photochemistry, the science of using light to change the chemical composition of matter. The change that light caused in the silver-laden molecules in film could be fixed with chemical developers, projected onto photographic paper, and then reconstituted into a picture using dyes.

Then came electronics, the controlled, monitored movement of electrons through matter in patterns that carry information. Electronics created new photographic display opportunities, such as television movies. It also allowed companies like Kodak to introduce increasingly sophisticated cameras at low prices by building in tiny semiconductors that controlled shutters and light exposures.

Electronics could also enhance photochemistry by making both the manufacturing and processing of photochemical products more exact. Indeed, the microprocessor controlling Kodak's high-performance business copier is described by the company as more powerful than most minicomputers.

Meanwhile, photochemical technology has become vital to electronics as electronics has advanced into microelectronics. Kodak and other photography companies found new markets for cameras and high-performance film that semiconductor manufacturers needed to design ever more powerful semiconductors in smaller and smaller sizes.

Eventually, microchips were designed that could handle so much information about incoming light that they began to compete with cameras in some image-sensing tasks, thus taking over markets formerly dominated by photochemical products. Television news today, for example, is virtually entirely dependent on electronic cameras that record images as magnetic patterns on videotape.

So far, experts give Kodak high marks for its understanding of the interplay between the two technologies.

There have been slips, of course. Polaroid's new Sun cameras make better use of electronics in instant photography to increase the ability of the camera to compensate for challenging lighting situations—when, say, the subject is in the shade while the rest of the scene is well lighted.

But Kodak designs and manufactures many of its own electronic components. In recent years, it has hired twice as many electrical engineers as chemists. And, two acquisitions—Spin Physics in 1972 and Atex last August—were clearly calculated to add specialized electronic cards to the company's deck. The former's newest product is the SP-2000 and the latter specializes in electronic systems used in preparing copy for printing in newspapers and magazines.

"Kodak is uniquely positioned to correctly assess the flow of technological change in this area," said Mr. Tremblay of Wellington Management.

Nevertheless, Sony's flashy press conferences in New York and Tokyo in October made some potential competitors wonder. Asked for his company's views on where the technologies are headed, Donald Dery, a Polaroid spokesman, said the company would not comment because "We have some disagreements here about how we would word answers to the most obvious questions."

And Thomas Henwood, an analyst at First Boston Inc. in New York, said that some stock portfolio managers have reacted by assuming, based on experience in other consumer product areas, that the all-electronic camera is bound to get steadily cheaper and more powerful. " 'Why bet against electronics?' is the way they view it," he said.

Of course, Kodak, while quick to dismiss suggestions that it is becoming an electronics company, adamantly denies that it is betting against electronics. "We agree with the growing conception of the TV as the center of things," said Mr. Thomas.

The difficulty is in defining what consumers want. Akio Morita, Sony's outspoken chairman, said at the Mavica press conference, "We did no market research." Pointing to his head, he added, "Market research is in here."

When told of the incident, Kodak's Mr. Thomas nodded approvingly. "People will almost never tell you they want something that doesn't exist," he said.

Kodak's guess is that consumers want to display photographs on television and to make high-quality prints of the same shots to send out with Christmas cards, carry on trips, and so forth. The key point to remember, in Kodak's view, is that film provides a far more sensitive light record than the charge-coupled device, the semiconductor on which light falls in the electronic camera. Film used in Kodak's inexpensive cameras records 10 times more information than the semiconductors, and 35-millimeter film, 40 times as much, Kodak claims. That makes for a higher-quality print.

Like Kodak, Sony believes that consumers will also want prints, or "hard" copy, of some of their electronic, or "soft" images, so it is working on a printer that it has promised to unveil in the spring.

But Sony sees the quality of the printed image as a secondary consideration for what it envisions as a new breed of photographer anxious to tie a versatile camera into television sets—most of which cannot use most of the added information from film in any case.

The all-electronic Mavica offers instant playback, the possibility of easily manipulating or transmitting the signals that make up the picture, and, most important, the opportunity to erase and reuse the videotape on which the picture is recorded. And, when hooked up to a videotape recorder such as the devices that 3.5 million Americans already own, Mavica becomes a movie camera.

"This is not competition for traditional photography," Mr. Morita told the New York press conference. "This is something entirely new."

Even if Sony is correct in its guess, however, Kodak can take comfort in the fact that it is ideally placed to make the printing devices to convert electronic images like those that Sony's Mavica will produce into high-quality hard copies.

Speaking more broadly, as Mr. Thomas, the Kodak research chief, said, the television set is only one of the crossover points between the two technologies that interests Kodak. Kodak researchers are "very interested in the idea of capturing images on film and then converting them to electronics for enhancing." Improvements in the sharpness and color of an image, and reductions in interference, or "noise," can be done both chemically and electronically, he noted, but it is easier with electronics.

"If you are involved on both sides of the aisle," he said, "it is a fascinating time."

8.3 Maybe There Aren't Any Product Revolutions for the Future

ROBERT B. CARSON

Turn to practically any business publication produced over the past decade and with painful regularity you will find articles or series of articles on "the impending computer revolution" with its great promise of uncounted new products. Indeed, a very great many of the computer-based products are now upon us—some perhaps already on the downside of their product life cycles. Video games, home computers, mainframe systems, information processors, telecommunications, CAD/CAM (computer assisted design/computer assisted manufacturing), robotics, and other examples of computer technology have been singled out as either examples of a new-product wave or as *the* new product that will produce a new era of investment, production, and selling. It is the stuff that corporate daydreams are made of: a brand-new beginning for investors, venture capitalists, entrepreneurs, managers, marketing experts, and so on. The daydream is particularly encouraging to a business community that has had little to cheer about lately. A decade or more of contraction in the "old reliable" basic industries of steel, autos, chemicals, consumer appliances, and, more recently, petroleum products firms certainly encourages the belief, or at least the hope, that American business stands on the threshold of a new-product era.

Hope, however, is not enough to make computer-based paraphernalia a large enough new-product wave to provide the boom American business desperately needs and wants. *The fact is, compared to past new-product revolutions, computer-based products will produce scarcely a ripple.*

Now that is definitely not a statement that has appeared with any regularity in business publications. In fact, some may think that it sounds so harebrained as scarcely to warrant attention. Yet, if we sit back, free ourselves of the "computer revolution" propaganda we have absorbed, and try, objectively, to consider the past history of other "new products," it is possible to conclude that such heresy has more than a germ of truth to it. Moreover, it is also possible to consider a future scenario for American business enterprise in which new products play a much diminished role.

The economist Joseph Schumpeter pointed out forty years ago that the great eras of business expansion have always been associated with a new technological development. This invention or innovation, like a snowball rolling downhill, gathered both momentum and mass as the initial idea and its exploitation created, through secondary and tertiary effects, new technological developments and new products in which to invest.

For example, consider the development of the steam engine. Simple by modern standards and not altogether obvious in its possible uses at the time of its appearance, steam power begat a host of related inventions and innovations. Within twenty-five years of James Watt's steam machine patent, steam began to replace water to power the looms of knit-goods factories. It also had been applied to transportation devices, such as railroads and ocean-going vessels. In turn, these industrial changes soon created a vast and growing demand for other products: coal for fuel and iron (and later steel) for tens of thousands of locomotives, millions of miles of railroad tracks, and thousands of ships' hulls. These railroads and ships in turn opened new areas to commerce and trade, building cities and dozens of other manufacturing and service industries that urban dwellers came to rely upon.

More recently, the development of the internal combustion engine and its application to the motorcar and motortruck stimulated the development of a countless number of new products. These ranged from products directly related to the building and using of trucks and cars—machine tools, petroleum, concrete, and chemical industries, for example—to the growing consumer products markets stimulated by the automobile's building of a suburban, single-family nation of consumers. Meanwhile, another innovation, the long-distance transmission of electrical energy, opened these new consumer markets for everything from radios and refrigerators to TVs and stereos. The steam engine, the internal combustion engine, and the long-distance transmission of electricity were indeed new-product revolutions, and in practically every way they lived up to their defenders' claims to revolutionize both business and society.

The impact of these monumental new products is a matter of historical record. These were products that could absorb—for a very long time—ever increasing quantities of capital investment, managerial skill, marketing guile, and, of course, workers. On this latter point, railroads alone employed one in every five industrial workers in 1900. The automobile industry in the broadest possible definition, including those who produced automobile parts as well as those contributing to their maintenance and operation, employed one of every seven working Americans in 1960. Only the most wild-eyed business optimists can foresee a similar employment effect generated by the computer revolution—a revolution, after all, whose whole purpose is systematically to reduce employment in all jobs.

However, we should not confuse issues. Important as it is, the matter is not concerned simply with the jobs impact of modern electronic developments as contrasted with that of earlier new-product booms. At stake is a more fundamental point: Are there really that many, or in fact any, new products that will have the capacity to absorb the resources of business in producing a sustained period of expansion like the railroad boom or the automobile boom? To put it more directly, might it be possible that there are no really important new products for the foreseeable future?

The thought is virtually unthinkable. Isn't progress natural and more or less continuous? Doesn't some new and better idea—another steam engine—always appear to replace an older and less desirable idea? Isn't it just as certain as the sun rising tomorrow that new products will come along to replace old ones on the declining side of their life cycles? After all, the steam engine replaced water power in the mills and freed plant location from the fall line on rivers. Steam railroads replaced the old and undependable canals. The internal combustion engine replaced the horse and in some respects the steam engine too. The refrigerator replaced the icebox. And so on. However, irrespective of what happened in the past with regard to the appearance of flourishing new products, there is simply no proof and very little empirical evidence to show that such a process must or can continue in the future.

In fact, if we examine the truly new products that have appeared over the past several decades, there have been only a few that stand out as revolutionary, and none have had a spinoff effect in creating entire new-product lines that compares with the steam engine, the railroad, or the automobile. The computer revolution, despite the ad man's tub-thumping, has changed our lives much less than many products that now are seen in decline. Will anyone seriously argue that the computerized radar range that talks to you while you set its dials is a quantum leap up from the ordinary electric or gas stove? Which has the greater impact upon business: the ability to move goods by rail or truck to any point in the United States in three or four days, or the capacity for instantaneous teleconferencing? In fact, is teleconferencing as big a jump past the telephone as the telephone was past the telegraph? Even the robotized assembly operations of the future promise a less-sweeping impact on factory labor and corporate profits than Henry Ford's assembly line produced.

Technological development hardly took place at all during humanity's first ten thousand years of more or less "civilized" existence. Only the last two centuries have seen great changes in transportation, communication, production, leisure time and consumption. The very success of our past new-product development, however, limits the prospects for useful new products. What in the communications realm could improve upon instantaneous communication? In consumer goods, what product or products do we really need to improve our lives? Would a ten-minute transatlantic crossing be that great an improvement over the Concorde's three hours?

Strange and uncomfortable as all this may sound, these observations should not be misunderstood. Of course there will be new products. Of course computer-based products are the most promising of the current new ideas, and computer technology will continue to spin off related new products for a long period of time. However, the revolutionary impact of any of these products is very small when we make historical comparisons. In other words, there is absolutely nothing on the horizon like the steam engine or the automobile as a propellant for business expansion. Indeed,

Doomsday advocates, looking at the world energy and resource crisis, often argue convincingly that the world cannot long sustain production of the goods we already have developed. But that is an entirely different argument from the one advanced here.

If there are no important new products to pump up investment and encourage marketing managers, where does that leave us? Well, we may be entering a long period of "making do with what we have." From a historical point of view, this is nothing very new. At least 100 centuries passed from the time humans domesticated the horse until we ceased basing all our land-travel calculations on how far and how fast horses could carry us. Yet, civilization did not stop progressing over that period. Human history did not move backward, but it did live without many new products.

"Making do" could take a number of forms. First of all, it could mean that the production and sales of goods will be simply a replacement operation—replacing worn-out goods and supplying new entrants into consumer markets with new commodities. Second, it could mean shifting efforts from making new products to making better old products. Third, it could mean shifting from products to services—a trend that has been under way and growing for the past three decades. And fourth, it could mean—and probably does—some combination of all these possibilities.

Such a scenario isn't very exciting by past standards, but it is a lot closer to the real world than the puffery of inspired business writers who now proclaim this good or that one as "the greatest new product since Henry Ford's Model T." And, it is a lot more honest than believing that business's recent doldrums will be washed away by some grand new innovation. Most important though, understanding such a scenario directs our attention to improving what we presently are doing, and there is the possibility of much reward to such a strategy.

Discussion and Review Questions

1. What is a product life cycle?
2. Pick five significant consumer products. Where would you locate each of these in terms of the product life cycle?

3. The home computer boom is well under way by now. How do you judge this product in terms of life cycle theory? Will it quickly reach the maturity stage, or will it be growing for a long time to come?

4. Brainstorm for a minute: What products do you see as growth products for the near future? Why?

5. Do you think Kodak's new camera will be a successful new product? Why or why not?

6. How do you react to the last article? Do you believe that the "new-product boom" era has indeed passed? If there is any truth to this point of view, what are the implications for marketers and, indeed, for all of American business?

PART 5

FINANCIAL PROBLEMS

ISSUE 9

Are the New Mergers Working?

Before examining the current merger trend, it is useful first to glance back at the past to obtain a perspective on modern-day merger activity. As we saw in the introduction to this book, one of the prominent themes in the development of American business enterprise has been the steady growth of ever-larger business structures. Whether measured by sales, profits, or assets, a large share of business activity is dominated by a comparative handful of giant corporations. For instance, in 1982, 62 percent of industrial assets and profits were controlled by the top 100 firms, compared to less than 50 percent a decade earlier. How shall we account for this continued tendency toward bigness?

The Impetus toward Bigness

Generally, two different explanations have been offered. The first holds, very simply, that profits are the driving force—that the large firm is a greater profit maker than the small enterprise. The second contends that expansion decisions are more concerned with providing the firm with greater strength and stability within its industry and within the markets it serves—that raw power is the objective. On closer examination, however, it becomes obvious that the second view is really very much like the first. To say a firm is only interested in its market position is a little like saying that the Los Angeles Dodgers really aren't interested in attendance, only in being in first place. But to baseball fans, it is obvious that being in first place greatly enhances baseball attendance. In business, the record speaks for itself. The bigger and stronger the firm, historically, the greater the rate of profits. Over the past twenty years, businesses capitalized at over $50 million have averaged profits of about 10 percent; businesses capitalized at $1 million to $10 million have averaged 7 percent. In the face of such evidence, it is hard to maintain that profits have not been the driving force for bigness. But how does size improve earnings?

Bigness provides a firm with greater profit potentials in two ways. First, increased size allows a firm to take advantage of economies of scale, which means that per-unit costs decline as the firm uses its plants, raw materials, personnel, management talent, and advertising space more intensively and more efficiently. Second, greater market size for a firm means protection from cutthroat competition and greater ability to set and maintain its own pricing structure. This freedom is not absolute, of course. Because too-extravagant a pricing policy will invite competitors to appear or will encourage government intervention, the firm, however large, sets prices under some constraints. The strategy, nevertheless, becomes obvious: The larger a firm, all things being equal, the greater the ability to widen the gap between total prices paid for its goods and total costs. The bigger the gap, the larger the profits.

Until comparatively recently, this traditional economic explanation of "bigness" has gone unchallenged; however, recent business studies indicate that perhaps most modern big businesses have exhausted their production and management economies of scale. While this may be the case, there is little evidence that business leaders themselves agree with this view. Bigness remains a characteristic trend in American enterprise.

Growth Strategies

A firm's growth can be facilitated in two ways. It can, like IBM, Xerox, and Polaroid, expand largely by using its own retained earnings (profits not distributed to shareholders) to finance its expansion. Or it can, like General Motors, General Electric, and ITT, expand by acquiring and absorbing other companies. Mergers, when one company acquires the assets and liabilities of another, have been the preferred route to bigness.

Three types of mergers are available to a firm:

1. Horizontal mergers combine companies that compete in the same market.
2. Vertical mergers combine suppliers and users in the production chain.
3. Conglomerate mergers join firms in totally unrelated fields of production.

Merger activity in the United States has taken place in four great waves: 1897–1914, 1920–1930, 1940–1947, and 1960–1970. The first three periods were dominated by horizontal and vertical mergers, and the most recent by conglomerate combinations.

As we have seen in our earlier historical survey, horizontal and vertical mergers were essential in assembling the great industrial giants during the first merger phase. Horizontal mergers built such giants as U.S. Steel, International Harvester, AT&T, General Motors, General Electric, and American Tobacco. Similarly, vertical mergers, although less obvious in their effects, were important in the corporate development of General Mills (milling and baking), Swift (meat processing and packing), Carnegie Steel (iron and coal mining), and hundreds of other firms. John D. Rockefeller's Standard Oil employed both devices as it grew to control over 90 percent of U.S. oil production, refining, and distribution.

Horizontal and vertical mergers continued in the 1920s and again in the 1940s, but not with the earlier vigor or importance. By the late 1950s, the impulse toward horizontal and vertical integration had practically ceased. Most of the desirable mergers, from the point of view of increasing efficiency and lowering costs, had been accomplished already. The remaining possible mergers among big businesses would have created such blatant monopoly power that they certainly would have led to government antitrust action. By this time the federal government, with considerable lobbying from smaller businesses and consumers protesting the decline of competition, had developed rather rigid guidelines in restricting vertical and horizontal mergers (see issue 10). Conglomerate mergers, however, presented new possibilities.

The Conglomerate Merger Wave

The decade of the 1960s was the heyday of conglomerate mergers. Putting together diverse firms under a single corporate leadership had several advantages. Older, established firms were able to diversify their operations and therefore hedge against the old problem of putting all their eggs in one basket. Classic conglomerate mergers included American Tobacco branching into foods by acquiring Sunshine Biscuit Co., Hunt Foods entering publishing by picking up McCalls Magazine, and Greyhound Corporation acquiring Armour meat packing.

Conglomeration also provided opportunities for new entrepreneurs. High capital requirements and considerable concentration in markets meant that about the only way a new enterprise could enter an industry was to pick up an existing firm. A new corporate empire could be put together by selectively merging firms from different industries. Moreover, the actual capital requirements for taking over a big firm were not as great as they might appear. Very often control of 20 to 30 percent of the firm's stock was sufficient. A small firm or group of investors with a healthy amount of working capital could very quickly acquire some industry giants. Old merger habits seemed to be turned upside down as little fish began to gobble up big fish.

The new conglomerate giants usually were led by a single driving personality, like Harold Geneen of ITT or James Ling of Ling-Temco-Vought. Between 1962 and 1970, Geneen merged 47 companies, including such firms as Airport Parking, Grinnell, Continental Baking, Canteen Corporation, and Hartford Fire and Casualty. Over the same period, ITT's assets grew from less than $1 billion to $4 billion. Ling-Temco-Vought's growth was more outstanding. Starting with skimpy assets of $94 million in 1960, James Ling put together a military-goods oriented conglomerate worth $2.5 billion, ranking fifteenth among U.S. industrials by 1970. Little LTV, like Jonah swallowing the whale, had even acquired the giant Jones and Laughlin Steel Corporation.

Although the conglomerate boom seemed to bottom out in the late 1960s, it began again in the late 1970s. This time much of the capital for conglomerate mergers was coming from abroad, as foreign firms such as Phillips (Netherlands), BP (England), Bayer (Germany), Nestle (Switzerland), and Renault (France) found good "buys" among American firms as the value of the dollar fell and as American stock prices remained depressed due to economic stagnation. Meanwhile, American energy corporations, suddenly bulging with profits, plunged back into merger activity.

How shall we evaluate the recent conglomerate trend? On the credit side, it can be argued that conglomerate mergers have strengthened firms by creating widely diversified product lines, insulating the firm from losses resulting from declining product demand in a single line. At the same time, conglomerates often pumped new management blood into faltering giants and provided capital for expansion that was not otherwise available. Sometimes mergers provided access to certain markets not otherwise available to a company. As our first article indicates, this was the inspiration behind the biggest merger on record, DuPont's $8 billion acquisition of Conoco.

While the first reading is generally supportive of the DuPont-Conoco merger, the second article takes a dimmer view of the recent merger wave. After surveying a number of the bigger mergers, it concludes that the acquiring companies often develop a case of "acquisition indigestion." In particular, the writer points out, shareholders of the acquiring firm have often seen their investments greatly diminish in value.

The third article opposes the merger boom from a somewhat different direction, arguing that bigness is a danger for American enterprise. Traditionally, economists have warned of the adverse effects of monopolistic power resulting from mergers. However, this article sees the bigness problem manifesting itself in growing corporate ineptitude and inability to manage rather than in dangerous monopolistic pricing practices. Viewing the future as a time when large companies will find it more difficult to adapt to quick and sweeping changes, it argues that we must distinguish between corporate expansion (merely accumulating the assets of other firms) and corporate growth (investing in brand-new production facilities). The suggestion is obvious: American corporations are squandering their cash and capital in unrewarding acquisitions when they should in fact be directing their funds to improve output and productivity.

The last article focuses on one company, Colgate-Palmolive, and its decision to move back from the merger frenzy by shedding some of its earlier acquisitions. Whether this approach will be the way of the future remains to be seen.

9.1   DuPont's Acquisition of Conoco: A Case Study Two Years after the Wedding

ROBERT B. CARSON

In the early summer of 1981, the financial pages of American newspapers carried stories on the continuing saga of Conoco Oil Company. Conoco, itself the nation's ninth largest oil producer and ranking fourteenth on the *Fortune* list of the nation's 500 largest industrials, was being courted, it seemed, by practically everybody. The object: matrimony through corporate merger. Conoco was, in the era of conglomerate mergers, a very attractive property. With energy prices high and rising and with a worldwide shortage of many minerals, Conoco's vast oil and mineral holdings were what a lot of people wanted. Its gasoline outlets, Conoco service stations in the United States and Europe and a string of economy gas pumping concerns in the southern and western states, may have been what made the company famous, but the oil and mineral properties were the cause for all of the merger activity.

The bidders were many and varied. Seagrams Ltd. of Canada, the whiskey people, opened the struggle with a bid of approximately $70 for a share of Conoco common stock. That amounted to $15 more than Conoco had been selling for at the time of the offer. Very quickly two oil giants made their moves; first Texaco (the 3rd largest producer of oil), then Shell (number 8), and Mobil (number 2). Then duPont Chemical Company jumped in. For several weeks, through May and June, the bidding was fast and furious. When duPont raised its bid to just over $90 for 50 percent of Conoco's outstanding shares, Conoco management accepted the inevitable and was absorbed by duPont.

When it was all over, it had been the biggest merger in American corporate history. In a complicated deal involving stock purchases and exchange of Conoco shares for duPont shares, duPont paid $7.8 billion for its new acquisition.

Why did duPont, skilled in chemicals but ignorant of oil, want Conoco? Well, there was Conoco's solid performance record (a 300 percent increase in its stock value over the previous decade), and there was also the prospect of continued rises in oil prices. But the real attraction to duPont was Conoco's oil and mineral properties. As duPont executives frankly explained, they were afraid that they might be closed off from their existing supplies of oil and minerals overseas and Conoco's domestic holdings were just too attractive to ignore.

Was it a good merger? Few Conoco stockholders were heard to complain. On the other hand, duPont had experienced a 700 percent increase in its debt, and its stock price soon tumbled, from $53 a share in early 1981 to $33 in mid-1982. However, as time has passed, the biggest corporate meal ever seems to be digesting rather well. Thanks to Conoco's operating profits, duPont's profits had doubled by 1983. Moreover, duPont felt well situated with regard to future oil and mineral needs, and that after all is what the company wanted in the first place.

9.2   Acquisition Indigestion

JACK EGAN

Do corporations know what they're doing when they buy other companies, through either hostile takeovers or friendly acquisitions? The incredibly poor experiences many well-known corporations have had with their once celebrated purchases makes you wonder.

The most dramatic example involves Inco, Ltd., the giant Canadian nickel company. Inco recently announced it was taking a $245-million tax write-off on ElectroEnergy Corporation (formerly E.S.B., Inc.), which it purchased for $230 million in 1974.

At the time, the deal was a landmark of sorts. Inco bought E.S.B., which makes Ray-O-Vac dry cells and Exide car batteries, after a fierce bidding battle with United Technologies. The deal put Morgan Stanley, Inco's investment banker, on the map as an orchestrator of hostile takeovers. Until then, few big companies had been willing to engage in such rough, acrimonious battles, but Morgan Stanley's representation of Inco gave hostile tenders respectability.

Inco is not the only company suffering from takeover indigestion.

R.C.A., in deep trouble, is trying to sell its Hertz subsidiary and has also reportedly put C.I.T. Financial on the block, but officially denies it. It bought C.I.T. only two years ago for $1.1 billion, a price that shocked analysts who were unimpressed by the rather sleepy financial-services company. I.T.T., the quintessential conglomerate, is now divesting itself of many of the companies acquired by its voracious former chairman Harold Geneen.

Other corporations, too, are getting socked on the bottom line by companies they bought. Mobil Oil, which has had such a hard time lately bringing off a takeover, is taking its lumps from its purchase of Montgomery Ward, which lost $160 million in 1981. And Exxon has not done well with Reliance Electric, which it bought for

$1.2 billion in 1979, claiming that the company had developed a revolutionary energy-saving motor. That dubious claim is still unproved. Philip Morris continues to lose money on 7-Up, a very costly acquisition, and General Foods is not getting much out of its purchase last year of Oscar Mayer for a very pricey $470 million.

Despite this extraordinarily sorry record for major acquisitions, some of the biggest takeover battles ever were waged last year. DuPont bested Seagram and Mobil to get Conoco in the biggest deal in history. U.S. Steel picked up Marathon Oil. And Fluor Corporation bought St. Joe Minerals for $2.3 billion.

It's still too early to predict the outcome of these takeovers, but the shareholders of the acquiring companies have taken a drubbing—one of the most overlooked aspects of the takeover game. The shareholders in a company that is bought almost always reap substantial rewards, the price of their shares jumping as soon as a bid is announced. But shareholders in the acquiring corporation often find their stock plunging after the takeover.

The shareholders of Fluor Corporation, the white knight that rescued St. Joe Minerals from the clutches of Seagram, have fared especially poorly. When Fluor announced its bid last April, its shares were trading at over $50. They haven't been that high since. Last week, Fluor was at $24, down 52 percent.

Shareholders of U.S. Steel and duPont have also taken a licking. Seagram wound up with 20 percent of duPont as a result of having bought Conoco shares in the bidding war, and has lost about $700 million on its holdings in just a few months.

Most of the concern and attention of government regulators focuses on the shareholders of target companies and whether they get a fair price. But they always wind up with a pretty good deal. And no one seems to care about the effect takeovers have on the shareholders of the acquiring corporations. In most cases, the shareholders don't even get to vote to approve the deals, even though the financial burden on them can be enormous. This makes a complete mockery of the idea that shareholders have a say in corporate decisions.

The rationale for many of these deals is that when shares of most companies are undervalued it's cheaper to purchase a whole corporation than to invest in new plants and equipment. But many companies end up paying such a high premium that earnings are reduced for years to borrow at astronomical rates to pay for their purchases. This reduces their credit ratings and makes future borrowing more expensive. Even duPont, one of the most financially solid corporations around, had its debt rating lowered from AAA to AA as a result of the Conoco deal.

Baldwin-United's current $1.2-billion offer for M.G.I.C. illustrates the gamesmanship that underlies many of these deals. Baldwin-United, a diversified financial firm, first claimed that it had enough money to finance the acquisition internally, but with the deal all but clinched it has announced—to the astonishment of everyone involved—that it must raise $600 million more. As Baldwin-United scrambles to come up with the money, shareholders in both companies are seeing their stock's value plummet.

To be sure, not all takeovers turn sour. United Technologies, under chairman Harry Gray, has pursued an aggressive acquisition policy, and the company has done well as a result. Obtaining Otis Elevator and Carrier has been beneficial; Mostek, a semiconductor maker, has proved less profitable.

To its credit, United Technologies pulled out of two bidding battles when it thought the price had gotten too high. One of these was against Inco for E.S.B. The other, in 1978, was for Babcock & Wilcox, a maker of steam generators for utilities. McDermott, Inc., ended up buying that company, and the weak demand for new generators has dimmed the purchase's glow.

In many takeover battles, the company that comes up on top is widely characterized as the "winner," while the company that pulls out is seen as a "loser"—even though the opposite is often the case. That is how many investment bankers, who do the deals and collect millions of dollars in fees, and arbitrageurs, who gather in the stock for astronomical personal gain, like to portray the struggle. They, after all, profit from the largest-possible transactions. The last thing they want is to encourage prudent bidding.

Lehman Brothers Kuhn Loeb ran an ad last year bragging that most of its clients who had attempted takeovers had succeeded. That's not necessarily something to brag about. After all, Lehman represented Fluor in the St. Joe acquisition, Philip Morris in the 7-Up deal, and General Foods when it bought Oscar Mayer. In retrospect, these companies would have done better by paying less or backing off entirely. Lehman also represented R.C.A. in the takeover of C.I.T., and collected a handsome fee in the process. Peter Peterson, Lehman's chairman, sits on the board of R.C.A. If and when R.C.A. rids itself of C.I.T., Lehman will represent it, and will again make a few million dollars.

Investment bankers are naturally reluctant to assume any responsibility for deals that go awry. Morgan Stanley absolutely refuses to comment on its Inco-E.S.B. deal, which turned out so disastrously.

But the top executives of corporations that make these dubious acquisitions must take ultimate responsibility. There is some risk in any business decision, but large-scale corporate acquisition seems especially perilous. Some deals can best be explained as ego trips on the part of chief executive officers. Takeovers, after all, are the corporate equivalent of war, and some of these executives like to play General Patton.

Mobil recently ran a sour-grapes newspaper ad complaining that the shareholders of Marathon Oil got a bad deal when Mobil was prevented from topping U.S. Steel's bid. The headline read: WHO LOOKS OUT FOR THE SHAREHOLDERS? But who, in fact, protects the shareholders of Mobil when it decides to diversify by making a crazy acquisition like Montgomery Ward? Debate about takeovers has always focused on whether they benefit the economy or merely increase corporate concentration. The issue of how well they serve the companies that make the purchases, and their shareholders, is usually ignored.

Takeovers will continue. But there should be a law requiring that they be approved by the shareholders of the acquiring corporation. They always pay the price of management's misguided decisions. The shareholders can't wait until the annual meeting to complain. By that time it's too late.

9.3   Bigness Has Weakened American Business

ARTHUR BURCK

To be sure, bigness in itself isn't bad. Many big firms are in industries where bigness is appropriate and necessary. But just as a huge truck-trailer is suitable for the New Jersey Turnpike but hardly for traversing the rush-hour traffic of downtown Manhattan, so unnecessary bigness can become a handicap in many sectors of the business world.

Excessive bigness often enables a company, by dint of size and money alone, to suppress its smaller competitors and thereby prolong its supremacy; in turn that can lead to stagnation and eventual vulnerability. The auto industry provides a classic example that I personally experienced from time-to-time for a quarter century.

In the early 1950s, far-sighted George Mason, head of Nash Motors, a predecessor of American Motors Corp., created a line of small compact cars that Nash-American Motors saw as the wave of the future in a world that already was clearly destined for energy shortages. Like so many other visionaries who were ahead of their times, Mason and his successor, George Romney, saw unsold Rambler small cars languish in showrooms, and by 1957 raider Louis Wolfson, AMC's principal stockholder, was threatening to take over, fire Romney and liquidate the auto business.

Romney was always sure that small cars would become winners, and he countered Wolfson by retaining me to arrange a "white knight" merger that would block Wolfson and keep AMC afloat until Rambler small cars became profitable. Before such a merger could be implemented, a "miracle" occurred. Ramblers started to sell as fast as they could be made, and with Romney assailing the Big Three's "gas-guzzling dinosaurs," AMC's new-found prosperity was reflected in AMC stock soaring from 6 to 90, one of the astounding turnarounds in history. Romney "cashed in" on his stock options and thereby became a multimillionaire, enabling him to leave AMC to become Michigan Governor and eventual presidential candidate. Without the irrepressible Romney to challenge the Big Three, AMC's crusade for small cars gradually petered out during the 1960s.

Moreover, with the Big Three muddying the waters with un- distinguished "me-too" small cars and other tactics that enable the mighty to suppress upstart competitors, it became clear that AMC lacked the financial muscle and small-car expertise needed to se- cure and widen its beachhead in the domestic small-car market.

I concluded merger with a foreign car maker was the only sure way to broaden the AMC beachhead. Since I had earlier tried to sell foundering Studebaker-Packard to the European car makers, I was aware that most European industry leaders were convinced that America was ready for the small-car age, and so in the early '60s, I traipsed from one end of Europe to the other talking merger with the major automakers, including Fiat, Volvo, British Motors and Renault (17 years after I first visited Renault in Paris, Renault started its takeover of AMC, but by then AMC was too far gone to be a viable base).

Why did the Europeans always stop short of the altar? When the chips were down, fear took over—fear of what might happen if they challenged on home grounds the massed might of the concen- trated American auto industry with its inexhaustible capital availa- ble to propagandize the consumer against small cars. They knew that the Big Three would tolerate a smallish American Motors, but were skeptical about what might happen to a strengthened AMC that presented a major challenge to Detroit's highly-profitable big cars.

Fiat's president put it graphically: "There is a certain amount of danger if one dances with the elephants."

The result was that throughout the 1960s and most of the 70s there was no competitor in our domestic market having the strength needed to force General Motors and Ford to join the small-car age—until it became too late.

As the consequence, Ford now faces the possibility that if things get much worse it might have to join Lockheed-Chrysler as a suppliant for taxpayer bailouts. That is what was predicted 11 years ago in my letter to Ford's management when I was working with Ford on a merger possibility:

> As I sit back and see the disdain of the younger generation for the Mark III and other standard cars, and how in preference they will seek out the VW, Fiat, Toyota or any *simple* car, I am thankful that I am not a substantial holder of Ford stock—or of any other U.S. motor company. . . . The U.S. car makers are in the same position as the railroads a generation ago. . . .
> I wish I could have your top officials review my Lockheed file. Suggestion after suggestion that could have changed the course of that once impregnable company always fell on deaf ears. . . . But please don't let me look back on the Ford file a decade from now and say: too bad, another Lockheed.

Why did the Big Three fail to take timely steps to effect an orderly transition into the small-car age? It is easy to blame management but that is not entirely fair; the reality is that Detroit managers had no choice. They were locked into a situation that resulted from the structure of the industry that was concentrated in the 1920s, largely through mergers, into one behemoth and two giants.

When companies get too big, they often lose the capacity to create new products or to launch replacements for the old. Why? As companies increase in size, there is a commensurate increase in bureaucracy, which becomes more and more inflexible. In the business world, change is the name of the game. Yet it is the very nature of bureaucracy to resist change.

Another factor that leads to corporate stagnation is that the larger the company, the greater its stock in the status quo. When investments in established products and methods run into billions of dollars, manufacturers are reluctant to retool and so the auto industry was slow to jettison the colossal investments in large cars.

The failure to innovate or otherwise change then opens the door to destructive competition. We then pay the penalty for having permitted many of our basic industries to become concentrated, usually as the result of mergers, many in the musty past. In concentrated industries, there is often no domestic competitor in a position to bring about innovative change, just as with autos. The vacuum is then filled by foreign competitors.

It wasn't only in autos that this was happening—steel, tires and consumer electronics are just a few of the staid industries where once-respected giants were relegated to second-rate status by nimble foreign competitors. The fact that U.S. Steel had $11 billion in assets and Bethlehem Steel $5 billion didn't prevent agile foreigners from obsoleting their technology and plants—indeed, it was their very size in a concentrated industry that made them vulnerable.

We all grew up in the belief that big companies were as much a part of America as apple pie. Bigness in business had been sort of a sacred cow, and until recently deservedly so; one can't overlook that large firms were creators of wealth and jobs. Then why are huge companies now failing us? Why have they lost their capacity in recent decades to innovate and change?

Through much of our early industrial history when the nation was booming and expanding, our giants prospered in concentrated industries because of relative insulation from major foreign competition. In most of our basic industries that had become "shared monopolies" through early mergers, their concentrated little "clubs" were never really invaded by aggressive foreigners; they were able to innovate and change at their own pace.

Thereafter our insulation—our privileged position—was extended for another half century by the happenstance of two world wars, and their recovery aftermaths. That left us relatively alone with undestroyed plants, advanced products and established markets.

So it was not until the 1950s, when the industrial nations began to recover, that giants first felt the impact of aggressive foreign competition. In retrospect, it is not surprising that the giants were unable to make alert response since never having experienced such aggressive competition from within their concentrated industries, they were burdened by lethargic habit patterns formed for another time and era. In other words, they were victims of the easy one-way street that was enjoyed by American business after World War II.

In view of the wreckage we now see everywhere on our industrial scene, we now have ample proof that the huge industrial bureaucracies have outgrown their day of usefulness in a hotly competitive world where innovation is the name of the game.

The clear lesson is that in today's changed circumstances the nation is served only when there is the largest possible number of viable, independent companies engaged in vigorous competition.

For too long, we have worshipped giantism and the idolatry of "economies of scale." We now know that there can be no meaningful economies of scale when products face obsolescence; and in an uncertain world, the only certainty is that every product will eventually become obsolete.

The damage that the giants inflict on themselves is often matched by the devastation that they wreak on the companies they acquire. One of the best kept secrets, though the evidence is everywhere around us, is that most acquisitions of the giants do not work out; some experts say that as many as seven out of ten are failures. Although there are no precise statistics—in part because acquirers understandably do not go out of their way to publicize mistakes—my guess is that more than half of the tens of thousands of companies acquired in recent decades by the giants were weakened, damaged or destroyed.

Obviously, the giants do not do so intentionally; it seems unthinkable that they can pay millions—and even billions—for a company and then permit it to become tarnished or worse. What usually is not comprehended—often until too late—is that mergers are not abstract jig-saw puzzles or mathematical formulae; basically they involve complex human beings with fixed ways, attitudes and prejudices, and differing talents; even under the best of circumstances it is difficult to take two disparate and separate groups and blend them into one happy, motivated and smooth-functioning team. We know it is hard enough for two people to stay married; just imagine when two huge, huge families are involved.

Moreover, when a giant is the acquirer, its huge bureaucracy is often unable, like oil and water, to mesh with the managers of a fragile entrepreneurial company. When another giant is acquired, stagnation in time sets in if the newly-added layer of bureaucracy is left intact, but it becomes just as bad if there are the wholesale departures that follow a hostile takeover while those who remain vegetate rather than make waves.

What often happens following takeover was described by veteran acquirer William Norris, founder and CEO of Control Data

Corp., when he and I appeared in 1978 before the Senate subcommittee on antitrust and monopoly:

> The most serious economic damage results from the destruction of job-creating resources. Technological innovation is the wellspring of new jobs. . . . Immediately after a takeover an innovation-stifling process sets in. The aggressor blankets the other with bureaucracy, layer upon layer. . . . Proposals for new products languish. . . . The result is the dispersal of the entrepreneurial team, the major job-creating resource.

We have no way of measuring the impact on the nation's economy of the damage to the acquired companies—we are dealing with "might-have-beens" that are largely conjecture. Nevertheless, we must remember that the giants for several decades have been beating the bushes to find the most tempting takeover targets, the cream of the crop of emerging growth companies and leading independents. In other words, we have undermined a generation of our most promising companies, the industrial future of America.

In the meantime, our huge companies are bargained and sold with the same reckless abandon as poker chips at Las Vegas. Under today's lax rules, there is no more concern given to public welfare in the takeover of a billion-dollar firm than on the sale of the corner hot-dog stand.

When the history of our times is written, the unrestrained mergers of recent decades may well replace the debacle of the stock market of the 1920s as the cataclysm most destructive to the nation's financial and economic foundations.

Big companies will always be essential in some industries, but with that qualification it is hard to quarrel with the goals expressed by Ronald Reagan seven years ago in Chicago:

> I am calling also for an end to giantism, for a return to the human scale—the scale that human beings can understand and cope with. . . . It is the locally owned factory, the small businessman who personally deals with his customers and stands behind his product, the farm and consumer cooperative, the town or neighborhood bank that invests in the community, the union local. . . . It is this activity on a small, human scale that creates the fabric of community, a framework

for the creation of abundance and liberty. The human scale nurtures standards or right behavior, a prevailing ethic of what is right and wrong, acceptable and unacceptable.

The solution of course is simple: withdraw from large companies the tax incentives—interest deductibility on acquisition borrowings and tax-free stock swaps—that so long have fueled giant mergers. Taking away these tax breaks will have the long-range effect of shrinking the stagnant and declining giants that can grow only through takeovers; in time the problem of decadent giantism will recede into the background. Moreover, the companies that might otherwise be acquired and eventually eroded will be spared.

On the other hand, the vibrant giants such as IBM have negligible need for acquisitions, and if they do, they will have little problem in making whatever acquisitions they really need since the tax benefits for them are not important. After all, they will still have an advantage over smaller companies that lack tradable stock and that borrow on unfavorable terms.

As the consequence, the main activity will then shift to small and medium-sized companies. That is the sector where mergers are needed to keep our capitalism dynamic, to remove the imbalance caused by the burgeoning bigness of past massive mergers.

The industrial future of America lies not with the decaying giants but with the nimbler businesses that can open up new horizons and merger is often the best way to hasten the growth of these creative entities.

9.4   Back to Basics: Colgate-Palmolive Sheds Its Acquisitions

GAIL BRONSON

After much hard work, Keith Crane, the chairman of Colgate-Palmolive Co., and his household-products lieutenants have restored the company to just about where it was 10 years ago.

Regression may seem a peculiar goal. However, Mr. Crane took over in 1979 a company hobbled by misfit acquisitions and sparse top management. His predecessor, David Foster, had tried, unsuccessfully, to propel Colgate out from under the shadow of the industry's giant, Procter & Gamble, through additions such as sports, food and apparel companies.

In that shopping spree, Colgate managed to buy a lot of trouble. It was turned into a company sapping the profits of its traditional lines to acquire other businesses already past their peak profitability. Moreover, Mr. Foster, a flamboyant man renowned for his dictatorial style, was unable—by his own admission—to delegate authority. A further complication was rumors about his personal problems.

So calamitous did the situation become that the board of directors eventually demanded Mr. Foster's resignation—but not until the deaths of two directors, one of them a great-grandson of founder William Colgate, tipped the balance against Mr. Foster. In electing Mr. Crane, who had been named president in 1975 over Mr. Foster's objections, the board installed as chairman and chief executive a man as low-profile and even-keeled as Mr. Foster had been flamboyant.

"For the past five years, it has not been much fun to own Colgate stock, follow the company or work there," says Daniel J. Meade, a securities analyst at First Boston Corp. "After half a decade of milking the heart of its business—by cutting back advertising, underfunding research and limiting new-product moves—Colgate decided to support its operations and run its business for the long term."

Searing Retrenchment

Mr. Crane imposed a searing retrenchment. He severed most of Mr. Foster's $935 million of acquisitions—at a cost of at least $96.5 million in reported write-offs. The 60-year-old Mr. Crane terms the divestitures the first steps toward his goal of a minimum 14% return on capital, compared with 10.6% last year and 7.5% in 1979. He also reorganized management, revised advertising budgets and moved to strengthen basic product lines with a new emphasis on production and profitability. . . .

Mr. Crane still faces the same business problems that confronted Mr. Foster when the latter took charge of Colgate in 1971: the brutal competition in the soap, detergent and toothpaste markets and Procter & Gamble's dominant position. He also can fall back on the same strength: Colgate's ability to ferry its products through well-entrenched marketing channels in some 54 countries.

Beyond clinging to that advantage, Mr. Foster had taken a quite different approach. Described by a former colleague as "a man who liked being the center of attention at cocktail parties," Mr. Foster had emphasized marketing rather than developing new products. His strategy was to try to outflank P&G with noncompetitive products that could be dressed up with jazzy advertising. So he began an ambitious diversification plan to move Colgate out of its traditional household and personal-care products.

Earlier Optimism

"One of the most exciting and productive aspects of our company's new direction," he told shareholders in the 1972 annual report, "is the increasing emphasis on developing new product categories distinct from our traditional product lines, in which market growth is generally limited to the growth of the population."

But Mr. Foster's strategy backfired. After he acquired sports companies, sales of golf and tennis equipment hit a plateau. Riviana, an acquisition known for Carolina rice, was hurt by a decline in rice prices. Lums restaurants and Pangburn candy suffered widening losses. And the biggest blot on Mr. Foster's portfolio was Helena Rubenstein, the cosmetics company, which quickly fell into red ink.

"They were all vanity acquisitions," says an advertising executive who handled Colgate accounts during the Foster years. "After Kendall (a medical-supplies company) and Riviana, the rest was junkola."

Moreover, Colgate's efforts to introduce new products generally foundered during the Foster regime. Frequently, the company took a short cut in rolling out new merchandise; it acted as a mere distributor rather than developing its own products. For example, it sold Alpen, one of the first "natural" breakfast cereals, for Weetabix Co. of Britain. In its first year, 1973, the product's American sales reached about $17 million—a 1% market share, which was considered remarkable in the industry. But as competitors entered the natural-cereals field, Cogate fled rather than spend money on marketing, says Jack Salzman, an analyst at Smith Barney, Harris Upham & Co.

Also introduced in 1973 was Pritt Glue-Stick, which Colgate sold under license from Henkel Co. of West Germany. This product also was dropped after a few years.

In other cases, Colgate's marketing magic failed to stir consumer interest. For example, a detergent laced with blue dye colored all the laundry in test marketing. And a dishwashing detergent packaged in waxy cartons similar to those used for orange juice was rejected by test-market mothers in Buffalo; they feared a hazard to children, who might think that the containers held juice.

"These are mistakes that P&G would never make," a former consultant to Colgate says. "You learn in this market to make simple and functional products. Colgate went for additives."

Neither the former nor the present chief executive would reply to all the criticism. Mr. Foster, who lives in a condominium near Palm Springs, Calif., couldn't be reached despite repeated attempts. Mr. Crane declined to be interviewed for this article and denied access to other Colgate executives. One vice president supported this decision, saying, "We're a different Colgate every month. How can he talk about anything?" She later added that Mr. Crane would prefer to accomplish certain goals and then talk to the press.

Some Successes

The company had scored some successes, of course. Irish Spring soap, introduced in 1972, was one in the Foster years. Fresh

Start, powdered laundry detergent, was Mr. Foster's last project, although it went into national distribution in April 1980, after Mr. Crane had taken over. The detergent, cleverly packaged in a clear plastic bottle, has been a boffo success, with sales in the final seven months of last year topping $70 million. The product commands a 5% market share and could pull in sales of more than $100 million this year, says Hercules Segalas, an analyst at Drexel Burnham Lambert Inc.

But not everyone is impressed. "Fresh Start is another example of Colgate's effort to keep up a bold front that something's happening," a Colgate consultant says. "Colgate has yet to rectify its 'me-too products' syndrome. I can't think of a single technological innovation from that company domestically."

In swinging Colgate back to its basic businesses—toothpaste and soap—Mr. Crane is reaching back into its history. Founded in 1802 as a soap and candle maker, Colgate began making toothpaste, which initially was sold in jars, in 1877. In 1928, the company merged into Palmolive-Peet Co., whose Palmolive soap was then the world's top-selling brand.

Discussion and Review Questions

1. Explain the differences between horizontal, vertical, and conglomerate mergers. What are the supposed advantages of each?

2. Why did DuPont acquire Conoco? Do you think their decision was based on sound or unsound economic reasoning?

3. If, as the second article alleges, stockholders have benefited little from the recent giant mergers, why have corporations pursued the merger path?

4. What is the "economies of scale" justification for large enterprise? Do you agree or disagree with Arthur Burck's position that we have passed the point of large-scale economies?

5. What specific arguments does Burck make to uphold his thesis that "bigness has sapped the vitality of American enterprise"?

6. What was Colgate-Palmolive's experience with conglomerate activities?

7. Can you see any particular problems being posed for the American business system by the recent merger wave? Discuss your view.

PART 6

BUSINESS AND GOVERNMENT

ISSUE 10

Is Antitrust Law Outmoded?

Government regulation of the marketplace dates almost from the beginning of business itself. English common law (law based on the legal precedent of past court decisions) had long held that conspiracies by tradespeople to set prices or to diminish competition were illegal. Similarly, the courts held that where monopolies were permitted to exist legally, the monopolist had obligations to perform services without discrimination among buyers and without abusing the general public. These points are worth remembering, since many extreme opponents of business regulation give the incorrect impression that regulation is a very recent development.

The Rise of the Trust

Despite its long tradition in common law, the idea of maintaining competition among sellers in the marketplace was not spelled out in statutory law in the United States until 1890. During the post-Civil War years, there had been a vast growth of business enterprise. In railroads, steel, oil, sugar, lumber, and many other products, businesspeople had at first faced a highly competitive situation. For many firms, profits were hard or impossible to obtain as producers undercut each other in an attempt to sell their goods. Very quickly, some business leaders saw the advantage of banding together to set a single profitable price or to limit their production so as to keep their prices high. After its invention by Standard Oil Company in 1879, the "trust" became a favored form of protection from competition. In a trust, competing companies surrender their stock to an appointed group of trustees. The trustees act like the directors of an individual unconsolidated company, making business decisions, setting prices, collecting income, and distributing it to the separate corporations (prorated according to each participant's share).

Very clearly, the object of a trust was to end price competition and to keep prices high. The trusts created a strong negative reaction from the general public. Similarly, they were attacked by those businesspeople who were excluded from trust benefits and found their own production costs rising.

Government Begins to Attack Monopoly

In 1890, Congress passed the Sherman Anti-Trust Act, which declared (in Section 1) that trusts and other combinations to restrain "trade or commerce" were illegal and (in Section 2) that monopolizing or conspiring to monopolize is illegal. The intent of the law was clear enough: no informal arrangements among competing companies to have joint monopoly power *and* no monopoly control by a single company. However, beyond that the law did not define what "restraint of trade" was or even what "monopoly" was. Neither did it create any government agency to oversee business. Rather, the federal government had to go to the courts for an interpretation on a case-by-case basis. During the early years, court opinion varied, and usually the large firms evaded serious penalties.

Not until the trust-busting activities of President Theodore Roosevelt's administration in the early 1900s did the government and the courts begin to interpret and use the Sherman Act. Still, the act was not employed very vigorously. When Standard Oil and American Tobacco were finally found guilty of monopoly behavior, the Supreme Court introduced a doctrine that has remained an important element of American antitrust law. In 1911, Chief Justice White pronounced the two giants guilty because they had *unreasonably* used their monopoly power, not just for monopolizing. His "rule of reason" held that "bigness" alone was not proof of guilt, "badness" had to be proved. This shifted the burden of proof upon the government in all antimonopoly actions under Section 2 of the Sherman Act. For the next 35 years, until the Alcoa case in 1945 (see the first reading) the "Rule of Reason" prevailed, thereby limiting government anti-monopoly activity under Section 2. The Alcoa case, however, reversed this interpretation, holding that size alone was proof of monopolistic (undesirable) behavior. Recently, under the Reagan administration, the "Rule of Reason" has been returned to favor.

The Broadening of Government Powers

For sixty years after passage of the Sherman Act, legislative efforts to tighten the antitrust law and to close legal loopholes moved slowly and not very effectively. In 1914, the Clayton Anti-Trust Act closed some of the loopholes by specifying certain illegal practices. Under the Clayton Act it was illegal (1) to have "interlocking directorates," whereby directors of different corporations sat on the boards of competing companies, (2) to discriminate among buyers, and (3) to require "tying contracts" whereby a buyer was obliged to take undesired goods in order to get those that were wanted.

Also in 1914, Congress passed the Federal Trade Commission Act, which forbade firms to use "unfair methods of competition" and created a five-member commission and a staff to determine unfair practices and to enforce compliance with these interpretations and other antitrust laws on the books. The FTC was the Congressional (legislative) antitrust arm. The older Anti-Trust Division of the Justice Department was the executive arm of antitrust enforcement. Together these agencies looked, on paper at least, like a formidable antibusiness weapon. Practice was a different matter. First of all, the FTC had few investigative powers and no punitive (punishment) powers. They could merely *tell* violators not to repeat their offenses. At the Justice Department, meanwhile, the inclination to enforce antitrust law vigorously depended on the political outlook of the current White House occupant. Not until much later did the FTC get more power, at which time it and the Anti-Trust Division began to coordinate their antitrust policy.

In 1936, the Robinson-Patman Act was passed in response to pressure from small grocers who were opposed to "price cutting" by the big chains. The act made illegal any "price cutting" that was intended to be "predatory" or to suppress competition. The objective was noble, but, again, interpretations were vague and enforcement uneven.

In 1950, the Celler-Kefauver Act gave new life and direction to antitrust law. Celler-Kefauver closed the most glaring legal loopholes that had permitted the steady growth of monopoly power. Absurd as it may seem, before Celler-Kefauver, competing firms were prohibited from collaborating in price setting (under Section 1 of the Sherman Act) but could merge and then fix their prices (as long as they did not violate the "rule of reason" interpretation of Section 2 of the Sherman Act). Under Celler-Kefauver, competitive mergers and the purchasing of stocks and assets of a corporation were illegal if they "substantially lessen competition or tend to create a monopoly."

At the same time, the FTC was given a vast increase in investigative and legal powers. Under Celler-Kefauver, the FTC was granted authority to approve or disapprove mergers before they took place. After conducting an administrative hearing and reaching a decision, the FTC could issue an order that a firm could only reverse by successfully appealing to the courts. To give the FTC strength to use its new authority, Congress over the next thirty years increased the FTC budget twenty times over and tripled the professional staff. Today the FTC and Anti-Trust Division of the Justice Department work closely together as the two federal agencies enforcing antitrust law.

The Antitrust Balance Sheet

How has business recently fared under antitrust law, and what does the future hold? In the case of government efforts to break up existing monopoly power, business has been challenged but not seriously threatened. In 1982, the government dropped its long-time effort to break up IBM. Meanwhile, its decision to strip AT&T of its phone operations (decided also in 1982) actually was welcomed by many AT&T officials who frankly wanted to get out of the "regulated" phone business.

According to court decisions, conviction requires proof of (1) a monopoly control of a market, (2) monopolistic (unreasonable) acts, (3) exceptionally high profits, and (4) the fact that divestiture (breaking up the assets) will not harm stockholders or the economic performance of the company. Recognizing that such proof is hard to make and that companies will fight long and costly legal battles in any prosecution based on monopoly power (the recent IBM case had been in litigation since 1968), the antitrust authorities have backed off in this area of maintaining competition. It is unlikely a firm will be prosecuted in the future simply because it has a large share of a particular market.

In the area of merger policy, government has done much better in the recent past. Practically all horizontal and vertical mergers except those of near-microscopic proportions have been opposed successfully by the antitrust authorities. While regulation of conglomerate mergers is just developing, here too government has won cases where some threat to existing market balance could be shown or where the merger involved the wedding of two or more very large corporations. However, there seems to be a new antitrust position developing in merger cases. Faced with growing foreign competition in some cases and market contraction in others, firms have recently argued that reduction of the number of competitors in a particular market may actually "strengthen" competition. The failure to merge might mean the wholesale bankruptcy of many enterprises. The antitrust authorities have been disposed to accept these arguments, and the vigorous antimerger guidelines of the 1970s are being loosened. Even giant mergers (DuPont–Conoco and U.S. Steel–Marathon Oil, for instance) have been permitted.

The questions that arise at this point are: Should we rethink our entire antitrust and antimerger approach? Do the realities of modern technology, capital requirements, and foreign competition require a new direction that permits the growth of ever-larger and more powerful corporate giants? The first article in this section concludes that, indeed, there is a changing attitude in Washington toward mergers in general and bigness in particular. The second article examines one well-known example of this new antitrust approach, namely, the historic government action in the IBM case in 1982. The third article maintains that our approach to antitrust is both old and complicated, and it proposes a new, very simplified antitrust strategy.

10.1   Bold Departures in Antitrust Policy

EDWARD MEADOWS

The Reagan Administration's antitrust policy is beginning to come into focus, and it's a whole new picture. If it still seems blurry to a lot of businessmen, that is doubtless because William F. Baxter, the assistant attorney general for antitrust . . . has gone out of his way to tone down the differences between current policy and that of past Administrations. . . .

But in fact Baxter, a chain-smoking Stanford-trained law professor, departs dramatically from his predecessors on some very basic issues. He believes, for starters, that most mergers are a good thing. And he is a proponent of a relatively new and fundamentally different philosophy known as the Chicago School of antitrust law and economics—so named because it first emanated from scholars at the University of Chicago.

The doctrine is said to have been first enunciated by Aaron Director, a law professor there who in the 1950s held seminars on what was then thought to be a radical doctrine. By now, Chicago School theory has percolated through much of academia, at least in its mildest forms. But it is not yet generally accepted in most U.S. circuit courts, or by the Supreme Court, where antitrust case law is made.

Chicago School theory stresses the commonsense notion that trustbusters should devote primary attention to the prices consumers have to pay. The theory rejects out of hand the traditional notion that prices are necessarily strongly affected by how many corporate players are competing in a given market.

Rethinking Alcoa

This goes against the precedent set by Judge Learned Hand back in 1945 when he ruled that Alcoa's 90% share of the aluminum market was prima facie evidence that the company was anticompetitive and had to be broken up. Chicago Professor Yale Brozen, a Baxter soulmate, says Alcoa's only "crime" was to have created a demand for aluminum, which Alcoa then satisfied by having plants ready to produce it. As Brozen sees it, the court should have looked at the market for recycled aluminum, and at the markets for competing materials such as tin, zinc, and silver, before passing judgment on whether Alcoa really had a monopoly.

The static "big is bad" doctrine came to be applied not only to big companies and the mergers that would increase their share of a particular market, but also to "vertical" arrangements or mergers between a company and its suppliers or customers. More recently, the theory has been applied to conglomerate mergers.

Chicago School theorists believe the limits to absolute size are determined by the marketplace. Conglomerates can be said to be too big when their size results in diseconomies of scale that erode their profits, in which case they have to slim down. And vertical mergers—those between customers and suppliers—are often regarded as procompetitive because they can lower costs: when a customer joins up with his supplier, he'll usually get cheaper supplies.

Only horizontal mergers (those between companies in the same business) are seen as potentially anticompetitive. And here the case against bigness has to be proved, because the Chicago School is willing to see bigness not necessarily as a symptom of monopolistic power but as a result of a company's greater efficiency. That greater efficiency, deriving from economies of large scale, can even translate into lower prices for consumers.

These ideas rest on the findings of vast empirical research. To antitrust experts of whatever persuasion, a key economic relationship is that between corporate concentration and pretax profit margins. More than 100 studies conducted over the last few decades have found that, as concentration increases, margins widen. From this, traditional thinkers about antitrust concluded that concentration allows producers to raise prices. But on the basis of further research, Professor Sam Peltzman, a University of Chicago economist, produced convincing evidence in 1977 that margins widen not because prices go up but because costs go down.

Peltzman looks and dresses more like singer Bob Dylan than any economics professor, but his conclusions have gained wide acceptance among economists. ''I find concentration symptomatic of one company having a technological or product edge over others, thus being able to win a larger market share,'' says Peltzman. He adds: ''On balance, concentration brings progress and lower prices for consumers.'' That's because the efficiencies of concentration at least open the possibility that prices can decline.

Richard Posner, a leading antitrust lawyer and Chicago professor, feels Baxter has a historic chance to bring Chicago School doctrine into the legal mainstream. ''Baxter has a greater opportunity to turn antitrust policy around than anyone since Thurmond Arnold [Franklin Roosevelt's gung-ho trustbuster], because not only has academic thinking changed but so has political feeling.'' The Republican takeover of the Senate and the replacement of Senator Edward Kennedy with Senator Strom Thurmond as head of the Judiciary Committee will give Baxter plenty of maneuvering room. Thurmond has already taken the extraordinary step of abolishing the subcommittee on antitrust and monopolies—the bully pulpit from which Senator Kennedy used to rail against big business.

Baxter recently told *Fortune* that the most fundamental change he has made so far is to demand, for the first time, that Antitrust Division economists clear everything the division does. All decisions on what companies to investigate and what cases to pursue must now be carefully scrutinized by the economists to see that they are economically sound. ''If it doesn't make economic sense,'' says Baxter flatly,'' it doesn't happen.''

In fact, economists are in such ascendancy at Baxter's shop now that some of the division's lawyers are complaining. They joke that Baxter prefaces every statement by saying, ''Based on my 1,400 hours of graduate studies in economics, I can say that. . . . '' Some claim Baxter is like ''a converted Catholic'' in his zeal to inject Chicago economics into antitrust law. Baxter actually is a convert: although he emerged from his undergraduate economic studies as an Adlai Stevenson liberal, he came around to the Chicago School while studying price theory as a law professor.

To Baxter and the Chicago School, the assault by the Carter Administration on vertical, or customer–supplier, relationships was useless and possibly prevented competition. Under Assistant Attorney General Sanford Litvack, the Carter Justice Department began prosecuting companies such as Cuisinart, which was fined $250,000 because it had required its dealers to maintain a certain minimum price. Chicago's Brozen says that case, as well as a similar one brought against Mack Trucks, was itself a restraint on trade. "Why worry if a manufacturer tells a retailer he can't cut his price, or that he must restrict himself to an exclusive territory?" asks Brozen. After all, the argument goes, a retailer is free to switch suppliers if he doesn't like the restrictions. By keeping its price up, Cuisinart encouraged imitators—as a visit to any houseware store will demonstrate.

Baxter agrees. A few weeks ago, when he was summoned before the House subcommittee on monopolies and commercial law, he said he would eschew interference with "contractual vertical arrangements in distribution chains." As Baxter sees it, "A vertical problem is either a horizontal problem in disguise or no problem at all." For example, if a supplier agreed to deal exclusively with one customer, and vice versa, that would be anticompetitive only if, as a consequence, there was less price competition among the remaining suppliers or customers—a horizontal problem.

Price Fixers to the Slammer

Conglomerate mergers are going to be looked at far differently by Baxter. Traditional antitrust theory hypothesizes that by buying an established company rather than starting one, a conglomerate reduces potential competition in the market it is entering. The Chicago School's answer is that conglomerates don't buy businesses out of a desire to enter any particular market, but act when they see a chance to pick up poorly managed assets cheaply.

Baxter says unequivocally, "The intellectual underpinnings of the case against vertical and conglomerate mergers have been thoroughly discredited." But he takes pains to acknowledge that such mergers haven't been "a major enforcement focus" at Justice for several years. Baxter says he will concentrate almost exclusively on activities that increase the risk of collusive behavior. And he plans tough prosecution of old-fashioned price fixing. "We expect to press for actual incarceration rather than suspended sentences," he says.

Baxter has not made clear what kinds of horizontal mergers he won't tolerate. He did stall Mobil's momentum in its bid for Conoco by asking for more information. But that may not be particularly revealing. Abbott Lipsky, the bright young deputy assistant attorney general, who was a student of Baxter's at Stanford, puts it this way: "To say we found serious competitive problems with a Mobil–Conoco merger is a mischaracterization. We found enough policy questions to investigate that we were forced to ask for more information."

Baxter has ordered a drastic revision of the Justice Department's 1968 merger guidelines, to be finished by spring. He views the old guidelines, written when Ramsey Clark was Attorney General, as "seriously out of date." Based on the idea that market share alone is enough to demonstrate monopoly pricing power, the guidelines classify industries by "four-firm concentration ratios," calculated by adding up the market shares of the top four firms in an industry. Then the guidelines spell out precisely what is, and isn't, allowed. For example, a horizontal merger is presumed illegal if, in a market in which the top four have a 75% share, an acquiring firm has 10% of the market and acquires a firm with 2%.

Two Views of 60%

Baxter, like many academic economists, doesn't buy even the guidelines' arithmetic on concentration. He prefers using something called the Herfindahl Index, in which the market shares of the top companies are squared and then added up. The differences can be dramatic. For example, in a market where the top four companies each have 15%, the concentration level is 60%, but it also equals 60% if one company has 57% and the other three have 1% apiece. Four equal shares of 15% would yield a Herfindahl Index of 900, below the "danger point" of 1,000; but a market with one company at 57% and the others at 1% would produce an index of 3,252—worth noticing.

Baxter, who complains of the "talismanic reliance on a limited set of mathematical indicators," obviously won't rely exclusively on Herfindahl. He plans to put horizontal mergers through a number of tests that go beyond the traditional market-share test. Whereas in the past a market share of, say, 10% could by itself trigger scrutiny, now antitrust investigators will have to also ask about such matters as technological innovation in an industry (a fast rate of change is a sign of competition); the rate of sales growth (a rapid rate indicates a market will attract competitors); the amount of risk capital required to enter the industry (low capital requirements suggest ease of entry); the amount of excess capacity in the industry (lots of excess capacity indicates a weak market that could stand more concentration since excess capacity depresses prices); product durability (durable goods such as cars have strong secondary markets that increase competition).

Perhaps the most important factor of all, and the trickiest, is how to define a market. For example, in 1947 the Justice Department alleged that DuPont, with 75% of the cellophane market, was a monopolist. A district court disagreed, noting that DuPont had less than 20% of the wrapping-materials market, and the decision was upheld by the Supreme Court in 1956. In these days of heightened international commerce, the market often must be broadened to include not only product substitutes but also imports. The Federal Trade Commission's concern that the four main U.S. automakers monopolized the market for American cars hardly mattered any longer when foreign makes began taking a quarter of the U.S. car market.

Another Carter Administration concept that is getting short shrift under Baxter's regime is the idea of a "shared monopoly"— where a few companies constituting an oligopoly act in tacit unison as a single monopoly. The FTC accused the breakfast-cereal makers and oil refiners of this, and considered bringing a case against the auto companies until their troubles made such a case look so absurd it had to be dropped.

Tacit collusion is hard to prove. Chicago School scholars are fond of noting that it is hard enough to get companies to collude overtly. A favorite example: in 1971 when the Civil Aeronautics Board allowed airlines to get together to carve up 21 domestic air routes to make them more profitable, the airline executives had trouble raising a quorum. They held meetings on only 13 of the routes, and got agreements on only four.

Clues for Action

Just what actions Baxter and the Reagan Administration will take on some other important issues is still not known. But clues emerge from interviews with those familiar with Baxter's thinking:

THE ROBINSON-PATMAN ACT

Many antitrust scholars, including Baxter, believe the 1936 act, which prohibits price discrimination, probably prevents more competition than it promotes. Chicago School scholars believe a price structure that reflects the economies of high-volume transactions bolsters efficiency. So they favor allowing manufacturers to charge small customers more than big ones—a practice the act was designed to prohibit. Baxter says he won't initiate any move to repeal the law, though he thinks it's an awful piece of legislation. Instead he will ignore the act.

THE FTC'S BUREAU OF COMPETITION

Since 1976, companies with sales of $100 million or more have been required to notify the Bureau of Competition before acquiring another company with sales greater than $10 million. The bureau has effectively halted a number of mergers, particularly those of the conglomerate variety. The Reagan Administration has already tried to eliminate the bureau's budget. And Reagan's appointee to the FTC chairmanship, James Miller, is a conservative economist who now works in the Office of Management and Budget, the outfit that attempted to bankrupt the bureau. In his Senate testimony Miller evaded the question of whether he will move to eliminate the Bureau of Competition. But he called for a "major review" of its function.

Once Miller joins the commission, he will tip the balance on the five-person panel to the Republicans. But any effort to abolish the bureau will meet some opposition from Congressmen, who look on the FTC as their own little antitrust division, beholden to congressional interests rather than those of the White House. It isn't clear that the Administration will have the stomach for the battle.

TREBLE-DAMAGE AWARDS

The Clayton Act awards treble damages to private plaintiffs who bring successful antitrust suits. The law is good for plaintiffs' lawyers, but has made businessmen cautious—afraid to compete vigorously by lowering prices, for example, lest they ignite a flurry of suits against them. Defendants are prone to settle rather than risk the triple whammy of losing in court. Some people in the Justice Department have shown interest in a proposal that would instead award damages plus 10%.

THE IBM CASE

Baxter says it isn't too late to drop the Justice Department's 12-year-old suit. The case charges that once upon a time IBM monopolized the computer market by selling products only in packages and pricing its new equipment below cost. But with the present proliferation of computers, IBM hardly looks like a monopoly. Baxter is now reviewing the case, and it is very likely that he'll drop it. [Ed. note: He did drop it in early 1982; see the next article.]

THE AT&T CASE

This one charges the telephone giant with illegally using its monopoly powers, and the outcome of the suit will decide how, and whether, Ma Bell can compete in the telecommunications market. While AT&T is on hold, a lot of companies eyeing this field, or already in it, are living with a lot of uncertainty. Telephone-equipment makers, data-processing companies, and cable-television systems are finding it hard to plan without knowing what role the giantess will play in the industry. The Commerce Department is fearful that a long, drawn-out case will allow the Japanese to leap ahead in telecommunications.

On general principles, Baxter has no hesitancy about prosecuting AT&T ("to the eyeballs," even) because the case would allow him to attack alleged government-created monopoly power. But the Justice Department is now looking to Congress for a way out of the mess. If Congress passes sound legislation ensuring that AT&T won't overwhelm the new markets with its clout, then Baxter says he will promptly drop the case. [Ed note: In 1982, AT&T agreed to sell off its local telephone service units and operate competitively in long-distance telecommunications.]

OLD ANTITRUST JUDGMENTS

The Antitrust Division is examining certain judgments rendered in the past that prohibit companies from making vertical arrangements or going into new lines of business. The division may ask the courts to drop the judgments and may also try to vacate others that bar corporations from such activities as sharing research without getting permission from the Antitrust Division. Baxter's operation doesn't want that power.

In a nutshell, Baxter's Antitrust Division is putting its faith in the marketplace. And at least one band of scholars would argue it's about time.

10.2   The Antitrusters' Bust at IBM

HARRY ANDERSON, WITH HOWARD FINEMAN, ERIK IPSEN, AND FRANK GIBNEY, JR.

The small group of lawyers for the Justice Department looked glum, but the platoon of elegantly groomed defense attorneys didn't bother to conceal their glee, laughing and slapping each other on the back. Shortly after 4 p.m. last Friday, Federal District Judge David N. Edelstein entered his New York courtroom for yet another hearing of the lengthiest proceeding in the Justice Department's history. The 71-year-old judge, who had spent six years on the case, demanded to know why the government was not represented by its trust-busting chief, Assistant Attorney General William Baxter.

Three times the boyish government attorney, Abbott Lipsky, 32, tried to apologize for his boss's absence—but the angry judge cut him off. Finally Lipsky told Edelstein what he clearly did not want to hear: the government had decided that its chances of success were outweighed by the costs of continuing to prosecute. With that admission, the government's massive antitrust suit against International Business Machines Corp.—the so-called Methuselah case of American jurisprudence—was over.

Mistake: Announced four and a half hours after the Justice Department's settlement with AT&T, its IBM decision represented a semi-graceful retreat from what is widely regarded as the biggest antitrust mistake the government has ever made. The suit was filed on the last business day of the Johnson Administration. It charged that IBM had engaged in illegal acts to achieve and maintain a monopoly in the computer business. Last week, though, antitrust chief Baxter insisted that while there is some indication that IBM had engaged in "bad practices," there was only "flimsy" evidence that those practices had anything to do with maintaining a monopoly.

Regardless of the initial merits of the suit, during the thirteen years that the case droned through the courts, IBM's dominance was challenged on every front. Persistent competition from such aggressive outfits as Control Data, Amdahl, Honeywell and Japan Inc. cut the company's share of the mainframe computer market from about 70 percent in 1969 to an estimated 62 percent today. According to Baxter, even if the government had won its suit, it would have had difficulty deciding how to foster greater competition.

IBM's chief trial attorney, Thomas Barr, hailed the settlement as a "complete vindication" and later suggested that the case itself had been a complete waste of time. The measurable dimensions of the proceeding are awesome enough; 2,500 depositions, 66 million pages of documents and more than 300 lawyers employed on the case at one time or another, plus a small army of IBM paralegal staffers. By one estimate, the direct cost to the government amounted to $13.4 million, but because a company's legal costs are tax deductible, Barr argues that the taxpayers were in fact footing IBM's far greater legal bills, too. The psychological costs were equally taxing: at one point IBM tried to remove Judge Edelstein from the case on the ground that he was personally biased against the company. And no one can say for sure how much business IBM lost to distraction or uncertainty aroused by the suit.

Safety: But the losses were substantial. IBM had to defend itself not only against the Justice Department, but also against competitors whom the government's action prompted to file similar complaints of their own. Although most of the private suits were eventually settled in IBM's favor, the sheer weight of litigation frightened both shareholders and management. Suddenly IBM, famed for its bold marketing and pricing strategies, began to play it safe. Rather than trying to undercut its competitors' prices, it consistently charged more—allowing rivals to move in on IBM's traditional markets and carve out substantial positions of their own.

While new competition would have eventually sprouted as a consequence of exploding technological progress, IBM's lack of aggression accelerated the process. "I'm glad the suit was brought," says Marvin Kosters, head of the American Enterprise Institute's regulatory-analysis group, "and I'm glad it's being dropped. The computer industry appeared threatened in the late 1960s, and it is good to force dominant companies to be extremely careful about what they do. . . . But it is bad to punish successful companies merely because they are a success."

By the late 1970s IBM finally realized how costly its timidity had become and took off its legal gloves. "For the past three years, IBM has been operating as if the Justice Department didn't exist," says Paine Webber analyst Sanford Garrett. In 1979, for example, the company announced a new series of mainframe computers with prices so low that they cut deeply into the profits of competing manufacturers.

New Products: More recently, under the leadership of chief executive John R. Opel, IBM has concentrated on strengthening its marketing network and developing new products. The company has opened a series of "business computer centers" to attract the owners of small businesses, and its new personal computers will be sold through Computerland retail stores and a new chain of specialty outlets being opened by Sears, Roebuck & Co. Aided by a massive advertising program, IBM could soon be selling as many as 350,000 personal computers a year. Many analysts doubt that the antitrust settlement will make IBM's marketing efforts any more aggressive than they already are, but they fully expect the company to begin acquiring other high-technology companies.

Long-range strategies were far from the minds of the 200 lawyers, executives, secretaries and spouses who gathered at New York's glittery Régine's discothèque to sip champagne in celebration of the settlement. "It's like VJ Day back in '45," exclaimed one eleven-year veteran of the case. "Monday some people may have to think about going back to jobs they haven't considered in years." And that could be a sobering experience. Instead of confronting the Justice Department, IBM will have to face the newest behemoth in the computer industry—AT&T. And in that competition, IBM is by no means the odds-on favorite.

10.3 A New Approach to Regulation

LESTER THUROW

Where Do We Go from Here?

If we are to establish a competitive economy within a framework of international trade and international competition, it is time to recognize that the techniques of the nineteenth century are not applicable in getting ready for the twenty-first century. The late nineteenth and early twentieth centuries witnessed a two-pronged effort to create and maintain competitive capitalism. Antitrust laws were developed to break up man-made monopolies, and regulations were developed to make natural monopolies act as if they were competitive. While both of these approaches have had their problems, the time has come to recognize that the antitrust approach has been a failure. The costs it imposes far exceed any benefits it brings.

The futility and obsolescence of the antitrust laws can be seen from a number of vantage points. First, with the growth of international trade it is no longer possible to determine whether an effective monopoly exists by looking at local market shares. Regardless of the share of domestic production held by General Motors, General Motors is part of a competitive industry and must deal with strong Japanese and European competitors. In markets where international trade exists or could exist, national antitrust laws no longer make sense. If they do anything, they only serve to hinder U.S. competitors who must live by a code that their foreign competitors can ignore.

One could debate whether international antitrust laws would make sense, but this debate would be completely irrelevant from a practical perspective. In the absence of anything resembling world government, and in the presence of widely differing views on the usefulness of antitrust legislation, no enforceable, international antitrust laws are going to come into existence.

If competitive markets are desired, the appropriate policy should be to reduce barriers to free trade. Whatever good competitive effects the antitrust laws have had on the behavior of the U.S. steel industry, they are completely dominated by the bad competitive effects of the reference price system designed to keep foreign steel out of the United States. Whatever good competitive effects the antitrust laws may have had on the behavior of U.S. auto makers, they are small in comparison with the competitive pressures brought by Japanese and European automobile producers. If one measures the potential gains to be made by enforcing the antitrust laws, as opposed to reducing real barriers to international trade, it is clear that the large gains exist in the area of more international competition.

Second, as incomes rise it becomes less and less clear as to what is the relevant market to determine whether a firm has acquired a monopolistic position. Most goods we buy are not physiological necessities but luxuries that could be substituted by other goods to produce just as high a real standard of living. Rolls Royces and Volkswagens are both cars, but the two products are in no sense competitive. For those who buy an expensive car, the real trade-off may be with a swimming pool, a summer home, or a wide variety of other products. Rolls Royce may have a virtual monopoly position in the production of very expensive cars yet still not have a position it can exploit. If it prices its product too high, people will shift to different products.

As an illustration of the same problem at the other end of the price spectrum, consider the antitrust case in the breakfast cereals business. Let us assume that a few companies have established an oligopolistic position with respect to dry breakfast cereals and are charging more than would be charged in a competitive market. Since any individual consumer can, if she or he chooses, buy no-name brand corn flakes at a much lower price, the brand names must be yielding some psychic utility or brand name corn flakes would not be sold. Consumers may have been convinced of this psychic utility because of advertising, but so what? At the income level of most Americans, most wants have been determined by some explicit or implicit form of advertising. Physiological needs determine very few of our expenditure decisions. Individual consumers may be making silly decisions (buying products at prices higher than they need to pay), but it is hardly the appropriate role of government, much less the antitrust laws, to stop people from making silly decisions that do not affect anyone but themselves.

But let's suppose that the no-name brands did not exist. Since corn flakes are hardly a unique, patented, hard-to-produce product, the absence of no-name brand corn flakes could only mean that individuals are willing to pay for having brand-name corn flakes. People are allowed to pay for the brand labels of clothing designers. Why stop brand labels here? If the brand premium gets too large, others can easily enter the no-name brand corn flakes market. But even if no-name brand corn flakes could not be produced, there are still a great deal of other breakfast alternatives (bacon and eggs, no breakfast). These other products make the market a competitive market even if there is no competition within the dry cereals business.

Third, monopoly rents are inherently limited in an economy full of large conglomerate firms. Since established market positions are usually easier to defend than to create, oligopolistic firms may be able to extract a small price premium from their customers, but this ability is inherently limited by the ability of other large firms to enter the market. Excessive rates of return attract competitors, and potential competitors have the ability to enter all those markets that are not natural monopolies. While the conglomerate movement may have lumped activities together that are not the most efficient sets of activities to be lumped together (to the same extent this is a product of the antitrust laws), it has also created a set of large firms that scan a wide range of products and markets to search for profitable investments. Firms with no actual or potential competitors are few and far between. As a result, this apparent monopolistic position is actually vulnerable from both the demand and supply side of the market. Potential customers have alternative uses for their incomes and potential competitors are almost always waiting in the wings if profits appear too high.

Fourth, it is not obvious that anything of economic value is accomplished even if an antitrust case is won by the government. Consider the current IBM case. Suppose the government were to win and IBM were to be broken into three or four large firms (an outcome that is highly unlikely given recent antitrust experience). What characteristics of the industry would change? By now we should have enough experience to know that a three- or four-firm oligopoly does not act noticeably different from a one-firm monopoly faced with potential competition (the Japanese) in its main business and actual competition where it is weak (in small computers).

If you look at other industries where antitrust laws have resulted in the creation of new competitors (oil and aluminum) or where they have stopped inefficient producers from being absorbed by competitors (steel and autos), it is hard to argue that these industries are more efficient or less competitive than the computer industry. IBM has driven other large firms out of the industry (GE and RCA) through being able to provide a better product. If the case were to succeed, the most likely winners would not be computer customers but foreign computer manufacturers. No one questions that IBM has a dominant market position. But this is not to say that it has been able to extract crippling monopoly rents from computer customers. In some ways the case reads like a government sign saying, ''It does not pay to be too efficient.'' Yet in a larger context, this is certainly a slogan that we do not wish to issue if we are interested in long-run efficiency.

Fifth, the whole antitrust vision springs from a very narrow view of competition. Competition means price competition—nothing more and nothing less. Yet price is clearly only one of the many competitive weapons (advertising, product quality, and so forth) and in many areas not the most useful or used weapon. We have a vision in the backs of our minds that if we only create enough firms, firms will be driven to price competition and have to abandon other forms of competition.

There are several problems with this vision. Even if it were true, the required number of firms is so much larger than the number that would be created by an antitrust ''win'' that it has no relevance to antitrust legislation. But more fundamentally, it is not true. There are many industries with thousands of small-scale producers (real estate agents, lawyers, doctors, specialty shops) who do not compete based on price. Many customers would rather shop in elegant surroundings than buy at the lowest possible price.

Shopping and the thrill of being enticed may be a major part of the enjoyment of buying goods and services. To look simply at the degree of price competition in the economy is to grossly underestimate the degree of real competition in the economy.

Somehow lurking in the backs of our minds is the puritan idea that if we could only strip away advertising, fancy surroundings, nonessential product characteristics, and the attractive salespersons, we would get back to true preferences that would create more enjoyment. Most of us think that we are clever enough to avoid being duped into doing anything that we do not really want to do, yet we think that we must act to protect someone else from being led astray. Why? Let me suggest that there is no reason. Nonprice forms of competition are just as useful and valid as price competition. When industries do not engage in price competition, there usually is a perfectly good reason (other than monopoly) as to why they do not. It simply isn't the most efficient way to compete. As a result, we are not going to restore price competition and puritan simplicity through the antitrust laws.

Given our modern economic environment, antitrust regulations should be stripped back to two basic propositions. The first would be a ban on predatory pricing. Large firms should not be allowed to drive small firms out of business by selectively lowering their prices in submarkets while they maintain high prices in other submarkets. The second proposition would be a ban on explicit or implicit cartels that share either markets or profits. Firms can grow by driving competitors out of business or by absorbing them, but they cannot agree not to compete with each other.

Discussion and Review Questions

1. Briefly summarize the key points of American antitrust law. What activities of a firm are illegal under the law?

2. What is the "rule of reason"? How was it applied indirectly in the recent IBM antitrust decision?

3. In what ways did the Reagan administration change the direction of antitrust law? How do you react to the new direction emerging in Washington?

4. Do you believe the government's action in the IBM case was (a) consistent with antitrust law and (b) in the public's best interest? Comment.

5. How do you react to Thurow's argument that antitrust activities should be reduced to two simple legal rules? What are these legal tests?

6. How do you respond to the following statement: "What we need is more competition and that can only be obtained if we break up the giant firms and make the big boys little boys once again."

ISSUE 11

How Much Deregulation Is Desirable?

The question of government intervention in the various affairs of business naturally enough sparks much debate. As we shall see, there is considerable division of opinion among business leaders on this issue.

Basically, such disagreements reflect deep philosophical divisions. Those who generally identify themselves as "conservative" hold to the view that the least government is the best government. This group identifies closely with the traditional capitalist philosophy of relying upon the market to direct the social system (see issue 1). Those who more or less defend the extension of government into business and the marketplace usually are called "liberal." They hold that government is necessary to correct and offset the undesirable outcomes that often develop in a free economy.

Past "Tolerance" of Government Intervention

While it might be expected that all "true believers" in the American business system hold to a conservative view of the economic world, this simply is not true. Opinion surveys of business leaders regularly reveal a fairly tolerant attitude toward the growth of government in the economy. In general, American businesspeople have accepted the broad outlines of a "mixed economy." Few oppose, as a simple matter of principle, government's general activities in maintaining the economy's overall performance, policing market activities, and protecting the poor and wretched. In fact, many recognize that government's overall role in the economy is quite supportive of business enterprise.

Government, in the nineteenth century, provided handsome subsidies to build canals and railroads, was an important purchaser of business's products, protected businesses from strikers and from overseas revolutions, and provided liberal tariffs to protect American manufacturers. Even today, when "conflict" supposedly characterizes business–government affairs, billions are appropriated annually to build roads and power projects, to develop harbors, to subsidize a wide variety of firms ranging from small businesses and farmers to airlines and defense contractors, and to insure the operations of banking and financial institutions. Tariffs are still employed to keep out the goods of foreign competitors.

Recent Rising Opposition

The "liberal" tendencies of most business leaders to accept the "mixed economy," however, have been sorely tested in recent years. Many see the interventionism of the past couple of decades as going too far. As a consequence, a large part of the business community was attracted to the deregulation movement that was a central feature of Ronald Reagan's "supply-side" economic program. "Getting government off business's back" became a powerful and persuasive slogan in the early 1980s. Although a few business spokespersons criticize all areas of government protection activities as unnecessary and costly (to consumers as well as business), the primary targets are certain consumer affairs activities, environmental protection, and job safety.

CONSUMER AFFAIRS

Government involvement in consumer affairs is a mixed bag. In the areas of protective labeling and packaging, food inspection, expanded product information, and credit protection, most business leaders would admit that benefits have developed for consumers and producers alike. In these cases the law is clear and little government bureaucracy exists. However, where government agencies such as the FTC (Federal Trade Commission), the CPSC (Consumer Product Safety Commission), the NHTSA (National Highway Transportation Safety Administration), and the FDA (Food and Drug Administration) can require long delays in reviewing business practices or can suddenly change the direction or interpretation of past agency policies, consumer protection is viewed as being clearly antibusiness.

ENVIRONMENTALISM

Without a doubt, the EPA (Environmental Protection Agency) has been a special thorn in business's side. Industries' complaints generally are directed toward the agency's excessive zeal in enforcing the letter of the law or even going beyond the law in setting standards. The costs of meeting these standards have been staggering. Irving Shapiro, DuPont's chairman, has estimated that, through 1985, 30 percent of his firm's capital budget will go for pollution controls. Worse still, Shapiro argues that only a quarter of these expenditures actually will improve the environment, the rest being "inflationary and unproductive."

The burden of environmental protection falls unevenly on different types of industries and upon firms located in different areas. Paper companies such as Scott are hit harder ($24 million on one facility alone) than "clean" product assembly plants. Chicago-based firms get much more EPA attention than those based in Phoenix. The effect of EPA controls has been to close as many as 200 major production plants in the United States over the past decade. Moreover, operating costs have risen dramatically. Nevertheless, despite the loss of jobs and the adverse impact on prices of consumer goods, public support for environmental protection has remained strong, especially among young Americans. A recent study by Resources for the Future found that 53 percent of Americans believe that "protecting the environment is so important that requirements and standards cannot be too high and continuing improvements must be made regardless of cost."

Undoubtedly some rules may be relaxed in a sluggish economy to help certain distressed industries, such as automobiles. However, concern for the environment will not go away soon. Business can expect to be required to pay the environmental bill as long as the majority of citizens demand it.

JOB SAFETY

In the area of occupational safety, many businesspeople and not a small number of workers believe that OSHA (Occupational Safety and Health Administration) has caused more trouble than it has cured. Its mandatory approach to job safety rules has discouraged many industries from following their own voluntary programs. Thus, some employers and workers argue safety has not been improved. Statistics seem to bear this out. Since 1976, on-the-job fatalities and injuries have increased annually despite (some would say because of) OSHA's efforts. Moreover, expensive OSHA job requirements have forced the closing of many plants and doubtless increased national unemployment. Some experts argue that as many as half a million Americans are clearly safer as a result of OSHA's rulings—they are out of work.

OSHA still is supported by organized labor and by reform-minded members of Congress; however, the agency has been the favorite target of those urging deregulation in the economy. Its bureaucratic bungling and its nonrecord of success invites attack.

THE OLD REGULATORY AGENCIES

Another target of deregulation has been the older government agencies created specifically to control prices and competition in particular industries. The most venerable of these is the Interstate Commerce Commission—regulator of railroads since 1887 and buses and trucking since 1935. Other such federal regulatory agencies include the Civil Aeronautics Board (air transport), the Federal Power Commission (electric and natural gas transmission) and the Federal Communications Commission (telephone, radio, and TV transmission). Set up originally to establish federal control over financing, pricing, and conditions of service so as to maintain "the public interest," these agencies have seen their authority shrink. The new deregulation trend is toward reducing government intervention in all of these areas, maintaining that the public is best served by the market.

New Directions?

Taken together, these current trends obviously amount to rethinking not only comparatively recent expansions of government in the marketplace but also some long-held practices of using government to balance public and private interests. We are left to ponder a difficult question: What is the proper balance between government intervention on the behalf of special groups—consumers, workers, the environment—and the interests of private enterprise?

When Adam Smith laid down his arguments on behalf of a capitalist economic system in *The Wealth of Nations* (1776), he saw competitive pricing as the ultimate protector of all in the society. The market would be "the great regulator." There would be no need for public laws to protect individual interests if the market worked properly. Only goods that consumers desired would be purchased, and prices would be determined by consumers' willingness and ability to buy. Shortages would drive up prices, and gluts would drive them down. Wages, too, would be set by the laws of supply and demand. Costs and damages to third parties (e.g., the environment) were not a matter of concern at all.

The first article faithfully reports this conservative view as it attacks the "market interference of the Federal Trade Commission." Written before the Reagan victory in 1980, it reflects the strong antiregulation bias that became an important feature of the Reagan administration. The second piece argues that the drift into "decontrol" during the Reagan years is a dangerous trend, especially with regard to the environment. The third article offers the trucking industry as a recent case study of deregulation. It indicates that business is not of one mind in supporting deregulation.

11.1 Restraining the Regulators

DOUG BANDOW

Over the past century, a tide of bureaucratic tyranny has swept over the U.S., depositing an alphabet-soup conglomeration of federal agencies—ICC, FTC, FDA, CAB, EEOC, EPA, OSHA, CPSC—upon the average businessman and citizen.

However, this overregulation of American life, with its estimated $100 billion annual cost in money and inestimable cost in liberty, has sparked an even stronger tide of anger and resentment *against* government, a tide that is threatening now to overwhelm the Federal Trade Commission (FTC).

The FTC, a $60 million agency with some 1,750 employees, was created in 1914; its power has steadily expanded over the years. It is now divided into three bureaus: Consumer Protection (advertising and business practices), Competition (antitrust), and Economics (industry reports).

In 1969, the American Bar Association (ABA) concluded that the FTC should either be reformed or abolished. This and other criticism led to a drastic overhaul of the commission in the early '70s, changing its personnel, redirecting its purpose, and expanding its power.

The commission's activist revival was strengthened by the 1977 appointment of Michael Pertschuk, a former aide to Senator Warren Magnuson, as FTC chairman. Pertschuk pledged to be "bold, innovative, and risk-taking." And it is for risky innovations that the FTC has since invited attack.

Its most dramatic initiative is its proposal to regulate children's advertising, which one industry lobbyist called, with little overstatement, "perhaps the most blatant example ever of unsubstantiated bureaucratic overreaching and misuse of investigative power."

Indeed, it is this rule-making proceeding that has crystallized the opposition to the FTC, since, according to University of Virginia law professor Ernest Gellhorn, this "worst case provides a virtual catalog of the deficiencies often argued to be present in other FTC actions: a confused and confusing program is proposed even though it is inadequately supported and may be beyond the agency's authority or, for that matter, government's responsible role; although the rule is likely to have a profound impact on an industry, that possibility is not seriously evaluated and the proposal is passed with emotion and enthusiasm but with little attention to the basic requirements of fair play."

The FTC staff, in its 346-page report, recommended that all TV ads directed at children under the age of eight be banned; all ads for sugared products directed at children under the age of twelve be banned; and advertisers of highly sugared products be forced to fund health and nutritional messages.

The proposals are unprecedented, since the FTC is not dealing with advertising that can in itself be called deceptive. (The agency once tried to force Canada Dry to change its trade mark, as deceptively implying that its products were made in Canada.) Rather, the alleged problem, for which the advertisers would be held responsible, lies with those who are *receiving* the advertising.

The proposed regulations are built upon the claim that children are not sophisticated enough to understand the selling purpose of the ads. This contention is dubious at best—the evidence suggests that children are quite skeptical about advertisements.

More important, banning ads would trample over freedom of speech, and expressly empower bureaucrats to decide what information people were able to "cope with," and therefore what information they would, and would not, be permitted to receive. Indeed, the regulations would be an open invitation for the government to attempt to be a guardian for anyone else who the bureaucrats believe, because of excessive trust, gullibility, or naiveté, is incapable of making the "right" decisions.

The proposed rules also would interfere with the ability of children to develop, and of parents to guide the child's development. Indeed, banning ads would arbitrarily over-"protect" children from the real world, causing other problems.

Moreover, the real receivers of the advertising are the parents—they are the ones who actually buy the toys, decide on the meals, and control the use of the television set. They, and not some officious public intermeddlers, are uniquely qualified to judge the individual needs, desires, and sophistication of their own children, and to respond accordingly.

Banning ads for sugar products is even more ludicrous. Ads, of course, do not cause tooth decay or malnutrition—inadequate dental care and bad eating habits do. If individuals are no longer responsible for eating sugared foods, then presumably they are no longer responsible for eating cholesterol or salt-rich foods, or using risky products, such as motorcycles. Thus, the logical next step would be to suppress virtually every form of commercial expression that encourages anything one of our self-proclaimed guardians thinks is bad for us (and indeed, petitions have already been filed with the FTC to ban advertising of salted foods, ice cream, and hamburgers).

The final proposal, to require sugar-food companies to fund "good nutrition" ads is also unfair, since the companies do not cause nutritional problems and have no responsibility to tell individuals what to eat. Indeed, the principle could as easily be applied to ice cream producers and car manufacturers.

This arrogant elitism—the belief that those anointed by God to protect the rest of us should have the power to mold us into their own image—and its threatening assault on freedom of choice and speech are not confined to children's TV ads, however. . . .

The FTC has also angered many groups by attempting to control their business practices. For example, it originally proposed industry-wide rules for the funeral industry, including detailed disclosure and price itemization standards, as well as requirements to give information over the phone and not to disparage cheaper merchandise.

The commission finally dropped these proposals last spring. Chairman Pertschuk later admitted that some FTC staffers had had a "vendetta" against the funeral industry.

Similarly, the FTC has sought to control the business practices of the used-car market. The suggested rules, five years in the making, would require that dealers display information on an automobile's condition and defects, estimated costs of repair, prior ownership and uses, and warranties, if any.

These rules are a reaction to what the FTC estimates are the approximately 10 percent of the consumers who have trouble with used cars, trouble ranging from undisclosed defects to misunderstandings over warranties (and for which there are other legal remedies). Thus, the added cost of inspection and disclosure—estimates of which range from $15 to $30 according to the consumer-oriented Center for Auto Safety, through 3 to 4 percent of the vehicle's cost according to the FTC, to $200 to $600 according to used car dealers—would be involuntarily added to *everyone's* bill.

Moreover, most used car dealers, who depend upon reputation and credibility to build up a clientele, already list defects and offer warranties. It is this pressure, not federal rules that may be circumvented by the dishonest, that best protects consumers. But the FTC's staff report specifically attacked the idea of dealers relying upon reputation, despite its competitive value for consumers. . . .

The FTC has also pursued, since 1972, a unique antitrust attack on the three major cereal companies—Kellogg Co., General Foods, and General Mills—that account for 82 percent of the cereal sold. The FTC is seeking either to break them up or to license their major brand names to competitors. These companies were chosen for political reasons—former FTC staffer Charles E. Mueller has admitted, ''I didn't pick the auto or petroleum industry because they have too much political clout. The cereal industry didn't have the political muscle to muddy the water.''

There is no evidence of company misconduct; the FTC is simply claiming that the companies maintain a ''shared monopoly'' through product proliferation (providing consumers with more choices) and advertising (providing consumers with more information). Thus, the companies are to be punished for being *too successful*. They have satisfied the demands of a diverse population for many goods at low cost, but the FTC has decided that more companies, though perhaps with fewer products at a higher cost, is what Americans really need, and therefore will have. . . .

Finally, Pertschuk has talked of resuscitating the Robinson-Patman Act, which has lain dormant over the past decade. Termed ''horrendous'' by Gellhorn, this statute basically prevents ''price discrimination,'' that is, selling similar goods for different prices to different customers. Since this Act actually contradicts the Sherman Antitrust Act, no one can do business at all without violating one law or the other. This makes *all* businessmen into lawbreakers, and which ones the FTC wishes to prosecute can therefore be selected by arbitrary standards.

The FTC has also consistently conducted media trials of businesses. Chicago economist Yale Brozen notes, "The FTC has come up with the technique of unilaterally deciding what is deceptive, conducting a trial by press release, and demanding that the advertisers run ads admitting the deception. The burden of proving innocence is left to the advertiser, if he can survive the trial by . . . accusation and publicity—a complete turnabout from our judicial system, in which an accused is regarded as innocent until proven guilty."

Not infrequently, the FTC is found to be wrong; however, the publicity war can be devastating. In the summer of 1978, the FTC released a disputed evaluation of whole-life insurance, which greatly affected some companies' sales. Insurance companies found it hard to present their side of the controversy.

And among the most abused practices has been the FTC's information requests, some of which even the FTC admits were both costly and vague. According to the *Wall Street Journal*, "[t]he Commission's famous 'fishing expeditions' . . . [depart] freely from the legal principle that subpoenas should state clearly what law violation has allegedly occurred. The agency has had a great appetite for the private files of the private sector in its search for litigation and publicity."

Finally, the FTC spends hundreds of thousands of taxpayer dollars to fund an intervener program, under which representatives of the "public interest" (primarily those who agree with the commission) are paid to testify before it. For example, the FTC paid $336,000 to witnesses who favored restricting children's advertising.

These and other abuses have created an army of adversaries intent upon controlling the commission. Judicial scrutiny is being increased; Gellhorn notes that "surprising numbers" of the FTC's actions are being reversed on appeal, and "judicial confidence in commission processes is at a low ebb." One example of this heightened scrutiny is District Court Judge Gerhard A. Gesell's decision barring Pertschuk from further regulation of children's advertising because of his predetermined position. Though overturned on appeal, the higher court did uphold review for such bias.

However, the most significant attack on the FTC has occurred in Congress, where the FTC's disparate opponents have coalesced to create tremendous pressure for restricting the FTC. In fact, the FTC has been getting along on only interim funding for two years, because of continuous, though then unsuccessful, attempts to regulate it.

The funding bill adopted late this spring imposes a variety of controls, which fall into two categories. The first consists of an amalgam of a dozen specific restrictions, such as halting rule-making proceedings on children's advertising and the auto industry, stripping the FTC of authority to cancel a trademark or take antitrust action against agricultural co-ops, and restricting the FTC's use of the subpoena. The second allows a congressional veto of any FTC rule or industry-wide decision.

These restrictive measures have won support even within the liberal, consumer-oriented, community—from Senator George McGovern, for example—and they present an important opportunity to rethink the entire concept of a "national nanny."

Private codes of conduct can, and do, protect consumers. For example, the Television Code of the National Association of Broadcasters regulates—voluntarily—the conduct of broadcasters. Indeed, the industry itself has reacted to the pressure from the anti-children's advertising groups by prohibiting host-selling (where the star plugs the product), cutting the volume of children's advertising, and controlling the advertisement of vitamins, toys, and certain foods.

But the greatest protection for the consumer comes from competition, with the incentive to expose any fraudulent and inaccurate claims of competitors. Former FTC commissioner Lowell Mason reflected on his experience with complaints of false advertising: "For the most part, the government wins because competition fights its battle for it. The greatest protection against false claims is the rivalry among merchants for the consumer's dollar."

Of note is a 1973 survey by the Marketing Sciences Institute, which found that 64 percent of the public preferred private solutions (consumer activities, consumers individually, and business) compared to 19 percent who preferred government solutions, when asked which group should be primarily responsible for getting consumers a fair deal. In fact, consumer activists and government consumer affairs personnel also prefer private solutions, by margins of 62 percent to 27 percent and 50 percent to 35 percent, respectively.

The FTC has become a force unto itself—lawmaker, prosecutor, jury, judge, and parole officer—busily substituting the personal whims of its officials for the decisions of consumers. Indeed, what these officials seem to detest most is individualism, diversity, and a competitive system that allows people to succeed. It is time to consider abolishing this run-away bureaucracy. Its attempts to control our lives make it a greater menace than anything which it purports to protect us from.

11.2   Laissez-faire Landscape

RUSSELL W. PETERSON

The crystal ball I am gazing into is murky, not from the cloudiness usually associated with crystal balls, but from polluted air.

The year is 1990. The darkest fears of environmentalists have been realized. Ronald Reagan, elected for a second term in 1984, was able to complete his program of "regulatory reform" before riding off into the smog-shrouded sunset. His public-lands policies have been fully carried out. His "New Federalism" is firmly in place. Environmental protection laws are less stringent; agencies charged with implementing the laws have been reduced in size and scope, and actions needed to address pollution and resource problems have been largely deferred.

My crystal ball shows that acid rain is causing widespread ecological disruption. By 1990, the sulfuric and nitric acids formed in the atmosphere from industrial and auto pollutants, causing acid rain, have sterilized 273 additional lakes in New York State's Adirondack Park and killed the forests of red spruce that once cloaked the mountains' upper slopes. But the problem of acid rain is no longer just a regional one as in the 1970's, when the first serious damage in this country was being documented in northern New York.

The lakes and forests of Maine, Vermont and New Hampshire are suffering the same fate. The Appalachians, Rockies, Sierra Nevadas and northern Cascades, the lake country of Minnesota and Wisconsin, the north woods of Michigan's Upper Peninsula, and the reservoir containing the drinking water for Boston have all been stricken. To the north, in Ontario, 10,000 lakes are now dead; 40,000 more are expected to succumb by the year 2000. In Nova Scotia, 18 rivers that once teemed with spawning salmon are devoid of all fish.

The same sulfur emissions from power plants and smelters that cause acid rain have also aggravated respiratory and heart disease in many Americans. The number of premature deaths attributed to sulfur-related air pollution in the United States and Canada was estimated at 51,000 a year by the Congressional Office of Technology Assessment in 1982; instead of being reduced through mandated use of the best available pollution controls, that number has increased by several thousand annually as a direct result of the Reagan Administration's policy of regulatory relaxation.

The nationwide decline in air quality is most dramatic in the wide-open spaces of the West, where a 78 percent increase in sulfur-dioxide emissions has turned the Big Sky Country of Montana into the Dirty Sky Country. For half the days of the year, smog now blankets the Grand Canyon.

After an eight-year relaxation of Federal strip-mining controls, the Appalachian landscapes of Virginia, West Virginia and Kentucky resemble a battlefield where local residents and nature have taken a terrible beating. Mountain tops have been removed to get at the coal. Wastes have been dumped down mountainsides. Streams are clogged with sediment. Acid drainage has contaminated wells. Landslides frequently dam streams and cause flooding in the hollows. Many families, even entire communities, have been forced to move.

Our national forests have also changed. Logging activity has doubled since 1980. What remained of the virgin forests, and the complex communities of life that they supported, has been largely replaced (where reforestation was feasible) with single-species tree farms. Elsewhere, steep mountainsides lie bare and eroded, centuries of accumulated soil and decayed matter on forest floors having washed into streams that previously supported trout, small-mouth bass and annual runs of salmon.

What was left of unprotected wilderness in the lower 48 states (23.5 million acres of wild lands had statutory protection in 1982, but 36.7 million acres did not) has now been criss-crossed with logging roads and thus permanently disqualified—by dint of no longer being "roadless areas"—for inclusion in the wilderness preservation system.

Our National Park and Wildlife Refuge Systems, as envisioned by Congress in the 1970's, will remain forever incomplete. Many of the hundreds of thousands of acres once slated for permanent protection as new parks and refuges—or needed to round out existing units in the system—have been lost to development. Meanwhile, full-scale economic activity on the National Wildlife Refuges, such as logging, grazing and mining, has taken precedence over the original and primary purpose of these Federal sanctuaries: wildlife and habitat protection.

Because of changes in the Clean Water Act regulations, by 1990 some six million acres of formerly protected wetlands will have been drained and converted to soybean cultivation, housing developments and other commercial uses. Many species of birds, fish, reptiles and mammals that are dependent on wetland habitats have suffered severe declines in numbers, to the dismay of hunters, fishermen and birders.

President Reagan's crash program to open up the entire Outer Continental Shelf for oil and gas drilling has resulted in a scattering of new wells and a modest (and temporary) increase in domestic oil and gas production. But the price of not considering the full consequences of energy development in offshore areas has been high. Chronic oil leakage and several major oil spills have seriously affected Alaska's commercial fishing, marine mammals such as the bowhead whale and waterfowl.

The energy picture in 1990 is not bright. By stressing fossil fuels and nuclear power while ignoring the potential of the sun's renewable energy and the savings to be gained from more efficient use of energy, the Reagan Administration has set the country back a decade in its pursuit of energy independence. A comment made to me and other environmental leaders by the President's counselor, Edwin Meese 3d, at a White House meeting back in 1982, has returned to haunt the country.

"What can a few windmills do?" Mr. Meese asked, when we had pressed the case for solar energy.

Indeed, an Audubon energy study showed that we could have been meeting one-quarter of our national energy requirements with solar power, and with greater energy efficiency, by the year 2000. Now, in 1990, our crystal ball shows, that vital goal, on which our economic health and national security depends, is still almost two decades away.

Of course, crystal-ball gazing is not an exact science, and the foregoing, based on the best available projections, are estimates, not ironclad predictions. But the exercise does reveal some of what *could* happen if all the Administration's environmental policies were carried through to completion. However, my crystal ball has not taken into account the strong public support for environmental protection and the growing opposition to the Administration's efforts to weaken legislative protection of our air, land, water and wildlife, as reflected, for example, in a 1981 Harris poll that showed 80 percent of those questioned wanted a strong clean-air act. If that opposition continues to grow, I believe this worst-case scenario will not become reality.

Nor is the Reagan Administration's environmental record entirely negative. The Administration, including James G. Watt, the Secretary of the Interior, supported taxsaving measures that will help protect pristine barrier islands off our coasts from development; backed an international ban, to begin in 1985, on commercial whaling, and helped to stop Federal spending for a hydroelectric dam that would needlessly flood vast forested areas in northern Maine and destroy what many consider the finest wild river in the eastern United States, the St. John.

Overall, however, Ronald Reagan gets an F when it comes to the environment. No other President in my experience has seemed to be less caring about the need to protect the nation's natural beauty and natural resources, less aware that over the long run a sound economy depends on a healthy environment. No President has seemed less concerned about the quality of life we pass on to future generations.

President Reagan has cut environmental programs more vigorously than almost any other part of his budget. He has filled key environmental posts with people who have previously worked against environmental regulations. In an approach that seems more radical than conservative, Mr. Reagan has repudiated what I hold to be a Republican tradition of conservation and protection of natural resources that goes back to Theodore Roosevelt.

During the transition from President Jimmy Carter to Mr. Reagan, some of the nation's most respected and influential Republican environmentalists served on a task force that had been asked by the President-elect to make recommendations for an environmental program. The task force sought to maintain the momentum of environmental protection while allowing for some easing of regulation and for economic incentives for pollution control.

Its report was ignored. The Administration listened instead to the recommendations of the Heritage Foundation, an extremely conservative research group, which proposed all-out offshore oil development, transfer of Federal lands to the states and the private sector, a reduction in air-quality controls and faster licensing of nuclear power plants. These recommendations fit in better, apparently, with the new President's determination to "get government off the backs" of the states and to "restore balance" to the Federal regulatory system.

Balance, however, is in the eye of the beholder.

Starting in 1962 with the publication of Rachel Carson's "Silent Spring," the American public has become increasingly alarmed by growing contamination of our environment.

Moving to correct the imbalance, Congress passed the first air- and water-pollution control acts and then, in 1969, the National Environmental Policy Act, which declared a Federal intention to encourage "harmony between man and his environment." During the Nixon, Ford and Carter Administrations, a series of laws was passed to achieve this goal. Together, these measures add up to one of the great bipartisan legislative achievements of the 20th century, and they serve as a model for other countries trying to balance material progress with environmental quality.

Our air and rivers and lakes gradually became cleaner in many parts of the nation. Thousands of acres of parkland and wilderness—remnants of our magnificent natural heritage—were preserved for present and future enjoyment.

The free-enterprise system responded to the new market for clean air and clean water. Laboratories and factories produced the processes and products to meet the demand, and hundreds of new companies, providing hundreds of thousands of new jobs, were created.

The natural balance between human beings and the rest of nature, thrown out of whack by a century of rapid industrial expansion and population growth, was beginning to be restored.

All this has abruptly changed, however, with the arrival of a new Administration that regards environmental regulation as nonproductive and as a drain on the economy. Vice President George Bush, chairman of Mr. Reagan's Task Force on Regulatory Relief, vowed to reduce environmental restraints in order to "increase productivity and provide more jobs."

Yet a study in 1979 by the Council on Environmental Quality, which advises the President and Federal agencies on environmental issues, showed that the benefits of measured improvement in air quality since 1970 could be valued at $21.4 billion a year. Of this total, $17 billion represented reductions in death and disease; $2 billion reductions in cleaning costs; $700 million increases in agricultural output; $900 million prevention of corrosion and other materials damage, and $800 million increased property values. By 1985, benefits from water-pollution control would be worth $12.3 billion annually—not to mention the billions of dollars saved by avoiding crop damage and lost workdays, and the value of human lives prolonged and human suffering prevented.

A study of the Environmental Protection Agency estimated that 524,000 jobs would be created by 1987 if existing environmental standards were maintained. In 1981, the E.P.A. estimated the total employment in water-pollution control at 220,000 (half of these jobs in the private sector), and the Department of the Interior estimated that more than 120,000 people were employed in air-pollution control.

The federally funded Solar Energy Research Institute, whose funds were sharply cut by the Reagan budget ax, had reported last year that a concerted national effort to improve energy efficiency and to increase the use of renewable power could, over the next two decades, help the country "achieve a full-employment economy and increased worker productivity, while reducing national energy consumption by nearly 25 percent." The Industrial Union Department of the A.F.L.-C.I.O. estimated that 600,000 new jobs could be created by 1990 in the conservation and solar industries.

On the other hand, the cost of environmental controls was estimated by the Council on Environmental Quality in 1978 to be $26.9 billion. Employers have reported that a total of 32,611 workers have lost their jobs because of environmental laws, according to an E.P.A. survey earlier this year.

Richard Kazis and Richard L. Grossman point out in their new book "Fear at Work: Job Blackmail, Labor and the Environment" (Pilgrim Press) that many more jobs have been created by the national cleanup than have been eliminated by it. The net gain in employment is probably even greater than indicated, since some of the reported "lost jobs" resulted from plant closings for which Federal air-pollution restrictions were blamed, but where the basic problems turned out to be obsolescence and poor management.

But the Reagan Administration has chosen to ignore these findings and to reject the lessons of the past. Instead, this new team of top national officials professes an abiding faith that environmental problems, from cancer-causing asbestos in schoolrooms to wetlands losses in the Mississippi Valley to strip-mining abuses in Appalachia, can best be solved by allowing the private sector to operate without Federal restraint. Whatever environmental regulation is necessary, this doctrine holds, should be the business of state and local governments—even though it was the very failure of state and local governments to assume this responsibility that necessitated a Federal regulatory role in the first place. . . .

The Reagan Administration has, paradoxically, given the environmental movement a shot in the arm. During and after the Sierra Club's successful campaign to gather a million signers on "Dump Watt" petitions, the club's membership jumped from 180,000 to 320,000. The Wilderness Society has pulled out of a long slump, its membership growing by almost 50 percent, to more than 60,000, since the new Administration arrived. The National Audubon Society raised nearly $1 million in its 1981 appeal to members—10 times the response of the previous year—in a letter that called for a Citizen Mobilization Campaign, which is now working to counteract the Administration's assault on the environment.

The nation's leading environmental organizations have banded together to meet the current challenge. Earlier this year, 10 national organizations issued a report titled "Indictment: The Case Against the Reagan Environmental Record," laying out 220 charges of actions detrimental to the nation. A follow-up investigation has just been completed which identifies scores of specific cases of "trickle-down" environmental damage in states and communities around the country. . . .

I began with a worst-case scenario foreseeing a polluted, unhealthy country eight years from now. But the future is really up to us. The kind of environment we insist upon is the one that we and our descendants will get.

11.3 Rocky Regulation Road for Truckers

THOMAS L. FRIEDMAN

It happened to the airlines and now it is happening to the truckers. Deregulation, coupled with a downturn in the economy, has thrown the once-utility-like American trucking industry skidding into a wholly new world and has touched off a price war that makes the competition between airlines seem like light-hearted jousting among friends.

Some of the oldest names in trucking have gone by the wayside, while 5,122 new truck companies have registered with the Interstate Commerce Commission since formal deregulation was enacted 18 months ago. Unshackled from regulatory restraints, motor carriers have filed more than 18,700 applications for new routes on which to haul cargo, producing a bonanza for customers by driving freight bills down by 10 to 20 percent.

The shake-up in the industry has now even silenced the mighty and often-aggressive International Brotherhood of Teamsters, whose strikes in the past have crippled the economy and . . . whose wage gains had been running far ahead of most other industries. Ten days ago, the teamsters negotiated a tentative, three-year contract that freezes wages, allows less frequent adjustments for inflation and makes big concessions in work rules. The union board ratified it last week.

"Deregulation has turned the industry upside down and the recession has magnified the effects," said John Ruan, president of the Ruan Transport Corporation in Des Moines. "I haven't seen competition like this since the 1930's, before regulation was instituted to protect people from precisely this kind of cutthroat pricing."

Deregulation of the $48 billion-a-year trucking industry began informally during the late 1970's with rulings by an increasingly liberal I.C.C. and was accelerated and codified by passage of the

Carter Administration's Motor Carrier Act of July 1980. As a result, an industry that for 45 years was as controlled as a utility has been thrown wide open, creating free-for-all competition where before there was virtually none.

In the process, the nation's 16,000 motor carriers are being forced to rethink who their competitors are, what kinds of freight they want to haul and how they intend to sell their services in the "new" trucking industry. The shape of the trucking business is changing so fast that no one is quite sure what it will look like when things settle down.

"It is a totally different industry than it was five years ago," said Stephen P. Murphy, senior vice president of Yellow Freight System Inc., one of the nation's largest motor carriers. "And I am ready to bet against anyone's five-year scenario for the future. This business is in such a state of flux right now no one knows where it is going to end up."

The American Trucking Associations, an industry trade organization, has been monitoring the health of a group of trucking companies that have annual revenues of more than $1 million. In 1974, when the survey began, the group contained 338 companies; mergers and bankruptcies have reduced that number this year to 208.

Probably nowhere has the transformation been more apparent than in the attitudes of the union men who drive the rigs and load the crates of freight—the teamsters. Always demanding bargainers, occasionally violent, and never ones to put themselves in their employer's place, the generous concessions that the teamsters would wring from the truck owners every three years would set trends for the entire American trade union movement [see Figure 3].

In 1979, after a 12-day strike, the teamsters negotiated a whopping national pay increase of 35 percent, bringing union truck drivers' salaries into the $30,000 to $40,000-a-year bracket. But this is 1982. Before, truck owners could pass along the teamsters wage increases to shippers by simply raising the rates charged on their I.C.C.-regulated routes. Even the nonunion competition was not allowed to undercut them.

"There was no incentive for the management to play hardball with the union before, so teamsters wages got way out of line with

FIGURE 3   WAGES AND PROFITS IN THE TRUCKING INDUSTRY,
1975–1980

Wages
Wages in the I.C.C.-regu-
lated trucking industry have
been rising faster than
wages in most industries.

Profits
...And wages, along with
deregulation, have pro-
voked a sharp decline in the
industry's net income.

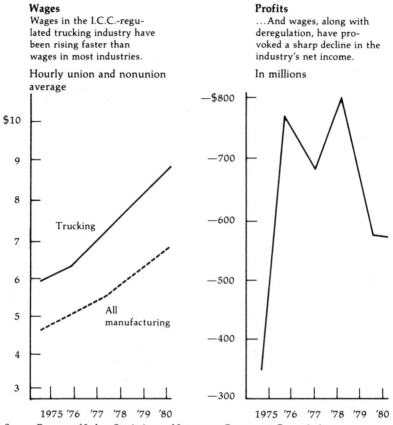

Hourly union and nonunion
average

In millions

Source: Bureau of Labor Statistics and Interstate Commerce Commission.

blue-collar standards for similar work,'' argued William M. Legg,
trucking industry expert for the brokerage firm of Alex, Brown &
Sons.

But since the onset of deregulation, the unionized truckers—
all the major carriers—have not been able to automatically pass on
their higher labor costs to customers, since shipping rates have
been allowed to float freely.

In addition, many of the new trucking companies have been
small nonunion shops, where wages run 20 to 30 percent lower

than at union companies—a cost advantage that under deregulation the newcomers can translate directly into lower freight rates.

The result: Union truckers have increasingly lost market share to nonunion shops, putting, by the teamsters' own estimates, some 20 to 22 percent of the 500,000 teamsters' drivers and dock loaders out of their jobs.

"The biggest enemy of our industry has been the international teamsters union, which ostensibly protected job security for its members but essentially destroyed it," said Arthur E. Imperatore, president of the A-P-A, Transport Corporation. "The union has priced us out of many markets."

. . . Mr. Wojak is president of Cooper-Jarrett Inc., a Morristown, N.J., common carrier with some 600 trucks, 1,150 employees and 31 terminals around the nation. Cooper-Jarrett turned 45 a few months ago, but this could be its last birthday, since on Dec. 28, it filed for protection under Chapter 11 of the Bankruptcy Act.

"It just became impossible to stay in business," Mr. Wojak said. "Competition has come down to one thing: discounting. We saw our rates falling to levels of a decade ago. In some cases rates went down so far, we were effectively paying a customer for the privilege of hauling his freight."

Mr. Wojak said his company made repeated attempts to merge with other trucking concerns, but each time potential partners were frightened off by a 1980 Federal law, steered through Congress by the teamsters, which stipulates that a union trucking company that decides to liquidate must pay the Federal Pension Benefits Guarantee Corporation enough money to back the pensions promised by the teamsters to union employees.

"We could never consummate a merger because nobody wanted to gamble on assuming our pension liabilities," said Mr. Wojak, who, like many analysts, believes that there are more than a few ailing trucking companies staying open and adding to overcapacity because they simply can't afford to liquidate.

To prosper under the new conditions, radical rethinking of market strategies is required by executives who for two generations have operated within the unimaginative world of regulated trucking.

For the largest truck companies—Roadway Express, Consolidated Freightways, Yellow Freight, Mclean Trucking and IU International—the most noticeable change has been in the size of the shipments they are hauling. This is crucial, since the size of the goods being picked up determines one's entire company structure.

Basically there are two kinds of trucking freight. "Less-Than-Truck-Load," or LTL, freight consists of a number of packages that cannot fill the back of one trailer. Those companies concentrating on LTL markets might have a truck make a dozen stops to pick up enough packages to make a truckload. The truck delivers the packages to a central terminal, where they are sorted like mail. Other trucks would then take the LTL packages to terminals in a variety of cities, where they would be put onto still other trucks for door-to-door delivery.

The other major type of freight is known as "truckload," whereby one truck picks up a truckful of goods from one shipper and takes it directly to the company it is to be delivered to in another city.

Most of the new companies are concentrating on the truckload business, which requires none of the overhead of LTL and can usually be run with nonunion labor or independents. The newcomers are effectively driving the majors out of the truckload trade, which they once dominated, and forcing them to compete all that more intensely.

"We are now looking at freight that we used to pass up on our way to work and we are bumping noses with people we never used to compete with before," said Roy Cayton, executive vice president of the Overnite Transportation Corporation in Richmond, the largest nonunion motor carrier. To deal with the new situation, said Mr. Cayton, Overnite has slashed prices in the last year by 10 to 15 percent.

"We had to cut our prices just to hold onto what we had," said Mr. Cayton. "We were being called by shippers every day, sometimes several times a day, asking us to meet the rates of our competitors. If we hadn't cut prices I would not be talking to you now. Before we used to sell service, now we have to be marketers as well. We have cut back our staff everywhere except salesmen. But even the salesmen have had to be retrained. They have to be skilled traffic specialists who can go out and explain the maze of new rates we have and tailor them to the customer's freight. It's just like the airlines."

In addition, all of the big companies are opening new terminals around the country in increasingly smaller cities in order to fill up their trucks with LTL freight. Whereas Overnite, for example, only had a terminal in Raleigh, N.C., it now has a small pickup and delivery terminal in Rocky Mountain, N.C., as well.

Raymond F. O'Brien, Chairman of Consolidated Freightways Inc., has dubbed this trend "The Federal Expressing of the trucking industry."

Even the small companies have to transform themselves into sophisticated marketing operations to survive. CRST Inc., in Cedar Rapids, Iowa, is typical of the new companies that have flourished under deregulation. For many years CRST was known as a specialized carrier hauling only steel in the Middle West. But when deregulation was instituted, the largely nonunion trucking company applied for a 50-state permit to carry whatever it wanted wherever it wanted. It concentrated solely on truckload traffic and with costs 20 to 30 percent below the union carriers it has been steadily "taking market share away from the big boys," said John Smith, CRST's executive vice president.

To hold on to these new-found gains, Mr. Smith said, CRST has "gotten into some marketing concepts pretty unique in the trucking industry." These included bringing out to Cedar Rapids the New York research company of Booz, Allen & Hamilton Inc. to analyze its markets and break down the cost of every single operation the company performed to create the widest scope for discounting.

"Before, we were operation-oriented," Mr. Smith said. "We worried if the shipper fit into our regulated structure. Now we have to be market-oriented and adjust our structure to fit the shipper's needs."

Which is just fine by the shippers, who, like travel agents, have had to become logistics specialists on all the new supersaver rates proliferating in trucking.

"We've been able to negotiate some very attractive contracts," said Warren S. Search Jr., director of transportation for Western Electric, which has been able to shave some 10 percent off its $220 million annual freight bill. "There is much more solicitation going on than ever before. The truckers are offering rates that reflect their costs, not the artificially regulated tariffs."

Just how long these bargain days remain depends in part on the willingness of the I.C.C. to interpret the Motor Carrier Act in the most freemarket fashion possible. Reese H. Taylor Jr., who was appointed I.C.C. chairman by President Reagan—some sources believe in exchange for support from the teamsters—was not known as a deregulation advocate by any means. Since coming in, his critics have accused him of trying to turn the clock back by tightening the restrictions on entry into trucking and making rate discounting more difficult.

Mr. Taylor declined to be interviewed, but his chief of staff, Robert Shepherd Jr., contended that the I.C.C. had no intention of trying to halt deregulation and was backing legislation to speed it up. Mr. Shepherd noted that the Motor Carrier Act did not totally deregulate the industry, although it substantially reduced regulations on entry and competition.

The consensus among the trucking executives interviewed was that the whole dispute over Mr. Taylor's views has become a bit of a red herring. Substantial deregulation, they note, has obviously taken place and it can't possibly be reined in now by administrative fiat.

"Deregulation is here to stay," said A-P-A's Mr. Imperatore. "The trucking industry has entered an age of entrepreneurism that will reconfigure the industry over several years. There is already a trend toward oligopoly which will continue. Most people won't be able to survive on their own, I can assure you they won't, especially if they behave like they have in the past."

Discussion and Review Questions

1. In what broad areas has governmental "social" regulation developed over the past two decades?

2. Do you believe there was good reason for this type of regulatory intervention? Philosophically, where do you stand?

3. Do you agree or disagree with the first article's contention that the FTC has gone too far in interfering with business affairs? Comment in some detail, defending your position.

4. How do you react to the argument that "without an effective Environmental Protection Agency, business will make more profits and

hire more workers *but* it will also lower the real quality of all of our lives?"

5. Why has the trucking industry responded so negatively to deregulation? Is it an exception, or do you think many other industries talk deregulation but privately want something else?

6. American automakers actually supported some of the early environmental protection and consumer safety requirements. Why? (Hint: What ever happened to the VW beetle?)

PART 7

AMERICAN BUSINESS AND THE WORLD

ISSUE 12

Has the Multinational Boom Ended?

Paralleling the stagnation of the domestic American economy in recent years has been the long contraction in international economic activity. The German economic "miracle" and the long booms in France and in other European nations had stalled by 1982 as unemployment edged toward double digits in practically all industrialized, noncommunist economies. Faced with shrinking markets at home, the international economy stood on the brink of all-out trade wars as nations went head to head in overseas price competition. Meanwhile, the less-developed nations suffered both from growing trade deficits and from the enormous burden of debts owed to the industrialized countries. After a long postwar growth in multinational corporate (MNC) operations, the bloom seemed to have passed. It is possible, however, that the trend was merely a temporary setback for MNCs.

Since World War II the level of involvement overseas by American enterprise has varied according to the size and nature of the firm. For most U.S. enterprises, international business activities are limited to a range of actions including active exporting; casual exporting; foreign licensing of patents, trademarks, and copyrights to foreign producers; and importing raw materials and semifinished or finished products for U.S. assembly and sale. Only a comparative handful of American enterprises are thorough-going multinational firms with their own overseas production, marketing, research, and even financial operations. Yet, in our era it is this handful that account for most of the nation's overseas economic activity.

The Rise of the Multinational Corporation

Strictly speaking, the multinational corporation is an old idea, dating back to the joint stock companies of the sixteenth and seventeenth centuries. Such operations as the British East India Company and the Dutch East Indian Company were highly profitable international business ventures in the early colonial period. However, while the idea is old, the modern MNC is truly a new kind of business undertaking. It began in earnest in the mid 1960s, and although corporations have trimmed down many of their overseas operations in the world recession of the early 1980s, the MNC strategy shows no sign of ending soon. America, of course, is not alone in this experiment. Such foreign giants as Royal Dutch Shell, Unilever, BP, Toyota, Hitachi, and Phillips rank along with Exxon, Mobil, GM, Ford, IBM, and GE as leading multinational enterprises.

In the simplest terms, an MNC is an enterprise based in one country but carrying on production, extraction, research, and sales operations in many other nations. In general, MNCs are highly integrated and diversified. Their large size and economies of scale in production are enhanced by their ability to shift capital assets and production according to profit objectives. The old constraints of geography and nationalism are minimized. Whereas national firms had to trade across national barriers and compete with foreign enterprises, the MNC can enjoy multiple national personalities in its day-to-day operations.

Sometimes the MNC can take the form of a single company, such as Pepsico. With a comparatively limited product line, Pepsico still ranks near the top one hundred of American manufacturing corporations. It manufactures Pepsicola in 114 foreign countries in over 500 plants, two-thirds of which are foreign enterprises. More frequently, the MNC takes the form of a giant international conglomerate such as Ford or General Motors. Ford, for instance, is much more than the Ford Motor Company. It is a combination of over sixty subsidiary firms, two-thirds of which are located overseas. Ford's activities range from automobiles to radios to machine tools.

MNC's Advantages and Disadvantages

One special attraction to multinational operation is the ability of the firm to avoid many of the restraints to trade that characterize purely national operations. Most multinationals have found that the old cultural and social conflicts faced by a foreign enterprise can be reduced by hiring foreign nationals to carry on important managerial duties in the production and marketing of products. Political difficulties often remain, but they doubtless are reduced because most MNCs have learned to create a local appearance for their operations. Occasionally, however, this has led to dangerous displays of corporate misbehavior, such as when U.S. firms accept the all-too-common habit of giving bribes to public officials when doing business with overseas governments. Nevertheless, American and European multinationals like Pepsico, Ford, and Fiat actually have been able to open operations in communist countries and to engage in expanded trade with Soviet-bloc nations.

Another advantage enjoyed by the MNC is its capacity to evade certain trade barriers. By locating its production within a high-tariff or protectionist area, the MNC can still obtain free access to local markets. Not only can the economic costs of tariffs be avoided, but the MNC, by locating its operations worldwide, can take quick advantage of changing market conditions—buying resources and selling goods in various countries as changes in prices and exchange rates dictate. With their battalions of financial managers, MNCs have become adept at shifting their financial holdings around from country to country to take advantage of changing interest rates and loan possibilities.

Most American MNCs also enjoy certain U.S. tax advantages that enhance overseas operations. Permitted to deduct foreign-paid taxes as a credit against a U.S. tax bill and to defer taxes on overseas profits not returned to the United States, as well as qualifying for Export–Import Bank loans and government insurance for foreign seizure (expropriation) of property, American MNCs receive special treatment from their government. Critics of MNCs, especially labor unions, see the multinational as "exporting jobs," but so far they have been unsuccessful in their efforts to end what they consider preferential treatment for the international giants.

Perhaps the biggest headaches for MNCs are caused in developing nations. A decade or two ago the threat was expropriation by a leftist government. Today that is less likely, but host-government intervention in a firm's affairs is still common. Quite naturally, most developing nations want access to the technology of the giant enterprise, since technology is the key to growth. Accordingly, some have demanded that production secrets be shared, apparently with an eye to the day when the foreigners can be thrown out and local enterprise can replace them.

Most MNCs have been able to adapt to these political–economic pressures, but some can't. For instance, Coca-Cola withdrew from the vast Indian market rather than reveal the ingredients of its secret syrup formula.

Another possible disadvantage to MNC operations involves an age-old economic argument: Can a firm become so large that its management ability is weakened and inefficiency grows? There is not much hard evidence to support this argument; however, in recent years a number of American multinationals have reported significant losses by some of their overseas subsidiaries. Partially, this may reflect economic conditions caused by the worldwide recession, but some experts feel that many MNCs mismanage their distant overseas operations.

Recent International Trends

American MNCs have slowed their overseas expansion in recent years. This reflects a number of developments. First, as we noted earlier, the American economic contraction of the 1970s and 1980s has spread worldwide, with rising prices and unemployment (and lowered sales) a characteristic of practically all economies in the world. Second, many of the best and most obvious overseas expansion possibilities have already been undertaken. As one MNC expert observed: "There really isn't all that much left to internationalize." Third, most of the more expansive MNCs have been petroleum-based operations. In the early 1980s era of recession, energy conservation, and falling energy prices, the will *and* the ability to expand have been curtailed for such firms.

On the other hand, MNCs from other countries recently have been active in undertaking investments in the United States. During the 1970s, as domestic inflation drove down the buying power of the American dollar, the exchange value of the dollar declined. Foreigners found that high-priced marks and yen could buy a lot of low-priced dollars. Thus, with the dollar depressed, it became wise to take advantage of the bargains in U.S. corporate stocks. Accordingly, the A & P Company was picked up by the Tengelmann Group (Germany); Nestle (Switzerland) bought control of Beechnut and Stouffers; and the Frederick Flick Group (Germany) took over W. R. Grace. By 1982, however, the bargain hunting was ending as the dollar strengthened and many nations watched their own currencies fall in value. Nevertheless, the attraction of American industry to foreign multinationals is not simply a matter of exchange rates. The political stability—even in bad economic times—of the United

States makes it much more attractive than expanded overseas investments in less-stable areas, even if such investments are more immediately profitable.

Looking to the the future, it appears that the bonanza years in MNC development are largely over, yet the sheer size of the world's MNCs and the volume of their international output and sales will maintain their importance in international business. The modern internationalizing of business operations is no passing phenomenon. The return to trading on a small, national scale is virtually unthinkable. As a result, in terms of business activity, we are left with a smaller, more interdependent economic world than before the MNC boom in the 1960s. Whether the modern multinational firm actually will break down the old nationalistic character of the world remains to be seen, but some enthusiasts believe that the development of the multinational corporation is perhaps the greatest deterrent to the trade wars and the resulting shooting wars of the past.

This view, however, scarcely seems supported by current international business trends. The first article, by the chief executive officer of American Motors, is a shrill attack by a representative of one nation's more active multinational segment against the activities of another nation's multinational enterprise. The second article, by the chairman of President Reagan's Export Council, worries about a full-blown trade war breaking out among the industrial nations that would interrupt multinational and international business operations. The last article turns to another area of multinational activity—operations in third-world nations—and offers a blueprint for improved business success.

12.1 The Japanese Are Not Playing Fairly

W. PAUL TIPPETT

During the two decades of domestic growth and domination of world markets, U.S. industry appeared to ignore the fact that foreign companies were investing in new plants and new technologies. We confidently rested on our laurels, increasing the volume of production but working with an aging national industrial plant dating back to World War II. We failed to upgrade our plant, technology and products as quickly as possible—sometimes funneling the profits that could have gone into such projects into higher wages for the work force and non-productive plant and product alterations dictated by government regulations.

Equally important, we minimized the possibility of other nations penetrating the U.S. market. "Made in America" was the standard all other countries aspired to match. Who would have dreamed that American consumers would buy automobiles or steel or machine tools made in Japan? . . .

Twenty years ago, imports accounted for just four percent of the U.S. auto market, but today their share has soared to 32 percent. In 1981 Honda, Toyota and Nissan had combined profits from U.S. sales of $890 million, while the U.S. auto industry posted a loss of $1.3 billion.

The U.S. auto industry reacted to the challenge of foreign competition by cutting costs to the bone and investing in retooling and new technology on a massive scale. In the past four years, the industry has made more progress in design, technology and productivity than it did in the previous four decades. As a result, vehicles made in America today can match those coming from any country in the world in terms of quality, durability and fuel efficiency. The one area where we still lag is in our manufacturing costs vis-a-vis those of the Japanese. *That* is an area sometimes beyond the U.S. industry's control, and I'll turn to it shortly.

Along with the current technological revolution, we are undergoing a more subtle but ultimately more far-reaching transition. Major growth markets of the future will be beyond our borders—just as they have been for the Japanese auto industry for the past two decades.

Today, there are a total of more than 320 million motor vehicles in the world. The Motor Vehicle Manufacturers' Association projects that by the year 2000, there will be more than 600 million—if that isn't a *growth* industry, what is?

Where do we expect this growth to occur?

In 1960, North America accounted for roughly 60 percent of all vehicle sales, but by 1980 that proportion had declined to 37 percent. Putting it another way—North American vehicle sales grew by 39 percent between 1960 and 1980, but European sales grew 188 percent and Latin American sales grew 600 percent during the same period.

In short, much of the growth of the U.S. auto industry will be in export markets. The successful companies will be the ones which think globally. Global markets, global supply links and global manufacturing plants. . . .

The companies which succeed long-term in foreign markets should be the ones that make commitments to create jobs and contribute to the economic growth of the countries where they sell their products. In this era of economic interdependence, no major company should expect to participate in a foreign market if its activities are limited to selling imports and taking the profits home, without investing in the host country.

But not everyone is willing to play by the rules of responsible, cooperative international trade. The Japanese have adopted just the opposite attitude—one of conquest rather than cooperation—in entering foreign markets. This is the greatest single threat to the U.S. auto industry as it undergoes the transition I've just described.

Many have attributed Japan's success in the U.S. auto market to a more efficient and more productive work force coupled with superior management techniques. The fact is that U.S. labor and management are just as dedicated and innovative as those of any country in the world. Japan's success in the U.S. market stems largely from differences in the two countries *political* treatment of industrial growth and foreign trade, not differences in culture or management style.

The number one difference in Japan's approach to world trade is the so-called targeted industry strategy, which has been the way of life in Japan for more than three decades. Key industries with high export potential are identified by the Japanese government and then nurtured domestically in a hothouse environment until they are strong enough to compete overseas. The Japanese government prohibits foreign competition in the home market hothouse through tariffs, quotas and restrictions on foreign investment. Companies are also often encouraged by the government to set production quotas, establish special supplier relationships and fix prices.

When these companies are ready to enter foreign markets, they enjoy such advantages as accelerated depreciation and special reserves for tax purposes, exemption from antitrust laws, subsidized low-interest loans, government-funded R&D programs and an under-valued currency—advantages no American company can either obtain or effectively compete with.

This spring, one U.S. company got fed up and decided to take on the Japanese single-handed. In a 700-page petition filed with the U.S. Trade Representative, Houdaille Industries, Inc., a Florida-based manufacturer of numerically controlled machining equipment, documented how the Japanese have used their unfair trade advantages to capture a major share of the U.S. market for such equipment. That petition is. becoming one of the best-read publications in Washington.

Let me touch briefly on just three of Houdaille's findings:

First, the Japanese Ministry of International Trade and Industry—MITI—forced low-volume machine tool makers out of certain market segments. Their market share was then turned over to a limited number of larger producers who formed a government-sanctioned cartel free of domestic competition and able to concentrate on exports.

Second, in the 1950's, MITI granted sugar import licenses to the remaining members of the machine tool cartel. The cartel members were allowed to buy sugar at the low world market price and then sell it in Japan at a much higher controlled price. The resulting profits were used to subsidize machine tool sales at extremely low prices in export markets. Thus, innocuous sugar licenses were used to support machine tool dumping.

Third, the Japanese government used money from betting on bicycle and motorcycle races to subsidize their R&D for the machine tool industry. Money collected from these races went to two institutions, innocently named the Bicycle Rehabilitation Association and the Motorcycle Rehabilitation Association. Under order from MITI, these two organizations funneled millions of dollars into the coffers of the machine tool cartel.

These kinds of actions have not been limited to the machine tool business. And what has been the U.S. response? For the most part, endless debate that has achieved little or nothing. During a congressional hearing a few weeks ago, Secretary of Commerce Baldrige admitted that 18 months of negotiations have failed to make a dent in Japanese trade policy.

I agree with the Secretary. The Japanese have been slow-walking our own government to death in trade negotiations. The Japanese won't change their trade policy unless they receive a clear and strong signal that we are serious.

I'm not suggesting that the U.S. should legislate hothouse protection for our industries. Instead, the Congress and the administration must make it clear to the Japanese that the days when they could get a free lunch in our market are over. Several possible vehicles to convey this message are already at our government's disposal—among them, limited local content requirements. The conveyance of this message should receive *top* priority when the new Congress convenes next January.

The new Congress must ask itself: How long can *any* of our country's basic industries—not just the auto industry—continue competing against the Japanese if the Japanese are allowed to use advantages not available in a free market?

All other industrialized countries in the Free World have perceived the threat of unfair Japanese competition for what it is—a concerted attack on their basic industries. Those countries have acted accordingly. The Common Market members for example, in order to offset Japanese subsidies, have a tariff on automobiles more than three times higher than ours.

The Japanese have accepted these restrictions and continue to do business in Europe. No trade war has occurred. If they can play on European turf by European rules, why shouldn't we get the same chance? That's all anyone in the automotive, steel, electronic or any other U.S. industry should get—a level playing field that still preserves the right of choice for the American consumer.

As I said earlier, in this era of economic interdependence, no major company should expect to participate importantly in a foreign market if its only strategy is to sell products and take the profits home, without investing in the host country. This principle has been the spirit behind Renault's business alliance with American Motors.

No responsible company should expect a long-term presence in a foreign market if it enjoys unfair political and economic advantages that are denied the host country's own basic industries. The impact of such advantages on *our* basic industries is all too evident in the Japanese-made products that line our shelves and in the long unemployment lines in our cities.

In sum, it's high time we woke up to the realities of the importance of international trade and the threat of Japan's unique trade policy. To fail to think globally in our own industrial planning or to refuse to confront the Japanese in our own market would be . . . foolish and suicidal. . . .

We can't afford to let our basic industries die. They are the backbone of economic productivity. Without them, this country would become a second class world citizen both economically and politically. . . .

Dr. William Abernathy of Harvard, a leading authority on industrial productivity, predicts in his worst case scenario for the U.S. auto industry that Japanese imports could completely displace automotive manufacturing in this country within the next 10 to 15 years. We can't afford to let that happen—not to our auto industry or to any of our basic industries. Such erosion of our industrial base would multiply our current economic problems and dangerously debilitate our national defense capability.

It's not too late to reverse the trend. There *are* measures we can take to counter the threat of unfair foreign competition. But the time for just talking about the problem is long passed. We have to accept the seriousness of the threat and take action now.

12.2 "I'm Worried about a Full-blown Trade War"

U.S. NEWS & WORLD REPORT AND J. PAUL LYET

Q Mr. Lyet, American businesses today appear to be getting squeezed out of foreign markets. Why is this happening?

A The problem of trade worldwide right now is one of barriers. Protectionism is gaining favor all over the world—indeed, even in our own country. Some of it, unfortunately, has assumed demagogic overtones.

Q Which countries are the worst offenders?

A No one's hands are clean. The European Community directly subsidizes farm exports. The Canadians have all kinds of restrictions on foreign investments. And the stories of Japanese protectionism are legion. They have quotas that limit beef and orange imports. They have a monopoly on tobacco and salt. Some of their amateur baseball leagues keep out American-made aluminum bats.

The problem isn't really high tariffs as much as it is nontariff barriers. The Japanese have a complicated system of inspection, for example, on many products that come in. I've heard that, if we were to use the inspection techniques that they require on some products, we would be taking Toyotas off the ship one at a time at our ports and the ships would be backed up for miles.

Q Hasn't Japan promised to remove some of these barriers?

A Our government has exercised a great deal of patience. Commerce Department and other U.S. government officials have made trips over there, and the Japanese have made a list of things they were going to do. But time marches on, and it's becoming particularly difficult for members of Congress from areas that have been severely hurt by imports not to vote for protectionist legislation in Congress. Even Japanese leaders recognize that protectionism is harmful, but I think they're getting a lot of pressure, too, from their smaller businesses and farmers.

Q How much is the low value of the yen against the dollar responsible for our trade troubles with Japan?

A I don't think it reflects the true value of the currencies, and it gives the Japanese a very real advantage in selling their products to the United States. I understand that the Japanese government is not intervening in the market for the yen.

Q Could it be that the U.S. created this problem by permitting the dollar to remain high against other currencies?

A The high value of the dollar is not all of the problem, but it's certainly a big part. The dollar is high in large part because of high interest rates. I think that the decline in interest rates is probably going to reduce the relative value of the dollar.

Q How can this country compete with smaller countries, such as South Korea, Singapore and Taiwan, where labor is cheaper and governments promote certain industries?

A We can't compete on the manufacturing level in many industries, especially those which are labor-intensive. But we can compete in service industries—such as transportation, banking and insurance—and we have to work to reduce protectionist barriers there. For example, many countries do not allow foreign banks to be set up in their countries.

One of our objectives is to have service industries, which are not covered now, on the agenda at the trade ministers' meeting on the General Agreement on Tariffs and Trade in late November. That is the organization that sets many of the rules for international trade. I cannot overemphasize the importance of that meeting.

Q How can we get developing countries such as those in Latin America, Asia and Africa to buy our goods and services?

A Our trade with developing countries is now greater than the combined trade with both the European Community and the Japanese. Yet some of these smaller countries are in trouble. Many of them had to borrow money from banks to pay for the high cost of energy as they tried to develop industry. So what are the U.S. banks doing? Now that these countries have run into trouble, the banks are cutting back on their loans. This is being done in large measure to protect their depositors.

These nations are going to need a lot of help, and there are more implications to this than trade. You've got to think about the political aspects—the destabilization that can result from economic collapse. It is not politically popular in the United States, but these countries may need direct foreign aid.

Q Are imports to blame for the slump in some of our heavy industries, or have these companies brought it on themselves?

A I think American industry has to plead guilty to the charges of poor quality and poor product planning in some cases, compared to our foreign competitors. From 1977 to 1981, foreign-auto imports increased 300,000 cars per year, while domestic production declined many times that amount. Hopefully, as interest rates fall and American manufacturers produce increasing numbers of quality, fuel-efficient cars, their sales and market share will rebound to previous levels.

Q What else can the U.S. do to promote exports?

A I think we are doing virtually as much as we can; the individual companies are the ones that really have to do the promoting. The foreign-commercial counselors in the Commerce Department are one big help. They are sort of an advance guard for the small businessman to show him the opportunities and take him by the hand in finding distributors.

I also think the new export-trading corporations are going to be a big aid. In addition to facilitating exports for smaller business, they will enable firms working with banks to sell goods and services overseas without running afoul of antitrust laws. But the bulk of the exports that are done in this country are done by relatively few big companies.

Table 2   The U.S. and Its Trading Partners

In the first eight months of 1982	U.S. Exported to	U.S. Imported From
European Community	$ 32.5 bil.	$ 29.6 bil.
Japan	$ 14.0 bil.	$ 27.7 bil.
Canada	$ 23.1 bil.	$ 31.3 bil.
Latin America	$ 24.3 bil.	$ 25.8 bil.
Eastern Europe	$ 2.9 bil.	$ 0.8 bil.
Rest of world	$ 49.6 bil.	$ 56.8 bil.
Total	**$146.4 bil.**	**$172.0 bil.**

Source: U.S. News & World Report. Basic data: U.S. Dept. of Commerce

Q   Are we providing enough low-cost financing to countries that may want to buy from us?

A   No. It's the biggest problem. For some reason, this administration has shown a notable lack of perception when it comes to the Export–Import Bank. Because of budget cuts and other restraints, the agency is not able to offer our potential customers the same low interest rates and terms that competing nations are willing to provide.

Q   Why not just leave it to the marketplace?

A   Let's take the example of the Canadian-subsidized sale of subway cars to the New York Municipal Transit Authority. The Canadians offered New York financing at a 9.7 percent interest rate if it would buy Canadian cars. That's lower than a United States supplier was able to produce. An international agreement was reached recently to make financing more uniform, but we have yet to see that work in practice.

The thing about Americans is that we are a market economy and we expect everyone else to act like a market economy, but others don't. The French and Japanese, for example, target industries for special treatment. Others say: "Sure, we'll buy your product. But you've got to buy so much back from us in countertrade."

Q   How does a country "target" industries?

A   They'll say at the government level: "Let's get together, guys, and work this thing out. What are the hot fields for the future?" Maybe it will be genetic engineering or computers or microelectronics. And then they really go about protectionism—subsidizing with research and development, direct grants, forced buyouts, forced mergers and everything else to do it.

You try and sell a computer in France, and it's nearly impossible because of protectionist practices. The French customer often prefers the American product, just as the Japanese like to smoke American cigarettes. But the Japanese put a 60 percent duty on the cigarettes coming in. You've got to sell them through the monopoly.

Q   What can the U.S. do to counter protectionist practices by other countries? Should we be retaliating?

A   Back in the early 1930s, we went to retaliation. Without thinking much more about it, we decided: "We're a big nation; let's let them have it, boys. Put the barriers up." We found other countries putting up barriers, too, and it was a fiasco. If the country was staggering and reeling under the Depression, this was the final kick in the pants that kicked the economy right in the gutter.

I'm worried about us getting into a full-blown trade war. We want to see the international-trade mechanism that does exist, imperfect as it is, maintained. We often forget how important exports are. At Sperry Corporation, where I served as chairman, about 43 percent of our business is outside of the country, and a substantial portion is exported from the United States.

Q Is talking enough, or do we need something further?

A It is argued that the Trade Act of 1974 already gives a President plenty of authority to act against unfair trade practices. At the same time, there is the view widely held that if, indeed, you were to pass some sort of reciprocity legislation, it would be an attention getter, causing them to say: "Now, look, they really mean it. What will the U.S. do next? We'd better ease up." I suppose it would not do any harm if it were the right kind of legislation.

Q What if the bill is amended further to require that cars sold in the U.S. have a certain share of parts made in this country?

A This so-called local-content requirement may be the worst piece of legislation introduced in more than 50 years. If you were to say that all parts and things that go into automobiles in this country have to be made in this country, it would be a very simple thing for the Australians to say, for example, that all farm machinery made in Australia has to be made from Australian parts.

The legislation could threaten any of a long list of products that are exported from the United States—machine tools, communications gear, computers, the whole works. It's protectionist legislation of the ugliest kind. Sometimes out of frustration you want to say, "Sock them and sock them good!" You get a lot of satisfaction out of kicking something, but then you pay later, no matter what it is.

Q Are we doing anything now that you would consider protectionist—in restraint of trade?

A We aren't as blatant in subsidizing exports of agriculture as the Europeans, but foreigners often point to our price supports and a variety of things we do to make our farmers economically healthy.

Q Some make the case that we need a national capability to

produce some products, such as steel, for national defense—

A   Yes. I think there are certain essential core industries in the United States that could be completely wiped out by the operation of the free-market system. At what point in a free-market society do you intervene? If you intervene, you protect an industry that, perhaps, will thereafter be less efficient than it otherwise would be under the constant pressure of competition. On the other hand, you risk being left vulnerable from a defense standpoint. So, on balance, some strategic core industries, such as steel, must be protected and made more efficient.

12.3 Six Challenges to Global Corporations

JAGJIT BRAR, R. DAVID RAMSEY, AND PETER WRIGHT

The rise of global corporations based in the third world has joined with consumerism and organized labor as a major force countering corporate power based in the West. Western-based corporations have long viewed the third world as a lucrative market, but they have failed to perceive fully the vulnerability of their own Western markets to competition from third-world multinational corporations. In the 1980s the growth, stability, and, in some cases, even survival of Western firms will depend on their success in re-orienting their roles and strategies.

Western-based global corporations will need to meet the challenges of the 1980s in the following six important arenas: management of foreign-denominated liquid assets, expansion or growth policies, decentralization of the production process, automation of assembly lines, re-evaluation of corporate–labor relationships and "globalization" of consumer tastes.

Management of foreign-denominated liquid assets. Almost daily, global corporations receive and pay large sums denominated in monetary units of several different nations. Since the institution of floating exchange rates, uncertainty in international money markets has grown significantly. In the 1980s, with heightened political tensions, international money markets will tend to become more nervous, perhaps even turbulent. A small, unforeseen, unfavorable change in exchange rates could have a major impact on corporate-earnings. Thus, in the years ahead, global firms must shelter their earnings not only from competitors, but also from the whims of international money markets. Decisions concerning the best currency mix in which to store short-term liquidity will certainly occupy more of a management's attention.[1]

Expansion or growth policies. Global corporations have consistently given much thought to charting and pursuing growth paths, but these decisions will be among the most difficult to make in the 1980s. The unpredictability of national political and economic alliances, combined with growing trade deficits in most of the third world and in some Western nations, will make the growth policies a balancing act; an act of expansion with enough leverage for retrenchment. Some U.S.-based firms which "rushed" to the People's Republic of China when Sino-American relations improved around 1972 are now finding retrenchment expensive.[2] Furthermore, several nations, because of their deteriorating international-reserve position, will take measures to encourage importation of foreign corporations and to discourage importation of foreign goods.

Historically, Western-based companies have relied heavily on capital from the host countries for construction of manufacturing facilities.[3] In the 1980s host countries will become less willing to raise capital and more demanding of foreign firms to share tax burdens.

Decentralization of the production process. Corporations will also need to establish foreign subsidiaries specializing in components rather than the total product. To a limited extent such specialization is already occurring in the electronics and automobile industries. The trend will continue because gaps in factor-price ratios among nations will widen and also because global firms will become increasingly hesitant, in view of potentially sudden political and economic developments, to put all their eggs in one basket.

Global-corporation strategies will shift away from product specialization toward component specialization. The global production process will become more "disaggregated" or decentralized. Since not all product components can be produced with equal efficiency in the same place, subcontracting with locally-owned, smaller firms will become more economically viable. Such complementary manufacturing will also enhance acceptance of foreign-owned global companies in the host countries.

Automation of assembly lines. The process of manufacturing certain products will change in yet another drastic way. Monotonous, arduous assembly-line tasks subject to human error will be undertaken by robots. Japan already "employs" approximately 50,000 robots, most of them in car manufacturing. There are roughly 5,000 robots in the U.S. In the 1980s cost reductions and increased consumer demand for uniformity in product quality will cause assembly-line automation to come up more frequently in boardroom discussions.

Re-evaluation of corporate–labor relationships. Automation will have implications far beyond the assembly lines. It will combine with another market phenomenon, the emergence of the third-world-based corporation, to redirect corporate–labor relationships. Executives of Western-based firms will undertake every effort to "educate" organized labor that the corporate–labor relationship should be more symbiotic than adversarial. Hesitancy by either management or labor to recognize this newly evolving symbiosis could be indeed very costly to both of them.

"Globalization" of consumer tastes. Another development which will receive more attention in world markets is the globalization of each nation's consumers. The growing world-wide craze or craving for designer jeans and Western fast foods exemplifies this phenomenon. The difficulty is that the astute global marketer will face greater challenges in searching for varied marketing strategies.

He will be faced with consumers who can buy the same products all over the world but who come from different geographic regions, religions and social, economic and cultural backgrounds. The marketer seeking world-wide success had better not have a Brooke Shields display her wares in Iran or Saudi Arabia.

In this decade global corporations, as an agent of change in world economic conditions, will come under closer scrutiny from the nationalistic fundamentalists; those who are the guardians of the *status quo* in national values and moral mix. Thus, the future success and stability of the firms will also depend upon their ability to avoid stepping over the subtle line that distinguishes economic progress from socio-cultural change.

Global businesses are important agents of economic development. But the firm which fails to appreciate fully the possible future consequences of economic development on its own operations, and which is unable to restructure corporate strategies in time, will find itself sailing upstream. In certain areas of national interests, the 1980s will present opportunities as well as dangers. The corporate leadership which is most alert to the nature of the challenges will deal most effectively with its opportunities and dangers. The astute executive can turn new challenges into new opportunities. The new opportunities will certainly breed newer challenges.

Notes

1. For related reading see, Waseem A. Khan, "Interest Rates and Current Exchange Rate Behavior," *The Collegiate Forum*, Winter 1981/82, Dow Jones and Co., Inc., p. 7.
2. Frank Ching, "As China Retrenches, Many U.S. Companies Cut Their Staffs There," *The Wall Street Journal*, March 25, 1981, p. 1.
3. Stephen Hymer, "The Efficiency (Contradictions) of Multinational Corporations," in R. E. Baldwin's *International Trade and Finance*, J. D. Richardson, editor, Little, Brown and Company, 1974, pp. 300–311.

Discussion and Review Questions

1. What is a multinational firm? How does it differ from most firms of twenty-five years ago?
2. What are the advantages and disadvantages to a firm's going multinational?
3. What is an international trade war? How would American business be affected if one breaks out?
4. Looking to the future, what challenges confront American global corporations for the rest of this century?
5. What is the attitude of host countries toward most multinationals? Why do they feel this way? What can the MNC do to smooth the waters?
6. How has the recent decline in the world economy affected U.S. firms—both those operating overseas and those at home? Explain.

ISSUE 13

How Can We Increase American Productivity?

For the worrier, there is much to be concerned about when looking down the road at the future of American business. While many enterprises remain strong and profitable, others are in trouble. The automobile industry, once the backbone of the American economy, employing directly or indirectly one out of every seven workers, has been in a ten-year nosedive. Indeed, across the nation, the old "smokestack industries"—steel, farm machinery, rail equipment, etc.—all seem to be in serious trouble. Small business, also a bulwark to the American business system, produced record failures in 1982 and 1983. The nation, once the leader of the world in standard of living, had fallen to tenth by 1982. Everywhere there are dark and forbidding signals. None are more forbidding than the decade-long decline in American productivity—the basic barometer of business performance.

The Importance of Productivity

Any human undertaking can be examined in terms of inputs and outputs. Inputs of hard work, dedication, and skill are required for academic success, athletic achievement, or simply making an "affair of the heart" (love, in other words) succeed. Obviously, when the inputs are greater and more painful than the resulting pleasures and rewards, we recognize that the activity is "unproductive" or simply not worth the effort. In other words, the return doesn't justify the effort, time, or whatever else is expended. Business is guided by very much the same principles. Here, the object is to combine the productive factors (labor, raw materials, capital, and management skill) in such a way that we have something for sale at the end of the process that is greater than the costs we paid at the beginning. How well we succeed in raising output as a ratio of inputs is called "productivity." A higher productivity ratio means we are getting more for less—that we are producing more goods at the same costs or the same amount of goods at lower costs.

The search for profit that is the eternal and central feature of a business society is simply an expression of the productivity problem. Profits will be higher when productivity is higher; lower when productivity is lower. The past successes of American enterprise and of the nation as a whole have been tied to our success in increasing productivity.

The interconnectedness of national economic growth and productivity is apparent if we look at the American case. What we find is two disturbing trends. As Table 3 indicates, the long-term growth trend of the United States, has, until recently, compared quite well with the other noncommunist industrial nations. Only Japan exceeded our performance over the one hundred years after 1870, and that mostly reflected the abysmal poverty from which the Japanese started. However, over the past two decades, all the industrial economies except the United Kingdom exceeded our performance. Worse still, if we focus only on the dismal years since 1970, we have averaged less than a 3-percent growth rate. The downward trend in growth, of course, means each of us on the average can expect smaller annual improvements in our standard of living.

Table 3.   Growth of Real GNP Per Capita in Selected Countries

	Growth rates of real GNP		Growth rates of real GNP per capita	
	1870–1969	1960–1977	1870–1969	1960–1977
United States	3.7%	3.6%	2.0%	2.4%
Japan	4.2	8.7	——	7.4
Germany	3.0	3.8	1.9	3.2
United Kingdom	1.9	2.4	1.3	2.1
France	2.0	4.9	1.7	4.0
Italy	2.2	4.4	1.5	3.7
Canada	3.6	5.1	1.8	3.4

Source: U.S. Department of Commerce, *Historical Statistics of the United States: Colonial Times to 1970* (Washington, 1975), p. 225; and *Statistical Abstract of the United States, 1979*, p. 437.

Figure 4 shows the underlying cause of the nation's declining growth and our sagging productivity performance compared to other nations. American productivity, quite simply, is in a nosedive. Although other nations' productivity rates also have fallen in recent years, they remain superior to ours. With greater output in comparison to similar inputs, these nations are successfully challenging American industry in world markets, as well as in our own back yard.

The Roots of the Problem

Although output per hour of labor is the usual basis for measuring productivity, it is obvious that the American productivity problem goes much deeper than the question of how hard the individual American works. After all, workers can be more *or* less productive if they have more *or* less capital goods (machinery) to work with. An hour of work by a person with a pick and shovel will not challenge the output of an individual with a backhoe. All of this leads to another dimension of the problem: Is the capital being used, even if it is of great quantity, to reflect the highest level of available technology? And of course, we then might ask: Is the available technology the best we are capable of producing? Overarching all of these components of productivity is the question of management skill: Is American industry managed in an intelligent and efficient way that will assure the best decisions about what is produced, how much of it, and under what productive arrangements?

As our earlier discussion (Introduction) of reindustrialization suggests, the honest answering of these questions should be *no*. We are not using the best capital and equipment. We are not improving our technology fast enough. And we are not managing our enterprises as efficiently and intelligently as possible. To be sure, we are doing better than the Russians and a lot of noncommunist countries, but by the standards of our past performance and our own expectations, we must do better. We must improve our productivity performance. Productivity is the lynchpin that holds the entire business and economic system together. Productivity, as a matter of business concern for the future, is not just *on* the agenda, it *is* the agenda.

Unless we improve our productivity and increase our output through a new business program, we are left with only two choices: First, we, each of us, can adjust calmly to a shrinking economic pie, accepting

FIGURE 4   HOW U.S. PRODUCTIVITY LAGS IN MANUFACTURING

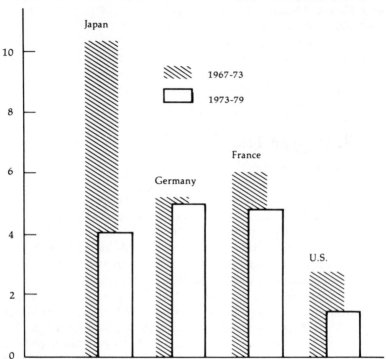

▲ Average compounded annual
percent increase

Data: Bureau of Labor Statistics
Business Week, June 30,1980, p. 65.

as our historical fate the fact that we booked tickets for the Titanic—and third-class tickets at that. Or, second, we can fight among ourselves, individually or in interest groups, for a bigger personal slice of a shrinking pie. This means some will have increasingly more while others have less. It will breed social and political disorder as the struggle between the haves and have-nots gradually tears the society apart. Such a situation invites a totalitarian political solution. Right-wing or left, it makes no difference. Neither capitalism, nor business, nor democracy, nor personal freedom could survive.

Thus, it all boils down to increasing the pie, to raising output and productivity. That is the next challenge to the American business system. Business enterprise and practically everything else we hold of value depends on our ability to meet that challenge.

While almost everyone can agree that there is a pressing need to raise productivity, there is less agreement on cures. The first reading places much of the productivity crisis at the feet of government, arguing that we have gotten into the mess through government—not market—failures. The second selection argues that there is no single cause for our productivity problem but that a very big cause has been business itself—particularly business's poor investment decision making and its failure to learn from the successes of our foreign competitors. The authors, in turn, call for the development of greater business and government cooperation in developing a "national industrial policy" (remember issue 1?). The third article takes a more hopeful position arguing that the new "high technology" will wash away our productivity problems in the near future.

13.1   Declining Productivity Is Government's Fault*

Frequently the decline of American productivity is approached as if it were the root of our economic problems. Such a perspective is mistaken; falling productivity is the result of our economic problems. To be blunt and direct, low productivity is the price an economic and social system must pay when it ceases to be organized solely to satisfy the objectives of profit making. The political and economic impulse to ''improve upon the market'' has been virtually irresistible over the past fifty years. These interferences with the market, however, have had a very simple and, if honestly considered, obvious effect: We systematically have shifted resources and concerns out of productive sectors of the economy into nonproductive sectors. The result has been to stifle initiative and efficiency and to encourage waste and economic decline.

The Role of Government Tax and Spending Policies

Government's role in reducing productivity can be categorized into at least two general areas of incorrect actions: (1) the actual physical expansion of the government's claim on the nation's output and (2) the various interventions of government into resource markets, social policy making, and pricing decisions that affect the activities of what remains of the private sector.

The growth of government's share of the Gross National Product from a mere 7 percent in 1902 to more than one-third today is not simply a matter of cutting up the total economic pie in different proportions. To follow the analogy, the aggregate growth of government activities has altered the recipe of the pie and interfered with the cook's ability to bake it. The growth of a government's budget, of course, has two sides—revenues and expenditures.

*Note: This selection has been taken from *Economic Issues Today*, 3rd ed., by Robert B. Carson, which presents Conservative, Liberal, and Radical points of view. This excerpt offers the Conservative point of view, but does not necessarily represent the view of the author.

Each must be examined separately to see how government interferes in microeconomic decision making.

REVENUES

First of all, the immense taxation necessary to sustain the government sector interferes directly with the industrial production and allocation decisions of enterprises. There is simply no such thing as a neutral tax policy. Worse still, even if some tax policies were less biased than others, American tax programs of the past fifty years have been constructed purposely by Liberal social engineers *not* to have unbiased effects. Taxes have been used for many other things than just collecting revenues to finance bloated budgets. In particular, taxes have been used as tools to redistribute income, converting the earnings of the more productive members of the society into outright gifts to the least productive. It should be noted that such penalizing of the productive elements of a nation and rewarding the nonproductive gives precisely the wrong signals in a society worried about improving productivity.

The decision to tax upper-income groups very heavily is among the most dangerous of Liberal aberrations. The usual economic justification for higher taxes on upper incomes is that they are relatively "painless," falling on individuals who have a diminishing value (marginal utility) for each additional dollar received. However, the national economic effects are not painless. Such taxation reduces the nation's fund of savings, which is mostly supplied by the well-to-do. Savings are, of course, the source for investment funds; therefore, reduction in the nation's savings limits the ability of business to expand and it ultimately lowers productivity. Only in recent years, with the growing understanding of "supply-side economics," has this obvious but long-overlooked result of our tax policies been given much consideration. However, recognition is one thing and changing policy direction another. The need for policy redirection is evident in Figure 5, which shows American investment rates shrinking compared with those of other industrialized countries.

Complementing our foolish personal income tax policies is our corporate tax system. Again, our search for a neutral and painless tax has led us to grief. Taking nearly half of all corporations' net

FIGURE 5   THE SHORTFALL IN U.S. SAVING AND INVESTMENT

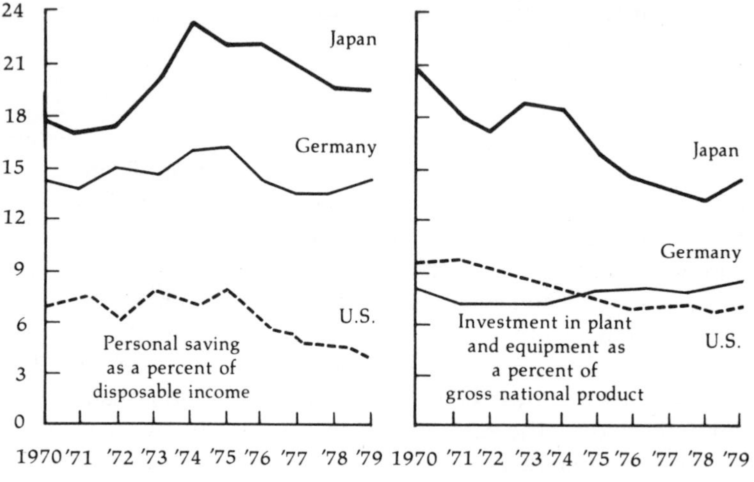

*Percent

earnings in tax revenues is scarcely neutral and can only restrict an enterprise's ability to make new capital investment. Corporate taxation policies, apart from robbing firms of necessary capital resources, have other undesirable effects. By taxing profits, losses actually become less of a problem. In some cases, profit-making firms actually seek to acquire losers. After all, an approximately 50-percent corporate profits tax also means a subsidy of 50¢ on the dollar for any losses incurred in operations. While the long-run effect of operating a firm at a loss is obviously bankruptcy, the creative accounting encouraged by our corporate profits tax produces substantial short-run benefits to a firm's income statement and balance sheet. Yet, the short-run advantages are still a matter of subsidizing inefficiency. Firms and industries that should be allowed, even encouraged, to be swallowed up by what Joseph Schumpeter called capitalism's "gales of creative destruction" are kept alive for tax purposes.

Not all tax policies have unintended negative effects on productivity. Some tax policies are created consciously to discourage efficient business decision making. The best example is the long-time AFL-CIO/Liberal effort to contain the investment of American firms within the United States by placing prohibitive taxes on multinational businesses. Reformers argue that productivity and employment are falling in the United States because some American firms are able to obtain better returns on their capital overseas. So-called "runaway firms" supposedly are starving their domestic production facilities on purpose. Never mind that unions, through outrageous labor agreements, have priced American workers out of world labor markets and placed important restrictions on the ability of business to innovate and introduce new capital-intensive production methods. Never mind that practically the only American corporation to show steady improvement in earnings and productivity are the very ones that have exploited multinational investment, production, and sales. We are asked to disregard all this and to tax the efficient firm so it will stay home and remain inefficient.

To recapitulate, under current government tax policies, capital and technology sources for productivity growth are made scarce. At the same time, corporations are discouraged by tax policy from acting wisely as profit managers. Instead of heeding the market command to close down unproductive operations, tax policies gentle and hide the market signal.

EXPENDITURES

On the expenditures side of government operations, the shift of resources from productive to unproductive agents is even stronger. The social expenditures made in the name of a better life for "working Americans"—everything from welfare to unemployment insurance to Social Security—have the ironic effect of discouraging work altogether. With greater numbers of the labor force artificially insulated from the market forces of supply and demand, the desire to work, and especially the desire to work very hard, is deeply eroded. Nonwork, after all, is to be rewarded and no one can slip through the "safety net," however hard they try.

From the point of view of productivity, this situation, along with the excessive power of labor unions to write their own work rules, means that labor inputs in production are vastly changed from earlier presafety-net and pre-union days. Quite simply, we all have become accustomed to working less diligently. The decline of the "work ethic" is of course not all bad. Few Conservatives will defend the 72-hour week and the intolerable working conditions of a century ago. But we cannot have it both ways. Increased productivity has made possible better hours and better wages; however, better hours and better wages are not possible in the future unless our output increases. If we choose to work less while at the same time we are producing less, then we must accept living on less. There is no such thing as a free lunch.

Lowered worker productivity is not the only outcome of government spending programs. Transfers to undeserving corporations . . . and subsidies to nonproducers similarly are a method of taxing the productive sectors of the economy to benefit the unproductive. They are not "free rides," but entail a cost we all must pay.

The Role of Government Social Policy

Apart from budgetary actions, government also has reduced productivity by its direct intervention in business affairs through misguided social policies. The list of such offenses against market efficiency is virtually limitless. and we have discussed several in earlier issues, so a few cases must serve to point out the problem.

Environmental protection remains very high among the American people's priorities. As social objectives, clean air, water, and earth, and conservation of resources for future generations are certainly noble concerns. Indeed, environmental protection can be had without abandoning the market system—if we understand it is not a free good and are willing to pay the price. Trouble arises when we believe there are no costs or when we fail to calculate the costs accurately. In terms of the productivity problem, our non-calculation of environmental costs and our failure to assign these costs in some rational manner to consumers of goods has had the effect of undermining the ability of American enterprise to produce efficiently. The Environmental Protection Agency's overly zealous efforts in the 1970s to end industrial pollution caused many firms to take actions that limited their productive ability. Capital investment required to meet EPA emissions controls reduced the amount of capital available for new investment and for research and development. Some production operations were closed altogether when business enterprises determined that cleanup costs exceeded profit possibilities. The air got cleaner in many American industrial cities during the 1970s precisely as the lines at the unemployment office grew longer. By singling out business as the cause of the environmental problems and by placing heavy cleanup burdens upon business enterprise, we traded off jobs and productivity for a cleaner but very expensive environment. While actual job losses are difficult to estimate, *Forbes* magazine calculates that meeting government environmental standards between 1972 and 1977 caused from 500 to 1000 plant closings and lowered productivity by 1.3 percent.

Similarly, the two-decade struggle to end racial discrimination through certain economic contrivances has not uplifted many minorities or female workers, but it has raised the cost of government administration and created at the upper levels of employment a "reverse discrimination" hiring effect. Those who condemn a free economy's inability to absorb minorities and women quickly into mainstream employment fail to understand the problem. Most workers who are allegedly "discriminated against" do not in a real economic sense deserve, here and now, to be in the mainstream. Only in the simple-minded thinking of Liberals and Radicals does it make economic sense to promote unqualified and inexperienced workers and upper-level managers, over more productive "mainstream" employees. While many white males may rejoice at such an observation, they should not misunderstand it. Claims to jobs or to promotions depend solely upon one's efficiency and diligence. If any other criteria are used, then both reason and order cease to exist in labor markets; and as labor market disorder grows, output shrinks.

It should be obvious that the list of recent social engineering efforts that lower output and raise costs goes on and on. It also should be obvious that none of these efforts, however well intended, will succeed if the nation is unable to increase productivity.

The Problem of Choices and Expectations

The productivity enigma points up a fundamental economic principle (really *the* fundamental economic principle) that always is taught rigorously in economics courses but is forgotten so easily in ordinary life: *opportunity cost*. Everything, absolutely everything this side of the land of the tooth fairy, costs something. The decline of American productivity is not the result of some twist of fate. It is not caused by the Japanese or the Germans or even the Russians. It is not, as too many believe, unexplainable. Our lowered productivity is the result of our decisions, collectively and individually, to opt for more nonoutput. Rarely does the decision present itself this way, but that is exactly what we are choosing when we choose clean air over industrial smoke, affirmative action over free-labor markets, a subsidized early retirement over work, keeping Chrysler alive rather than letting it fall into bankruptcy, taxing the rich heavily to sustain the nonrich, and so on.

From a Conservative point of view, many of the nonoutput decisions are defensible, so long as everyone agrees to the objectives and understands that the result will be a lowered standard of living. However, most of our nonoutput decisions are imposed by the few on the many. That is pure tyranny—not democratically defensible on any grounds. Philosophically, it is wrong. Economically, it is disastrous. Unless we realize soon that our unrealistic expectations about the "good life" for everyone (deserving or not) and our reliance upon government to painlessly fulfill these expectations only produce the opposite of the intended effects, productivity declines will continue. And as the economic pie shrinks and expectations stay the same or rise, the economic truths of the market will be superseded by the reality of raw political power and force. In such a world, freedom, individualism, and democracy have ceased; and economists, already hard pressed to explain what principles guide their thinking, will simply be trotted out to bless whatever particular tyranny is in authority.

The Conservative scenario for improving productivity is, by this point in the text, self-evident: Rely on the market forces to organize and direct production. Artificial interventions by Liberal social tinkerers, by manipulative labor unions, and by well-organized minority issue groups prohibit market efficiency. They shift investment in and rewards to the unproductive elements and activities of the society. The market cannot resolve instantaneously all of the social problems, real and alleged, that exist. But in the long run, as the illustrious past record of American productivity and growth shows, the market will decide the *what, how,* and *for whom* questions much more efficiently than can government or some weird mixture of government and the market.

Declining productivity is the result of a failure of the market produced by the failure of government. The continued decline of productivity will produce the failure of everything that we hold of value. Without continued growth, we all must have less, which we are not prepared by our nature to accept. This paradox is the central economic and political fact of our time. It will be solved one way or another, for better or ill.

13.2 Declining Productivity Is Business's Fault

IRA MAGAZINER AND ROBERT REICH

Rampant inflation and high unemployment are symptoms of economic stagnation. Our standard of living is no longer rising. In 1980, our median family income declined 5.5 percent in real terms. In contrast with the 25 years following the Second World War, when the real goods and services we could purchase for every hour we worked steadily increased, the past decade has witnessed a decline in our productive growth. . . .

The most obvious culprit has been the cost of energy. Sudden and significant rises in oil prices in 1974 and again in 1979 seriously affected our economy. And yet, rising energy prices constituted less than 15 percent of our total inflation during the 1970s. More importantly, other industrialized countries that were more dependent on foreign oil managed to confront the energy crisis more successfully than we, maintaining better productivity growth and more rapidly rising living standards.

A less obvious, but perhaps more important factor has been our increasing integration into the world economy and our failure to maintain international competitiveness.

The value of imports and exports together now equal almost 40 percent of the total value of all goods produced in the U.S. In 1969, they accounted for only 16 percent. During the past decade in the United States, nearly 2 million manufacturing jobs have been lost, a situation that is directly due to increased imports. Only costly protectionist measures, which have raised prices for American consumers, have prevented even further losses. Over the same period, the share of the world market claimed by U.S. manufactured goods has declined by 23 percent. Over 20 percent of our domestically sold autos are now made abroad, compared to 8 percent in 1970; 14 percent of our steel, compared to 9 percent in 1970; over 50 percent of our consumer electronics products, compared to 10 percent in 1970. The list goes on, growing longer year by year:

hand calculators, cameras, metal-forming machine tools, textile machinery, tires, watches, footwear, electrical switching equipment, and motorcycles—a sizable percentage of all these manufactured goods are made abroad.

In too many industries, U.S. companies have not remained competitive with foreign rivals. In certain cases, this lack of competitiveness was inevitable; some countries can exploit indigenous raw materials that are inherently superior and more accessible than ours, others can depend on an abundance of low-wage labor. In most cases, however, our lack of competitiveness has stemmed from our inability to improve productivity and deliver higher-quality products for a lower price than competitors in other high-wage industrialized economies. This decline of relative productivity is the major *reversible* cause of our present economic woes.

Today there is an emerging consensus on this diagnosis, but sharp disagreement remains about what government and industry in the United States should do to remedy the problem.

Some argue for preserving economic relationships as they were. This means controlling price increases, erecting further tariffs and quotas against foreign imports, preventing factory closings and relocations, limiting direct investment abroad, and investing government funds into bankrupt companies. While a few of these measures might be of limited use as part of an overall industrial development program, in the aggregate they are counterproductive. Markets, unlike Brigadoon, cannot be frozen in time, however much we may yearn for years gone by. Indeed, restrictions such as these might have the perverse effect of stifling economic growth while imposing substantial costs on the economy.

Other people blame our declining competitiveness on government interference in the economy. They call for greater private capital investment, to be achieved by lowering taxes for individual savers and companies and at the same time reducing the rate of growth of public expenditures for social security, health, and welfare programs. Further, they seek curtailment of government regulations pertaining to environmental protection, occupational safety and health, and consumer protection—measures, they allege, that have diverted large amounts of resources to nonproductive uses.

At the very least, such adjustments in government intervention would have inequitable effects. Because the ability to save is greater for the rich than for the poor and middle classes, a tax cut for savers and investors would be likely to result in a regressive shift of the tax burden.[1] Moreover, a decline in spending on social services might reduce the standard of living for a substantial number of our citizens who, because of age, ill health, or lack of job training, must rely to a significant extent on public assistance. Lower- and middle-class citizens are also more dependent on clean air, safe working conditions, and consumer protection. Our wealthier citizens can compensate by living in less polluted neighborhoods, drinking bottled water, vacationing in scenic environments, opting for safer jobs, and purchasing higher-quality products.

Proponents of these so-called "supply side" solutions argue that the sacrifices and inequities are short-term conditions that are necessary to stimulate overall economic growth, which will improve everyone's living standards in the long term. They also claim that many government services are now so inefficient that some cuts could be made without dire consequence.

Surely government can be more efficient. And perhaps some short-term sacrifice is warranted for the sake of long-term gains. But the fact is that increased competitiveness will *not* result from reduced government intervention in the economy. Our failure of competitive strategy, not government interference, has been responsible for our decline. For example, Japanese steel companies are far more productive than their American counterparts, yet they have spent far greater sums on pollution control, provided better working conditions, and paid higher taxes than our steel companies. Meanwhile, over the past 20 years, American steel companies have spent more than $60 billion (1978 dollars) in capital investment. If our steel companies had had more liberal tax deductions or fewer environmental mandates, would they have invested more heavily? If they had increased their investments by 10 or 20 percent, would their competitiveness have improved? We doubt it. Their declining competitiveness has been due to poor investment strategies: an unwillingness to use new technologies or to undertake more fundamental investments, a lack of aggressiveness in managing their overheads, and a failure to push for exports.

---

[1] Ed. note: Under a regressive tax system, those with lower incomes pay a higher tax rate.

In any event, the relationship between aggregate capital investment and increasing productivity is unclear. Between 1967 and 1973, our rate of productivity growth declined, although the rate of growth of capital formation was stronger than it has been at any time in the postwar period. In the last five years, a larger share of our national product has been devoted to business investment than at any other time since the Second World War. Our annual investment in manufacturing as a percentage of manufacturing output has increased steadily over the decade. Highly touted statistics about our low level of investment compared to that of other countries are misleading because they fail to take account of differences among economies. Our economy has a large service sector and a high proportion of knowledge-intensive industries that are not dependent primarily on capital investment. Moreover, our manufacturing companies lease a significant percentage of their equipment and invest a significant proportion of their total investments abroad; such expenditures are not counted in comparative investment statistics.

By contrast to economic policies that focused almost exclusively on the management of aggregate demand, supply-siders are now asking how investment can increase our standard of living. The question is appropriate. It is their answer that is wrong.

We offer an alternative view of how to increase national wealth. We focus on increasing the *competitive* productivity of our industry. We suggest that U.S. companies and the government develop a coherent and coordinated industrial policy whose aim is to raise the real income of our citizens by improving the pattern of our investments rather than by focusing only on aggregate investment levels. Our country's real income can rise only if (1) its labor and capital increasingly flow toward businesses that add greater value per employee and (2) we maintain a position in these businesses that is superior to that of our international competitors. Our companies must undertake appropriate strategies in line with these goals; our government must have explicit policies to promote this industrial restructuring and competitive productivity.

The guiding discipline for both business strategy and government industrial policy derives from the international competitive marketplace. Success depends on gaining and sustaining a competitive advantage in specific business segments. The means to accomplish this vary from business to business, depending upon its cost structure, growth rate, and the evolution of technology and markets. Generalized solutions to the problem of our declining competitiveness are inappropriate.

Once dominant in most of the world's businesses, many U.S. companies have not kept pace in recent years with changes in the international competitive environment. Our systems for evaluating investment decisions have not sufficiently considered the competitive evolution of businesses. Our accounting systems have given managers incorrect signals about investments. Our systems for measuring total product costs have misallocated manufacturing and distribution overheads and have failed to provide accurate information on the total costs of improvements in process and quality control. Our pricing policies have allowed foreign competitors to gain strong footholds in U.S. markets. We have allowed foreign competitors to gain advantages in other national markets from which they can better penetrate the U.S. market. In managing our international businesses, we have overemphasized the importance of cheap labor in production at the expense of productivity improvements and long-term market penetration. We have failed to give workers a stake in productivity improvements. Finally, we have paid too much attention to rearranging our industrial assets and too little attention to building our industrial base.

The U.S. government has also failed to help our companies gain competitive productivity in world markets. Hundreds of government programs directly or indirectly affect both resource-allocation decisions across industries and competitive positions among firms. But no government program has been viewed as part of a coherent industrial policy.

The federal government affects the pattern of industrial investment through a wide variety of tariffs, quotas, orderly marketing agreements, special tax laws and rulings, loan guarantees, targeted subsidies, patents, and export promotion and financing programs. Usually developed *ad hoc*, often in response to political pressures, these programs have affected industrial development unevenly. In many cases, they have retarded the flow of capital and labor from more productive uses. In those cases where the programs have contributed significantly to advancing the competitive position of U.S. producers, this effect has often been accidental.

By contrast, Japan and many European countries have adopted explicit policies for promoting selected businesses. In some instances, these policies have resulted in misallocations of resources, but our trading partners are becoming more sophisticated about how they selectively assist industrial development. Increasingly, their industrial policies enhance the creation of wealth by improving the international competitiveness of a number of growing businesses and by easing the transition of declining businesses.

The debate over industrial policy in this country has been more ideological than pragmatic, framed in terms of the ideal relationship between governments and markets rather than in terms of the hard realities of international competition. Surely the market decisions of countless consumers and investors are generally preferable to government direction for determining which goods and services should be produced in the economy and how investment should be allocated. These transactions provide a rich source of information about the size and competitive potential of various businesses, and they spread the results of mistakes and poor decisions among all actors in the market instead of focusing them in one place.

But the practical choice is not between government intervention and nonintervention. To a significant degree, the governments of all industrialized countries, regardless of political ideology and rhetoric, inevitably affect the pattern of investment in their economies through procurement, tariffs and quotas, guarantees, and various selective tax breaks and subsidies. In the U.S., these measures are usually formulated by agencies and Congressional subcommittees in response to special pleadings from well-established and politically powerful industries. Other nations understand that the only real alternative to developing a rational industrial policy that seeks to improve the competitive performance of their economy in world markets is for the government to cede the formation of policy to the politically strongest or more active elements of industry.

Industrial policies are necessary to ease society's adjustment to structural changes in a growing economy. New products are discovered and others become outmoded; productivity improvements reduce employment in some factories and increase output and employment in others; some industries migrate to low-wage regions or to developing countries, while technological breakthroughs create new industries in high-wage countries; some skills become obsolete and new ones are needed. Harsh social dislocations can result when workers lose their jobs and communities lose their industrial base. The speed and incidence of new industrial developments may not automatically remedy these declines. Unless government affirmatively acts to ease the adjustment, affected groups may seek to resist economic change through political means.

An effective industrial policy ensures that no group is driven to oppose economic change because it fears being forced to bear an unfair share of the burden of that change. Through programs of retraining, relocation, and targeted public investment, hardships caused by industrial restructuring can be remedied in ways that do not hinder economic progress. Countries that have anticipated and planned for changes in industrial structure have avoided the industrial costs associated with massive layoffs and plant shutdowns, such as paying large subsidies to dying companies. . . .

The course currently being pursued in U.S. economic policy will require great sacrifices from those in our society who can least afford them and will jeopardize many of the values we as a nation have come to hold dear. These sacrifices are justified as being necessary to regain economic prosperity. But these policies will not bring prosperity. Prosperity can be achieved only by means of an industrial policy carefully geared to international competition. . . .

13.3   The Promise of Hi-Tech

ROBERT JASTROW

Each explanation for our ailing productivity has its proponents, but none fits the facts. Yet the ailment is real; the economy is stagnating. What is killing our productivity? If we could identify the villain, we could cast him out.

I believe the System Dynamics Group at MIT, and a few scattered economists and business experts, have hit on the answer. There is no villain. The trauma we are passing through now is not a depression, but a natural interlude between two great waves of economic growth. American industry is shedding its skin, casting off old technologies and developing new ones. But the new skin has not yet hardened. Industries based on the new technologies—mainly computers and microelectronics but also robots, fiber optics, long-distance communications, biotechnology, and exotic new materials—are still young. They have not yet developed to the point where they can take up the slack in employment and industrial output created by the decline of the aging enterprises—the smokestack industries of steel, chemicals, autos, and so on.

Double Wallop

The potential for growth in the new hi-tech industries is mindboggling in terms of new jobs and new wealth. The computing industry alone is expected to grow from its current $50 billion to at least $100 billion a year in 1986, making it the biggest business in America. The market in long-distance communications is about $50 billion and growing at the rate of 18 percent a year. Robots, another major new industry, pack a double wallop. Not only do they increase industrial productivity, but the construction of robots itself is showing phenomenal growth, from $200 million in 1980 to a projected $2 billion by 1985.

Fiber optics is another rapidly growing technology. These light-pipes, made from glass fibers the thickness of a horsehair, can carry voices and data in a stream of tiny laser pulses at the rate of millions of pulses a second. AT&T plans to use a message-carrying light-pipe in a telephone cable between Boston and Richmond. The new cable would have taken 2 million pounds of copper with the old-fashioned wire technology.

There is little question that growth in the hi-tech industries will more than make up for the decline in the smokestack industries. Projected growth of $50 billion in the computing industry alone in the next four years is enough to offset the combined losses in the shrinking steel and auto industries. And new jobs go with the growth—easily sufficient to replace the jobs lost in the smokestack industries. Hewlett-Packard, one of the medium-size hi-tech companies, employs 57,000 people, Xerox more than 100,000. Two more Hewlett-Packards and a Xerox in the 1980s will make up for all the jobs lost in the auto industry.

Other countries will vie with us for a share in the wealth generated by the new technologies. Japan is the most formidable competitor. That nation graduated 87,000 engineers in 1980, compared with 63,000 in the United States, and is rapidly closing the gap in total numbers of scientists and engineers engaged in R&D in industry. The Japanese built their initial successes on technology borrowed from the United States, as we once borrowed our technology from Europe. Now, still following in our tracks, they are working very hard to acquire their own base of innovative research in semiconductors, computing, robotics, fiber optics, super-plastics and biotechnology.

I would bet my money on America in this competition. The Japanese have the advantages of long-range planning and very productive management of people. But their industrial organization tends to stifle initiative, especially youthful initiative. "The nail that stands up gets hammered down," says a Japanese proverb. Conformity and respect for elders are highly valued traits in Japan.

We Americans have the advantages of an open society and an upward mobility that gives free rein to the innovativeness and entrepreneurial energy of human beings. This is what counts most of all—human capital, and a society in which it is utilized to its maximum potential.

A small army of inventors and entrepreneurs is America's greatest asset. New businesses spring up like mushrooms; half a million were formed last year. Three out of 4 will fail in 5 years. The survivors are the great men of America. They create jobs, wealth, a bigger GNP, and a higher standard of living for everyone.

The business firms that make up the *Fortune* 500—mature firms like GE, duPont and IBM—created essentially no new jobs from 1969 to 1976. Young, hi-tech companies like Digital Equipment and Data General, founded by inventors and entrepreneurs, generated new jobs at the astonishing rate of 40 percent a year in the same period. The inventors and entrepreneurs also generate wealth.

In 1968, two engineers borrowed $2.5 million and formed Intel Corporation to manufacture semiconductors. Today, Intel's revenues are heading for a billion dollars a year. A billion dollars a year out of a few million! Where did that money come from? It didn't come out of the ground, but out of the brains and entrepreneurial energies of those men.

Another story, one of many. Kenneth Olsen, 31-year-old engineer, started Digital Equipment Corporation in 1956 in an abandoned textile mill. Today, Digital Equipment revenues are approximately $4 billion—a nice addition to the GNP. Still another example: the Xerox machine was invented by Chester Carlson, working in a little room behind a beauty parlor in Flushing, New York. Xerox revenues were $8.7 billion last year. Other examples abound. The list of modern innovations created by the solitary American inventor is impressive; not only Xerox but also the FM radio, Kodachrome, Polaroid, ballpoint pens, the zipper, cellophane, Bakelite and many others.

Why does the system work so well in America? Part of the answer is entrepreneurial zeal, fanned by the promise of huge profits. Nolan Bushnell started Atari on $500 and sold the business for $30 million. Part is the creative satisfaction to the inventor in seeing his brainchild make its way to the marketplace.

But creativity and the desire for wealth are found in other nations. The big difference in America is venture capital—money available to be invested at great risk in the testing of a crazy idea. The Japanese are our peers in technology and our superiors in education and industrial organization, but they lack venture capital and a system that could exploit it if it were available. Accordingly, they lack the army of entrepreneurial inventors that created America. The Japanese system funds innovations through the government and big business. It has no way of funding entrepreneurs and therefore it has none.

Capital Gains

The United States is awash in venture capital, thanks to a change in the tax laws in 1978 that lowered the tax on capital gains. Venture capital, which had been at the level of about a quarter of a billion dollars in previous years, doubled after the change in the capital gains tax, and then trebled and doubled again, reaching an estimated $6 billion in 1982. Venture capital, and the entrepreneurs it funds, are the secret weapon of America in the coming competition with Japan. The Japanese are aware of their weaknesses in this area, but they may not be able to do much about them, because the American way would go against the grain of their whole society. That is why I am betting on America.

Discussion and Review Questions

1. How has America's recent growth rate compared with other industrialized nations? Comment.
2. Why is productivity an important issue?
3. Do you think government or business is the primary cause for our productivity dilemma?
4. According to the first article, what particular problems have been caused by government?
5. The second article points the finger of blame at business's own failure to act responsibly, and it argues for a national industrial strategy of business and government working together to raise productivity and U.S. competitiveness in the world. How do you react?
6. How do you react to Jastrow's argument that our productivity problems will be eliminated by a movement toward hi-tech? Is there sound basis for this view or will high technology simply create other problems—jobs lost and industries closing as the result of technological changes, for instance?

Suggested Readings

Despite the length and breadth of the foregoing collection of current business writings, they indeed only scratch the surface of a study of modern American business enterprise. The challenges facing the American business system are many and varied, and we have only inquired into a few of the more obvious and troublesome themes. For the serious student of business, more is needed to gain a sense of mastery over the subject matter. The following bibliography has been organized for those who wish to go a bit deeper, to sharpen up their general and specific thoughts on how a production-for-profit system operates and where such a system in fact is heading during the waning years of the twentieth century.

The following selections of suggested readings are grouped loosely into headings roughly equivalent to the topics we have examined. For the most part, the bibliographical selections are recent studies. Where it was thought to be essential, some older "classics" have been included. All of the readings listed are books; nevertheless, the reader should be aware of the important contemporary business reporting and critical analyses that may be found in such periodicals as *Barrons, Business Week, Dun's Review, Forbes, Fortune, The Harvard Business Review, Inc., Nation's Business, The New York Times, The Wall Street Journal, U.S. News & World Report,* and other publications. Doubtless, some readers will find the following list incomplete, possibly omitting a favorite or well-known title. My only excuse is that this is simply a beginning bibliography, a representative starting point for a deeper study of business institutions. From the great wealth of business books, I have tried to select a mere handful from which to begin a critical study of American business enterprise.

History, Ideology, and Organization

Bluestone, Barry, and Bennett, Harrison, *The Deindustrialization of America* (New York: Basic Books, 1982).
Chandler, Alfred, *The Visible Hand* (Cambridge, Mass: Harvard University Press, 1977).

Friedman, Milton, and Friedman, Rose, *Free to Choose* (New York: Harcourt Brace Jovanovich, 1980).

Heilbroner, Robert L., *Business Civilization in Decline* (New York: W. W. Norton, 1976).

Kroos, Herman, and Gilbert, Charles, *American Business History* (Englewood Cliffs, N.J.: Prentice-Hall, 1972).

Simon, William E., *A Time for Truth* (New York: McGraw-Hill, 1978).

Thurow, Lester, *The Zero-Sum Society* (New York: Penguin Books, 1981).

Social Responsibility

Blake, David, et al., *Social Auditing: Evaluating the Impact of Corporate Programs* (New York: Praeger, 1976).

DeGeorge, Richard, *Business Ethics* (New York: Macmillan, 1982).

Sethi, S. Prakesh, *Up Against the Corporate Wall*, 3rd ed. (Englewood Cliffs, N.J.: Prentice-Hall, 1977).

Silk, Leonard, and Vogel, David, *Ethics and Profits: The Crisis of Confidence in American Business* (New York: Simon and Schuster, 1976).

Management

Blanchard, Kenneth, and Johnson, Spencer, *The One Minute Manager* (New York: William Morrow, 1982).

McGregor, Douglas, *The Human Side of Enterprise* (New York: McGraw-Hill, 1960).

Maslow, Abraham, *Motivation and Personality*, 2nd ed. (New York: Harper & Row, 1970).

Ouchi, William, *Theory Z* (Reading, Mass.: Addison-Wesley, 1981).

Marketing

Hartley, Robert F., *Marketing Mistakes* (Columbus, Ohio: Grid, 1976).

Kotler, Philip, *Marketing Management*, 3rd ed. (Englewood Cliffs, N.J.: Prentice-Hall, 1976).

McCarthy, E. Jerome, *Basic Marketing: A Managerial Approach*, 5th ed. (Homewood, Ill.: Irwin, 1975).

Finance

Black, Stanley B., *Foundations of Financial Management* (Homewood, Ill.: Irwin, 1981).

Ewing, H. Griffin, *Innovative Corporate and Executive Strategy* (Chicago: Nelson-Hall, 1982).

Nader, Ralph, and Green, Mark, *Corporate Power in America* (New York: Grossman, 1973).

Government and Business

Buchholz, Rogene A., *Business Environment and Public Policy* (Englewood Cliffs, N.J.: Prentice-Hall, 1982).

Kahn, Herman, *The Future of the Corporation* (New York: Mason and Lipscomb, 1974).

Weidenbaum, Murray L., *Business, Government, and the Public* (Englewood Cliffs, N.J.: Prentice-Hall, 1981).

Production and Productivity

Reich, Robert, *The Next American Frontier* (New York: Times Books, 1983).

Ross, Joel E., *Productivity, People and Profits* (Reston, Va.: Reston, 1981).

International Business

Heller, Robert, and Willott, Norman, *The European Revenge* (New York: Scribners, 1975).

Kahn, Herman, and Pepper, Thomas, *The Japanese Challenge* (New York: William Morrow, 1982).

Magaziner, Ira, and Reich, Robert, *Minding America's Business* (New York: Harcourt Brace Jovanovich, 1982).

Acknowledgments

ISSUE 3

David P. Garino, "A Case Study in Successful Entrepreneurship." From "Zippered Pocket Gives Firm Niche in Crowded Shoe Market" by David P. Garino, *Wall Street Journal*, November 22, 1982. Reprinted by permission of *The Wall Street Journal*, © Dow Jones & Company, Inc., 1982. All rights reserved.

Arthur Levitt, Jr., "In Praise of Small Business." From *New York Times Magazine*, December 6, 1981. © 1981 by The New York Times Company. Reprinted by permission.

Business Week, "Big Business Has Lost Its Entrepreneurial Instincts." From "Managers Who Are No Longer Entrepreneurs." Reprinted from the June 30, 1980, issue of *Business Week* by special permission, © 1980 by McGraw-Hill, Inc., New York, NY 10020. All rights reserved.

ISSUE 4

David Vogel, "America's Management Crisis." From *New Republic*, February 7, 1981. Reprinted by permission of *The New Republic*, © 1981 The New Republic, Inc.

Steve Lohr, "Overhauling Management." From *New York Times* Magazine, January 4, 1981. © 1981 by The New York Times Company. Reprinted by permission.

ISSUE 5

William Ouchi, "The Japanese Management Model." From *Theory Z: How American Business Can Meet the Japanese Challenge*, © 1981, Addison-Wesley: Reading, Massachusetts. p. 43–47. Reprinted with permission.

Edgar H. Schein, "Maybe the Japanese Model Won't Work in America." Reprinted from *Sloan Management Review*, Fall 1981, pp. 82–87. Copyright by the Sloan Management Review Association. All rights reserved.

L. Erik Calonius, "Trying Japanese Management in America." From "In a Plant in Memphis Japanese Firm Shows How to Attain Quality," *Wall Street Journal*, April 29, 1983. Reprinted by permission of *The Wall Street Journal*, © Dow Jones & Company, Inc., 1983. All rights reserved.

ISSUE 6

Joseph E. Richardson, Jr., " 'I Said We'd Never Have a Union.' " From *INC.*, November 1979.

AFL-CIO Federationist, "Labor in Defense of Unions." From "A Short History of American Labor," *AFL-CIO Federationist*, March 1981.

Charles G. Burck, "What's in It for the Unions." From *Fortune*, August 24, 1981. Reprinted by permission of *Fortune* and Charles G. Burck. © 1981 Time, Inc. All rights reserved.

ISSUE 7

Carole B. Allan, "Over 55: Growth Market of the 1980s." Reprinted by permission from *Nation's Business*, April 1981. Copyright 1981 by *Nation's Business*, Chamber of Commerce of the United States.

Arlene Hershman, with Mark Levenson, "The Big Clout of Two Incomes." Reprinted with the special permission of *Dun's Business Month* (formerly *Dun's Review*), April 1979, Copyright 1979, Dun & Bradstreet Publications Corporation.

Sandra Salmans, "New Trials in Test Marketing." From *New York Times*, April 11, 1983. © 1983 by The New York Times Company. Reprinted by permission.

Curtis Hartman, "Future Shop." Reprinted with the permission of *INC*. Magazine, November 1982. Copyright © 1982 by INC. Publishing Company, 38 Commercial Wharf, Boston, MA 02110.

ISSUE 8

Peter Nulty, "The Computer Comes to Main Street." From *Fortune*, September 6, 1982. © 1982 Time, Inc. All rights reserved.

Barnaby J. Feder, "Kodak's Quest for a Camera." From *New York Times*, December 6, 1981. © 1981 by The New York Times Company. Reprinted by permission.

ISSUE 9

Jack Egan, "Acquisition Indigestion." From *New York*, February 22, 1982. Copyright © 1983 by News Group Publications, Inc. Reprinted with the permission of *New York* Magazine.

Arthur Burck, "Bigness Has Weakened American Business." Reprinted by permission of "Vital Speeches of the Day," February 1, 1983, pp. 238–42.

Gail Bronson, "Back to Basics: Colgate-Palmolive Sheds Its Acquisitions." From *Wall Street Journal*, September 23, 1981. Reprinted by permission of *The Wall Street Journal*, © Dow Jones & Company, Inc., 1981. All rights reserved.

ISSUE 10

Edward Meadows, "Bold Departures in Antitrust Policy." From *Fortune*, October 5, 1981. © 1981 Time Inc. All rights reserved.

Harry Anderson, with Howard Fineman, Erik Ipsen, and Frank Gibney, Jr. "The Antitrusters' Bust at IBM." From *Newsweek*, January 18, 1982. Copyright 1982 by *Newsweek* Magazine. Reprinted by permission.

Lester Thurow, "A New Approach to Regulation." From *Zero Sum Society* by Lester Thurow. © 1981 by Basic Books, Inc. Reprinted by permission of the publisher.

ISSUE 11

Doug Bandow, "Restraining the Regulators." From *The Libertarian Review*, Summer 1980. Copyright 1980 by *The Libertarian Review*. Reprinted by permission.

Russell W. Peterson, "Laissez-faire Landscape." From *New York Times Magazine*, October 31, 1982. © 1982 by The New York Times Company. Reprinted by permission.

Thomas L. Friedman, "Rocky Regulation Road for Truckers." From *New York Times*, January 24, 1982. © 1982 by The New York Times Company. Reprinted by permission.

ISSUE 12

W. Paul Tippett, "The Japanese Are Not Playing Fairly." Reprinted by permission of "Vital Speeches of the Day," January 1, 1983, pp. 106–79.

U.S. News & World Report and J. Paul Lyet, " 'I'm Worried about a Full-blown Trade War.' " Reprinted from *U.S. News & World Report*, November 29, 1982. Copyright 1982 U.S. News & World Report, Inc.

Jagjit Brar, R. David Ramsey, and Peter Wright, "Six Challenges to Global Corporations." From *Collegiate Forum*, Spring 1982. © 1982 by *Collegiate Forum*. Reprinted by permission.

ISSUE 13

Ira Magaziner and Robert Reich, "Declining Productivity Is Business's Fault." Reprinted with permission from *Minding America's Business*. Copyright © 1982 by Law & Business, Inc., 757 Third Avenue, New York, N.Y. 10017. All rights reserved.

Robert Jastrow, "The Promise of Hi-Tech." From "Science and The American Dream," by Robert Jastrow. First appeared in *Science Digest*. © by the Hearst Corporation.